Well-Preserved Boundaries

Cappadocia was a place of cohabitation of Christians and Muslims until the Greco-Turkish Population Exchange (1923) terminated the Christian presence in the region. Using an interdisciplinary approach drawing on history, political science and anthropology, this study investigates the relationship between tolerance, cohabitation and nationalism. Concentrating particularly on Orthodox–Muslim and Orthodox–Protestant practices of living together in Cappadocia during the last fifty years of the Ottoman Empire, it responds to the prevailing romanticism about the Ottoman way of handling diversity. The study also analyzes the transformation of the social identity of Cappadocian Orthodox Christians from Christians to Greeks, through various mechanisms including the endeavor of the elite to utilize education and the press, and through nationalist antagonism during the long war of 1912 to 1922.

Gülen Göktürk received her Ph.D. in Political Science and Public Administration at Middle East Technical University, Turkey. She currently works as an Assistant Professor at Eskisehir Osmangazi University, Turkey. Her research interests include nationalism studies and Ottoman non-Muslim communities.

Birmingham Byzantine and Ottoman Studies
General Editors
Leslie Brubaker
Rhoads Murphey
John Haldon

Birmingham Byzantine and Ottoman Studies is devoted to the history, culture and archaeology of the Byzantine and Ottoman worlds of the East Mediterranean region from the fifth to the twentieth century. It provides a forum for the publication of research completed by scholars from the Centre for Byzantine, Ottoman and Modern Greek Studies at the University of Birmingham, and those with similar research interests.

For a full list of titles in this series, please visit www.routledge.com/series/BBOS

The Cult of St Anna in Byzantium
Eirini Panou

Eastern Trade and the Mediterranean in the Middle Ages
Pegolotti's Ayas-Tabriz Itinerary and its Commercial Context
Tom Sinclair

The Eloquence of Art
Essays in Honour of Henry Maguire
Andrea Olsen Lam and Rossitza Shroeder

Iconophilia
Politics, Religion, Preaching and the Use of Images in Rome, c.680–880
Francesca Dell'Acqua

Centre for Byzantine, Ottoman and Modern Greek Studies
University of Birmingham

Well-Preserved Boundaries
Faith and Co-Existence in the Late Ottoman Empire

Gülen Göktürk

LONDON AND NEW YORK

First published 2020
by Routledge
2 Park Square, Milton Park, Abingdon, Oxon OX14 4RN

and by Routledge
52 Vanderbilt Avenue, New York, NY 10017

Routledge is an imprint of the Taylor & Francis Group, an informa business

© 2020 Gülen Göktürk

The right of Gülen Göktürk to be identified as author of this work has been asserted by her in accordance with sections 77 and 78 of the Copyright, Designs and Patents Act 1988.

All rights reserved. No part of this book may be reprinted or reproduced or utilised in any form or by any electronic, mechanical, or other means, now known or hereafter invented, including photocopying and recording, or in any information storage or retrieval system, without permission in writing from the publishers.

Trademark notice: Product or corporate names may be trademarks or registered trademarks, and are used only for identification and explanation without intent to infringe.

British Library Cataloguing-in-Publication Data
A catalogue record for this book is available from the British Library

Library of Congress Cataloging-in-Publication Data
Names: Göktürk, Gülen, author.
Title: Well-preserved boundaries : faith and co-existence in the late Ottoman Empire / Gülen Göktürk. Description: First edition. | New York : Routledge, 2020. |
Series: Birmingham Byzantine and Ottoman studies ; volume 28 |
Includes bibliographical references and index.
Identifiers: LCCN 2020004621 (print) | LCCN 2020004622 (ebook) |
ISBN 9780367273385 (hardback) | ISBN 9780429296253 (ebook)
Subjects: LCSH: Cappadocia (Turkey)–History. | Cappadocia (Turkey)–Ethnic relations. | Religious tolerance–Turkey–Cappadocia–History. | Nationalism–Turkey–Cappadocia–History. | Toleration–Turkey–Cappadocia–History. | Turkey–History–1878-1909. | Turkey–History–20th century. | Turkey–History–Ottoman Empire, 1288-1918.
Classification: LCC DS156.C3 G65 2020 (print) |
LCC DS156.C3 (ebook) | DDC 305.6/81949509564109034–dc23
LC record available at https://lccn.loc.gov/2020004621
LC ebook record available at https://lccn.loc.gov/2020004622

Birmingham Byzantine and Ottoman Studies Volume 28

ISBN: 978-0-367-27338-5 (hbk)
ISBN: 978-0-429-29625-3 (ebk)

Typeset in Times New Roman
by Swales & Willis, Exeter, Devon, UK

 Printed in the United Kingdom by Henry Ling Limited

To my parents

Contents

List of figures viii
Acknowledgments x

   Introduction 1

1 Ottoman tolerance reconsidered 19

2 Maintaining boundaries: Faith and co-existence in late Ottoman Cappadocia 41

3 The path toward nationalism 74

4 *Halasane ta pragmata* (Things spoiled) 115

5 Tolerating the heretics: The distinctive case of the Greek Protestants 131

   Conclusion 155

Bibliography 161
Index 173

Figures

0.1 The Exchange Memorial at Neokaisaria. On its stone panel is written: "The live memory of Neokaisaria. Here and there. Never forgotten!" Photograph: Gülen Göktürk   2
0.2 Flyers of the fifteenth and sixteenth pan-Greek *Gavoustima* of Cappadocians organized by the "Cultural Society of Misti" and the "Asia Minor Society of Neokaisaria, Ioannina," respectively. I owe thanks to both societies for providing me with the posters of the *Gavoustima* gathering they organized   3
0.3 The Hasatani family in their local costumes, Sille, Konya. Source: Prodromos B. Spyrakos. Permission granted by the family   8
0.4 Map of Central and Southern Anatolia. Source: Η Έξοδος τόμος Β' (The Exodus Volume 2). Permission granted by Centre for Asia Minor Studies   9
1.1 A depiction showing Mehmed II presenting his "lost" *berat* to Patriarch Gennadius II. The Greek Orthodox Patriarchate, İstanbul. Photograph: Gülen Göktürk   32
2.1 Kayabaşı: An Orthodox Christian neighborhood in nineteenth-century Niğde. Photograph: Gülen Göktürk   51
2.2 A Greek-speaking Orthodox family from Ürgüp (Prokopi) in the late nineteenth century. Source: Photography Archive of Centre for Asia Minor Studies   56
2.3 An inscribed stone panel of a house door from Cappadocia: "the house of Tylkiar Anastas, Masallah, 1871." Photograph: Gülen Göktürk   63
2.4 The wedding ceremony of Rahil Loukopoulou in Nevşehir. Source: Photography Archive of Centre for Asia Minor Studies   69
2.5 St.Vasilis Church of Misti (Çarıklı) Niğde. The construction of the church was completed in 1922. The Orthodox Community of the village could only use it for two years (Karalidis, 2005, p. 99). It is

	enormous for the size of the village community at the time. Photograph: Gülen Göktürk	70
3.1	Tombstone of a tavern keeper's wife from Niğde in Karamanlidika in the yard of Zoodokhos Pigi Monastery in Istanbul. "In this tomb lies tavern keeper Savva's wife H. Vithleem from the village Iloson of Niğde. May god have mercy her soul. July 21, 1897." Photograph: Gülen Göktürk	83
3.2	Greek language teacher Phillippos Papagrigoriou Aristovoulos in Nevşehir. Source: Photography Archive of Centre for Asia Minor Studies	93
3.3	Teachers and graduates of the Theological Seminary (1908–1909). Source: Photography Archive of Centre for Asia Minor Studies	95
5.1	Greek students of the American College in Talas with their Greek teacher, H. Bogdanos (third from right, seated) and next to him, the American director. Source: Photography Archive of the Centre for Asia Minor Studies	137
5.2	The Oratory House of Evangelicals (Δζοαράν) in Zincidere with its congregation on the left (Source: Agapidis, 1950) and its current state on the right. Photograph: Gülen Göktürk	138
5.3	The American Hospital in Talas. Source: *The Missionary Herald*, 1914	140
5.4	Anatolia College, Merzifon. Source: *The Missionary Herald*, 1921	144

Acknowledgments

I am deeply grateful to Prof. Onur Yıldırım for his support and encouragement at every step in my academic life thus far. I still remember the very first time I knocked on his door in 2005 as a sophomore who wanted to become an academician. From that moment on he shared his knowledge and experience with me. Through times when I felt discouraged by unlucky experiences he never let me give up. I owe so much to him.

This book is essentially based on the archival collections of the Centre for Asia Minor Studies. I would like to express my special thanks to assistant director Stavros Anestidis for facilitating my research and to historian Dimitris Kamouzis for his valuable advice. I should like to thank the Turkish Scientific Council (TÜBITAK) for supporting me within "graduate student research program 2214-A" at Wellesley College in 2014. I wholeheartedly thank Prodromos B. Spirakos for unhesitatingly giving me precious photos of his refugee origin grandparents. I owe thanks to John Tsevas, the director of Greek Historical Evangelical Archive, for sharing with me documents and information about the Greek Protestants, and to Anastasia Papazoglou for hosting me many times in her village, Neokaisaria, and inviting me to an annual gatherings of Cappadocians in Greece. I would like to express that this book is also in memory of her lovely father Nikos Papazoglou who passed away a few years ago.

I would like to thank Eleni Patoucha for hosting me for months; for making her apartment home to me, for patiently teaching me Greek, for helping me in my translations, and more than that for being an elder sister to me. I am also grateful to the other members of my family in Greece, Andreas Baltas, Margarita Pavlou, Haris Mexa and Rudina Billa. My greatest debt is always to my parents. Without their support and patience, I would have given up long ago. They have always encouraged me with their unconditional love and never-ending effort. My history-lover and story-teller father inspired me so much to become an academician. He enjoyed the topic of my book as much as I did and took me to several Cappadocian settlements to track the traces of Anatolian Orthodox together. This book is dedicated to my parents Meral and Halim Sırrı Göktürk.

Introduction

I remember the summer I met an authentic group of Turcophone Greeks in a village called Neokaisaria (New Kayseri-Caesarea) in Ioannina, Greece. Until this encounter, I had always visualized these people as an extinct ancient community. They are not. Although spoken only by the elderly, Turkish is still alive among some second- and third-generation refugees. I distinctly recall attending a funeral that day. I was standing outside a funeral house with Maria, the daughter-in-law of the deceased woman. She was telling me how she feels when she speaks Turkish: "I speak Turkish from my heart, it is my mother tongue. I learned Greek at school, I just speak it." In the meantime, the familiar melody of lament rose from the house: *Keçi bağlarında dolanıyorum, yitirdim yârimi aranıyorum.*[1] That summer day was a magical experience for me. It was cloudy, and, in my imagination, the lament was heard from the mountains of Epirus and the Argaeus mountain greeted from far away the village of Cesareans. The guest room of the village church was decorated with photos of the ancestral land and the tiny memorial in the small square of the village was there to remind the villagers of their refugee origins. That day, I realized that my journey with these people was not yet over.

Three years after my first encounter with the Turkish speaking Greeks, I attended a festival of Cappadocians to continue my research. The festival was *Gavoustima*, the gathering of Cappadocians from all over Greece, which has occurred annually for almost two decades. *Gavoustima* is derived from the Turkish word *kavuşma*, meaning "coming together," and it was coined by the Cappadocian Greeks and given as a name to the festival (πανηγύρι), which each year is organized by a different local Cappadocian association and held in a different locality. Anything and everything recalling Cappadocia was there during the festival: music, dance, food, language, memories and stories from the family members about the old country. Only Cappadocia itself was absent from the picture. I tried to interview people, but our conversations were often interrupted by chit chat. I could not insist, and tried to enjoy the atmosphere. We were in Neo Agioneri, Kilkis, but it seemed to me that we were pretending to be in Misti, Niğde.

During the festival, I also noticed that the speakers addressed the audience as "the children of Cappadocian Hellenism," a title by which they distinguish themselves from the rest of Greek society in emphasis in their Cappadocian origins,

2 Introduction

Figure 0.1 The Exchange Memorial at Neokaisaria. On its stone panel is written: "The live memory of Neokaisaria. Here and there. Never forgotten!"
Photograph: Gülen Göktürk

but without putting in doubt their "Greekness." That is to say, they celebrate their origins with feelings of nostalgia; however, nationalistic feelings are not lacking.

Still, when I think about *Gavoustima*, I find myself lost between amazement and incomprehension. I wonder if it is really possible to miss a place you have never physically been to. It is like a craving for food you have never tasted. I do not, of course, doubt the genuineness of their feelings of nostalgia but I do question why second and third-generation refugees still have these feelings. Confused by this question, I recall the moment when I talked to a second-generation Turcophone refugee in Neokaisaria in 2009. He told me about his visit to Turkey. "Do you know, my daughter? I was asked to buy land from my village of origin in Kayseri," he said, "I refused. Why settle there? My home is here." Now I realize that the attendees of *Gavoustima*, when celebrating their origins, were not actually pining for their lost land. This ancestral land was actually alien to them, the land of their deceased parents and grandparents. They could happily visit these lands as tourists, but they would not live there. Their feeling of nostalgia in fact has nothing to do with lost land; it is rather a fantastical romance, a way of celebrating their differences from the rest of their society. As a consequence, I believe that my study has a contemporary resonance, despite focusing on the late nineteenth and early twentieth century.

This book investigates the relationship between tolerance, cohabitation and nationalism by focusing mainly on Orthodox–Muslim and Orthodox–Protestant practices in living together in Cappadocia in the last fifty years of the Ottoman Empire (from the 1870s until the Population Exchange between Greece and Turkey, 1923), mainly due to problems in obtaining sources outside of this period. It is also an analysis of the transformation of the social identity of the Cappadocian Orthodox Christians from Christians to Greeks through various

Figure 0.2 Flyers of the fifteenth and sixteenth pan-Greek *Gavoustima* of Cappadocians organized by the "Cultural Society of Misti" and the "Asia Minor Society of Neokaisaria, Ioannina," respectively. I owe thanks to both societies for providing me with the posters of the *Gavoustima* gathering they organized.

mechanisms, such as utilizing education and the press, and through all sorts of nationalist aggression during the long war (1912–1922). My greatest disappointment is that due to the absence of first-person testimonies reflecting the Turkish-Muslim perspective for cohabitation, the subject matter could only be examined through the Greek Orthodox perspective.[2]

The book includes many theories but essentially argues that the cohabitation practices of different communities in the pre-nationalism era provide clues to understanding how nationalism was embraced by the people. In other words, it affirms that nationalism falls into the pre-existing boundaries and dynamics of relationships between faith groups. This is not a primordialist argument that reduces national identity to Church affiliation; it investigates tolerance and competitive inter-faith living, and attributes special attention on the one hand to cultural flirting between religious communities, and on the other hand to ways of preserving boundaries and keeping the group (Self) intact in the face of the potential intervention of the Other. The center of attention is the microcosms of lay people rather than the macrocosms of rulers and Church authorities.

The unique quality of this book is that it does not focus on conflict, in contrast with the general tendency of nationalism studies to focus on conflict zones, considering the fact that the nationalist ferment can easily be nourished by controversy. History demonstrates that even in areas of relative peace, nationalism found ways to establish itself, and even penetrated places where there was no visible inter-communal conflict. Cappadocia was one of those places. Despite the confessional differences between religious communities, people were not in conflict, and they enjoyed common customs, religious rituals and a shared language, spoken by most of the Christians of the region. Nevertheless, even the Cappadocian Christians eventually nationalized in the first decades of the twentieth century, a period that I call the years of discontinuity, as it represented a detachment from previous epochs due to the strict nationalist policies of the Committee of Union and Progress (the CUP), never-ending wars and the eventual displacement of peoples with the Turkish–Greek Population Exchange in 1923. The elite endeavor to Hellenize the Anatolian Orthodox began earlier in the second half of the nineteenth century, but it was only successful in creating a sort of broader community consciousness, or proto-national bonds, if we follow Hobsbawm,[3] especially among the people who received an education in local community schools, and among Cappadocian immigrants in big coastal towns. I will most certainly discuss the various responses to the nationalization attempts of the elites. By pinpointing the traditional relations between faith groups in a relatively peaceful ecosystem in a pre-nationalism era, the book explains this seemingly inconceivable nationalization process and, in doing this, benefits from Robert M. Hayden's concept of "antagonistic tolerance" and Peter Van der Veer's "religious nationalism,"[4] two terms that complete one another. The former refers to competitive cohabitation, and the latter to the transformation of pre-existing religious belongingness to nationalist belongingness in some regions like India and the Balkans. In India, for example, dreams of nationhood always include religion as one of the main aspects of national identity.

This book ultimately aims to respond to current Pax-Ottomana romanticism through an investigation of a relatively peaceful region which had the potential to best exemplify the myth of "Ottoman multiculturalism," as well as through a detailed discussion of contemporary theories of accommodating plurality in order not to arbitrarily utilize concepts like tolerance, multiculturalism and justice. It is hard to deny that until recently the official historiography in Turkey was nation-state oriented; homogenization policies of the early republican era were almost never questioned, and the history of the Ottoman Empire was underrated. Nowadays the wind blows in the opposite direction; the Ottoman Empire is overly exaggerated and politicians and some scholars go even further, claiming that Ottoman plurality was "a pre-modern" or "a pre-nation-state" multiculturalism[5] and that the Ottoman Empire was a land of "tolerance."[6] This approach is flawed on several points. One is that it employs the term "tolerance" positively and, in fact, randomly, without any reference to tolerance/ toleration debates in liberal and critical theories of justice, and implies "peaceful living together" even though these two concepts are not equal. Additionally, it remains inadequate to answer such questions as: if the Ottoman Empire was an example of "peaceful cohabitation," why was it dissolved into several nation-states? Was there really a glorious past to which we can look for solutions to solve the problems of today? And how can we label a historical occurrence with contemporary concepts like multiculturalism? This book hopes to answer these questions with an approach that questions Ottoman romanticism through an examination of Cappadocia that might have suited the romanticist arguments. As we will see, however, even then cohabitation was highly competitive, if not actually conflictual, and cannot serve as an example for today.

Names and places

From the beginning of my research I knew that I was not in a position to invent borders within contemporary Greek society. The object of my examination is a historical group of people, not contemporary Greeks of Cappadocia origin, and I am by no means trying to question anybody's "Greekness." Additionally, I am aware that some historical debates one way or another have contemporary repercussions. With that in mind, during my continuous readings about the topic, I eventually decided to drop the term *Karamanlı* (pl. – lar), a label that is often used in historical and philological studies about the Cappadocian Orthodox. I myself also used the term in my previous studies. *Karamanlı* was a term that was historically used by some Orthodox Christians pejoratively to address the Turcophone (and even the Grecophone) Christians from the Ottoman province of Karaman, suggestive of being vulgar peasants and savages.[7]

Cappadocians themselves never used the term *Karamanlı*. Instead, they used phrases like Christians, Christians who inhabit the East, Anatolian Christians, Anatolian Orthodox and Anatolians when referring to their compatriots in their contemporary publications.[8] For Richard Clogg, the term *Karamanlı* was first used to refer to Turcophone Anatolian Christians in Greek texts of the eighteenth century, and possibly earlier. Clogg also cites a German traveler who recounted the presence of Turcophone Christians known also as "Caramanians" in Istanbul in the sixteenth century. It seems that the term *Karamanlı* was not coined in recent centuries;[9] it had in fact been in use for a long time. Some scholars have recently revived the term *Karamanlı* and established a new category for the history and publications of Turcophone Orthodox of Anatolia, separate from the general community of the Greek Orthodox of Asia Minor. The pioneer of studies of *Karamanlides* and *Karamanlidika* is Evangelia Balta, and several other scholars adopt the term *Karamanlı* in their studies.[10] Alternatively, Stefo and Foti Benlisoy seem to hesitate to use the term *Karamanlı*, especially in their later works, and instead refer to Anatolian Orthodox by the titles they used for themselves in their publications in the nineteenth century.[11]

6   *Introduction*

This study rejects the category of *Karamanlı*, and studies the Orthodox of the Anatolian interior (or Cappadocia) within the general framework of the Greek Orthodox Community (i.e., Rum) of the Ottoman Empire. There are two reasons for this. First, historically, they were offended by the term *Karamanlı* as it was a label to humiliate the Anatolian Christians. Second, speaking Turkish as a mother tongue was not peculiar to them; the Turkish speaking Orthodox did exist in other parts of Asia Minor in addition to Cappadocia.[12] Further to this, despite the common belief that the Anatolian Orthodox spoke Turkish, a special Greek dialect was still present in some Orthodox settlements in Cappadocia even in the late nineteenth century. Among all eighty-two Orthodox villages of Cappadocia, Greek was spoken in the nineteenth century in twenty of them.[13] Therefore, language on its own does not form a category. Last but not least, the written language called *Karamanlidika* was not only used in Cappadocia but also in Pontus[14] and in other regions of Asia Minor, and publications in this written language could reach many places in Asia Minor and be read by members of the general Orthodox public. In short, there is no need to put the Cappadocian Orthodox in a hypothetical cage and separate them from the rest of the Greek Orthodox Community. To put it differently, although the Greek Orthodox communities of each and every region had peculiar traits that differentiated them from the broader Community,[15] they were pieces of a whole. For example, the Pontic community was different from the Ionian community. Similarly, the Cappadocian community had distinguishing characteristics due to its peculiar geography, neighborly relations, socio-economic conditions and history. However, they all belonged to the Greek Orthodox Community. We can certainly distinguish and categorize them according to their place of origin and study a particular local community, but I disapprove of any approach that has the tendency to invent new "ethnic" groups within an "ethnic" group.[16]

As a general rule, the Orthodox communities in city centers were Turcophone. Greek was preserved predominantly in the villages. The more conservative the people, the more they tended to retain their linguistic identity. Since they dealt with economic activities in public places like markets and bazaars, men spoke Turkish, whereas women, if they did not live in a mixed village, continued to preserve and speak Greek and have a limited knowledge of Turkish. In the nineteenth century, however, this situation changed. As a result of male immigration to big cities, in poorer villages women started to work in Turkish fields and houses. Due to the fall in male population and female exposure to the Turkish language, the Cappadocian Orthodox faced a larger loss of linguistic identity than in previous centuries. Toward the end of the century, even in the few remaining Greek-speaking villages, Greek was replaced with Turkish.[17]

In light of the above-stated arguments, throughout the study I interchangeably use the terms Cappadocian Orthodox, Cappadocian Christians, Cappadocians, Anatolian Orthodox, Greek Orthodox of Anatolia or simply Orthodox and Anatolian Christians. Since their nationalization was in process and incomplete during this time period, I hesitate to use the term Greek since it denotes ethnicity and nationality. As for the other side, I either employ the term Muslim or Turk; in the prenationalism era both meant adherence to Islam and the concept of Turk did not have any ethnic connotations and was often used by non-Muslims for their Sunnite neighbors. Interestingly, the Anatolian Orthodox referred to the Alawite communities as Turkmens (Turcomans).[18] It seems that the concepts of Turk and Turkmen had solely religious meanings for them. Concerning the Protestant converts of Greek Orthodox origin, I have introduced the concept of Greek Protestants. Here, Greek refers to their previous membership of the Greek Orthodox congregation.

Another important point to clarify is the geographical term Cappadocia. As I mentioned, those Orthodox Christians also called *Karamanlı* were the inhabitants of the Karaman *Eyalet* (a subdivision of the Ottoman Empire), and they were named after their place of origin (the suffix *-lı* is used to denote place of origin in Turkish). Until the advent of the Provincial Redistricting Act (Teşkil-i Vilayet Nizamnamesi) in 1864, the Karaman *Eyalet* included seven *sanjaks* (provincial districts): Konya, Niğde, Akşehir, Beyşehir, Aksaray, Kayseri and Kırşehir, in line with contemporary Turkish administrative structure. The territories of the Karaman *Eyalet* were at the same time the land on which the Karamanid Dynasty had reigned (1250–1487). With this new Act, the Karaman *Eyalet* turned into the province of Konya (Konya Vilayeti). The province of Konya now consisted of the *sanjaks* of Konya, Isparta, Burdur, Antalya and Niğde. Kayseri and Kırşehir were now parts of the province of Ankara, along with the *sanjaks* of Yozgat, Çorum and Ankara. In short, the Anatolian Orthodox were the settlers of a union of Konya and Ankara provinces. The only missing area is the *sanjak* of Adana in considering the Orthodox settlements.

Anagnostopoulou maps out the regions where there was a high concentration of Greek Orthodox communities in interior Asia Minor, and employs Byzantine province names. There were two areas with a significant proportion of Greek Orthodox communities: Cappadocia and Lycaonia. Cappadocia included the *sanjak* of Adana from Cilicia and Kırşehir from Galatia. For her, Cappadocia and Lycaonia together were Greater Cappadocia. Balta, on the other hand, defines Greater Cappadocia in accordance with the settlements of Turcophone communities. In her explanation, it lay to the north as far as Ankara, Yozgat and Hüdavendigar, to the South Antalya and Adana, to the East Kayseri and Sivas, and to the West as far as the borders of Aydın province.[19]

The Cappadocian Orthodox were very few in number compared to their Muslim neighbors, and their settlements were very scattered. For this reason, we cannot possibly limit the borders of Cappadocia by the physical particularities of the region. Due to dispersion, the ecclesiastical division did not overlap with the Ottoman administrative structure. For example, a metropolis could contain two or three different provinces; conversely, there could sometimes be two or three metropolises in one Ottoman province.[20] For this reason, historians' descriptions of Cappadocia might seem confusing, because some are inclined to define it in accordance with the ecclesiastical division, and some with the Ottoman administrative division.

8 Introduction

This book is not particularly concerned with the Turcophone Orthodox of the whole Asia Minor but with the Orthodox of Cappadocia and draws the boundaries of Cappadocia as a union of the provinces of Ankara and Konya plus the sanjak of Adana in line with the 1864 Administrative Act. It focuses predominantly on the Greek Orthodox settlements in Kayseri, Niğde, Aksaray and Nevşehir. For the purpose of this book, in addition to the interviews with the refugees from these areas, the narrations of refugees from Keskin (Kırşehir), Gürümce (Adana) and Silli (Konya) are also utilized. Throughout the book, Cappadocia and interior Anatolia are used interchangeably.

By the time of the Turkish–Greek Exchange of Populations in 1923, the Orthodox communities living around Kayseri were Turcophone. The region was famous among the Greek Orthodox Community as the land of St. Basil the Great (fourth century AD), and was an old center of Christianity. The Metropolitan Bishop of Kayseri lived in Zincidere, thirteen kilometers north of Kayseri, a center of education and religion for the Orthodox since the Monastery of John the Forerunner, and the only Seminary located in Cappadocia. Unlike Kayseri, the Greek Orthodox communities of Niğde were mixed in terms of their mother tongue. Those who lived in the city center were Turcophone, but there were both Grecophone and Turcophone villages, as well as villages where people

Figure 0.3 The Hasatani family in their local costumes, Sille, Konya
Source: Prodromos B. Spyrakos. Permission granted by the family.

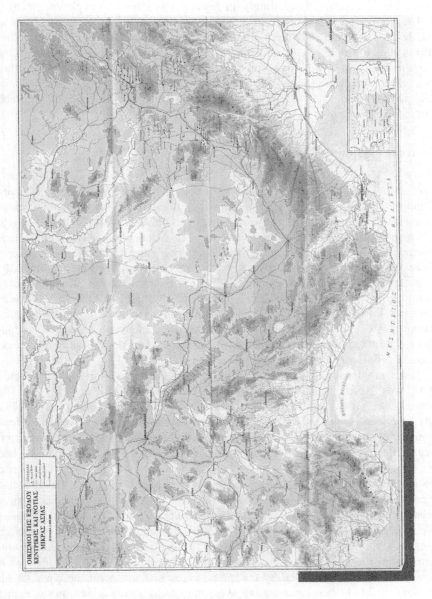

Figure 0.4 Map of Central and Southern Anatolia.
Source: Η Έξοδος τόμος Β' (The Exodus Volume 2). Permission granted by Centre for Asia Minor Studies.

spoke both languages. Interestingly, in Grecophone villages, people are reported to have sung their songs in Turkish. The Metropolitan Bishop of Konya lived in Niğde. As for Nevşehir, there were both Turcophone and Grecophone settlements. For example, the community of Sinasos was Grecophone, whereas the community of Malokopi was Turcophone. Lastly, the number of Greek Orthodox people in Aksaray was low compared to the other centers of Cappadocia. The most important Orthodox settlement was Gelveri with its four thousand Orthodox inhabitants.[21]

Sources and methodology

Early studies of the Cappadocian Orthodox have been very crucial for this book. However, in order to make a solid contribution to the existing literature I chose to dwell on the faces of the crowd and, therefore, devoted an enormous amount of my research time to examining the Oral Tradition Archives (Αρχείο Προφορικής Παράδοσης) of the Centre for Asia Minor Studies (Κέντρο Μικρασιατικών Σπουδών) in Athens, where I explored the testimonies of refugees from Central Anatolia and also utilized the library collection. Additionally, I made use of the rare books about individual Evangelicals and the missionary publications available at the Greek Historical Evangelical Archive (Ελληνικό Ιστορικό Ευαγγελικό Αρχείο). Finally, I delved into various *Karamanlidika* (i.e., Turkish in Greek letters) publications of the time, including almanacs, regulations of brotherhood organizations, newspapers, periodicals like *Anatoli*, *Terakki* and the missionary newspaper *Angeliaforos*.

The Oral Tradition Archives at the CAMS contains interviews conducted with over five thousand refugees from the early 1930s to the early 1970s. The project was initiated by a Greek aristocrat Melpo Logotheti Merlie (1890–1979). My first impressions of the oral tradition accounts were that I was in serious trouble, as the refugee testimonies were purely nostalgic; they were conducted years after the events and with people who had already passed away, so I had no opportunity to clarify any point I did not understand. Moreover, I also had no idea of the questions asked by the researchers of the CAMS to the refugees; I could only read the answers and then attempt to guess the questions as they related to topics like schools, migration, the Exchange of Populations, Turkish–Greek relations, nearby villages, etc. I read the accounts in Greek even though most of the refugees were documented as Turkophone, and I wasn't completely sure about the accuracy of the translations. For example, I had no idea what word would have been used by the interviewees in Turkish for the word Greek (Ελληνας) that I often came across. Were they using *Yunan* which means ethnic Greek or *Rum* which means Greek Orthodox Christian? With these questions in mind I read the writings of two scholars, namely Papailias and Kapoli who critically, even fiercely, evaluated the Oral Tradition Archives of the CAMS.[22] Their works helped me refine my thoughts about the Oral Tradition Archives and make my analysis carefully.

First of all, Papailias warns researchers about the founder of the Oral Tradition Archives Merlie's interpretation of Turkish–Greek co-existence, underlined as it is with a desire for a more tolerant future. For Papailias, Merlie encouraged her researchers to find signs of harmonious interethnic relations and not to highlight any Turkish violence against Greeks. What could be the reason for this stance? Was she a philanthropist, a humanist or just a liberal? It is a difficult question to answer, but it seems that it was mainly a romantic attitude, probably because she was fascinated by her encounter with the Turks in Cappadocia to where she had traveled on a center-sponsored journey, something she herself stated in her correspondence. In line with Merlie's interest, Cappadocia became the Centre's focal point and consequently thirty-four percent of the interviewees selected were Cappadocians. As mentioned, Cappadocia and/or Central Anatolia was perhaps the most peaceful region in the Ottoman Empire so an "Ottoman tolerance" or "peaceful cohabitation" discourse could easily be generated with reference to Cappadocia. According to Papailias, Merlie was well aware that Cappadocia would suit her objective of portraying harmonious cohabitation in the Ottoman Asia Minor. Papailias's warning drove me to be more cautious in evaluating testimonies heavily nostalgic for lost homelands (χαμένες πατρίδες) and for the "good Turkish neighbor."

Second, for Papailias and Kapoli, when the CAMS researchers knocked on the doors of refugees to gather information about their hometowns in Asia Minor, the stories that they were expected to tell were of their distant past and few of them were eager to narrate it. For many, it was "a lament over ruins."[23] They had relatively positive feelings about their life in Asia Minor, especially following the Second World War, Civil War and all the hardships of refugee life after their expulsion and the Exchange. Papailias's statements match my observations. I have not come across any testimony that argues that life in Greece was better than life in Asia Minor. Therefore, the refugees were recreating a world of peace in a distant past under the sway of the discomfort they felt in the conditions existing at the time they were interviewed, and looking back was a source of pleasure for them.

The interviews invented Asia Minor but not the land the refugees lived on. The source of their imagination was the difference between present and past. Their nostalgia harbored dichotomies like past and present, existing and non-existing, here and there, remembering and forgetting, us and them etc.[24] Similarly in the Oral Tradition Archives, there were good and bad Turk, Asia Minor and Greece, present and past, native Turks and refugee Turks, Asia Minor refugees and locals (ντόπιοι), Christianity and Islam, and the periods before and after the Young Turk Revolution of 1908. Almost every detail or experience was narrated in comparison to something else. The frustration of their present conditions was reflected as a longing for the past. Remembering the bad was always accompanied by remembering the good. Dichotomies are important in weighing refugee perceptions and making conclusions. For example, a distinction between good and bad Turks in a refugee narrative implies that Turk is the Other, an external actor, if not an enemy.

Many historians find memory as a source of history writing less credible since it is open to distortion more than written sources. Especially with oral histories, which deal with the distant past, there is the possibility of distortions influenced by changes in values and norms that might unconsciously change perceptions.[25] So, when CAMS researchers interviewed people about their life in Asia Minor, a lot of water had flowed under the bridge and memories were already reshaped by the recent past and the present. Another difficulty was raised by eighty-two-year-old Alexandros Yagtzoglou to a CAMS researcher in 1957:

> You should have come ten years before. In those years everything was fresher in my mind. Now it is late. Most of our people died and so did the brains of the remaining people, we are not able to tell anything.[26]

Yagtzoglou was right; their experiences in Asia Minor were now filtered by the years between then and now and now as they were elderly they could barely remember the details. All these are fair concerns for oral history in general and the Oral Tradition Archives in particular. A student of oral history should be clear about what (s)he looks for in oral history as a material for any academic endeavor because its credibility lies in the symbolism, imagination and meaning they include, if not in its adherence to facts.[27]

Memories are repetitions and since they are reproduced in very different systems of notions and at different periods of our lives, they lose the form and appearance they originally had. My personal stance is that memory is a reflection of societal norms and past experiences; so it is collective, but this does not mean that individuals are totally passive in this process. Memory is a social as well as an individual process, and the more significant a name or face is the more likely it is to be remembered, so memory depends on individual comprehension as well as upon individual interest. This is along the lines of what I observed in the oral tradition accounts. The presence of good interpersonal relations with a member of the Other positively affected the general perception of Turks in the eyes of refugees. Despite the hardships originating from nationalist CUP policies in the last two decades of the Empire, a relentless period that was lived through by the interviewed refugees, and despite the anti-Turk propaganda they faced after their expulsion, a refugee could say, for instance, "nowadays they say a lot about Turks; we never met such Turks. They must have been other people. They were good and respectful to women. I wish everybody would be like Turks."[28] Or, conversely, a refugee could label Turks pejoratively because of bad inter-personal encounters and antagonistic intercommunal relations in his/her locality, and so easily adopt "the bad Turk" image created by Greek nationalist propaganda. As in the lines of a refugee testimony: "When they saw us coming from a revelry, Turks would be jealous of us. They could initiate a fight. You could not say 'long live Greece!'"[29]

As previously claimed, the testimonies at the CAMS were overly nostalgic, and I initially regarded this as a pitfall for my research. Many scholars see nostalgia as "sentimental kitsch."[30] Nostalgia might distort past events, but it tells us about their meaning in the present time. It might also create a problem of anachronism since it informs about the past using feelings of the present. As an example, in the oral testimonies I looked at, refugees made distinctions about the years before and after the Young Turk Revolution (1908), where the Hamidian years were seen as relatively good in comparison with the hardships they went through afterward. If not approached carefully, the Hamidian years could be evaluated as the "good old days." However, it was also a period of censorship, Armenian massacres, forced conversions and Islamist policies, and most likely for Christians it was worse than the previous *Tanzimat* period. Since the testimonies in the Oral History Archives do not tell us anything about the years before the reign of Abdülhamit II, it would be easy (though incorrect) to conclude that the Hamidian period was a *belle époque*. In order to avoid such a conclusion, a researcher has to have a sense of history developed through supporting readings and comparative analysis of different areas of diversity.

Selectiveness is also an issue in research supported by and reliant on oral history and memory. It is often claimed that there are good memories and bad memories and memory mostly works in favor of good memories. However, the notion of good and bad differs from person to person. Remembering good or bad, I believe, is closely related to the respective intentions of the interviewee and the researcher. If a researcher conducts a study about the massacre of a particular group of people, for example, his/her questions would more often remind the interviewee of bad memories, and if an interviewee has bad feelings toward the people (s)he is talking about (s)he might stress the bad memories. Therefore, if forgetting and selectiveness are pitfalls, my suggestion to overcome these issues is not to focus on the interesting and rare stories of individual interviewees, but instead on the common things in different interviewees' narratives. After all, says Caunce, it is the ordinary events that shape our lives and for this reason a historian should be interested in typical events, not extraordinary ones.[31] To put it a different way, the collection and analysis of specific details of narrowly limited events, developments, or phenomena result in loss of perspective and neglect of context.[32] My study covers many interviewees, both urban and rural, from different settlements of Cappadocia, and I focus on the common points in their narratives because shared social frameworks of individual recollections constitute the basis of this book. This way I prevent myself from falling for the romantic vision that prevails in studies about Ottoman plurality. As for my book, I will try to complete the picture drawn by the Oral Tradition Archives through historical imagination in addition to two publications of the Anatolian Orthodox *Anatoli* and *Terakki*, as well as the missionary publications *Angeliaforos* and *The Missionary Herald*.

Except for *The Missionary Herald* all three of the above-mentioned publications were in *Karamanlidika* and emerged in the second half of the nineteenth century. "The teacher of Anatolia," Evangelinos Misailidis, started publishing *Anatoli* in Izmir in 1843 and after a break he continued to publish it in Istanbul starting in 1851. The newspaper survived until 1912 or 1922. Scholars do not agree upon an exact date. *Anatoli* was followed by *Nea Anatoli* which survived between the years 1912–1923.[33] *Anatoli* was one of the major and most circulated newspapers of the time among the Orthodox Community and contributed massively to the development of Turkish in the Greek alphabet. In time, the expression of Turkish sounds with Greek letters took a conventional form in the newspaper and became a source of reference for *Karamanlidika* for the Anatolian Orthodox, so that after a while the newspaper started to criticize those who made orthographical mistakes when writing Turkish in the Greek alphabet. Interestingly, the Turkish language used in the paper became plainer over time. It was first due to reader complaints since many of its readers were not familiar with Ottoman Turkish and could only speak simple Turkish. Second, it was a result of the general pattern of elimination of Arabic and Persian words and phrases in the language at the time. The readers of *Anatoli* were mainly the Turcophone Orthodox from Istanbul and interior Anatolia. For the purposes of this book, I have benefited particularly from the issues of *Anatoli* published in the last decade of the nineteenth century (1891–1897); however, I also examined a few issues from the period 1851–1854 to see how *Anatoli*'s purpose of emergence was portrayed during its initial years, and to cite some relevant examples. A whole book could easily be written just about *Anatoli*, but I never intended to dwell specifically on *Anatoli*, only to benefit from it.

The short-lived *Terakki* (progress) was another publication I perused and it was published in the heart of Cappadocia in Nevşehir in 1888. As can be understood from the title, it was aimed at the progress of Anatolia, as did *Anatoli*, and published articles about science, medicine, general knowledge, religion, history (including Ottoman history), morality, human development and concerns for the future of Anatolia.

Unlike these two, the missionary newspaper *Angeliaforos* was first published in 1872 by the American Board of Commissioners for Foreign Missions (ABCFM) in Istanbul in *Karamanlidika*. There were also Armenian and Armeno-Turkish versions of the paper, both of which were called *Avedaper* and emerged in 1855 and 1860, respectively. *Angeliaforos* means "the bringer of good news" or simply "the messenger." The paper is composed of three main departments, religion, education, and family, and concludes with a summary of both domestic and foreign news. For this book, I was able to study the issues of *Angeliaforos* published between 1889–1890 and 1903–1904. *The Missionary Herald* reported that, by 1903, the number of subscribers of the three versions of the paper was almost exactly two thousand five hundred (Barnum, 1903). Although the other two versions were bought by Armenians, this means that *Angeliaforos* was circulated almost double that of *Anatoli*, whose subscribers were five hundred by 1890 and three hundred by 1895.[34] The missionary newspapers *Avedaper* and *Angeliaforos* had the same content and they not only targeted the newly converted but also the large class of people who sent their sons and daughters to missionary schools and the people who never attended their services.

Another written source I have used for this book is *The Missionary Herald*, the magazine of ABCFM published in Boston. It reported from foreign missions in China, India, the Near East, Africa and Indigenous populations of the Americas, among others. This magazine covered a wide range of topics, including local customs, cultures, geography and history; success stories in topics regarding missionary work; and education and health missions or the reasons for their failure. For this book, I looked at issues it raised from the 1870s to 1922.

Themes

The book is ultimately a response to the Pax-Ottomana romanticism especially prevalent in current political discourse. This anachronistic perspective portrays Ottoman plurality as a pre-modern equivalent of multiculturalism, and seeks to cure current minority issues and identity claims of the country by referring to the "Ottoman tolerance" myth. I call it a myth since the term "tolerance" is used randomly without any reference to theoretical discussions about it. Similarly, multiculturalism is arbitrarily employed disregarding its fallacies.

I first analyze the term tolerance, and discuss the possibility of generating a new perspective of the term. I then continue with the Ottoman way of dealing with diversity, and open a debate about some free-floating terms like *millet* system and religious tolerance. I determine Ottoman tolerance to be negative, religious, and pragmatist (in times of crisis it could also be intolerant), and indifferent in nature.

I explore Ottoman tolerance at a societal level and consider the practices of living together in Cappadocia, because it is my contention that no other region of the Empire would be better suited than Cappadocia to buttress the romanticist thesis of "peaceful cohabitation." Nevertheless, a close-up study of Cappadocia illustrates that, even there, religion – the primary vehicle of border maintenance – sets the rules of rivalry between communities, and it was in fact this rivalry that provided a suitable setting for nationalism. There is a general misinterpretation that at a societal level tolerance is equal to peaceful living together. In an ecosystem where tolerance prevails, we often do not notice conflict until times of crisis, but little or no conflict does not necessarily equate to peaceful cohabitation. Although Cappadocia was one of the least conflictual regions of the Ottoman Empire, practices of living together were still highly competitive, rather than peaceful, indicating antagonistic tolerance at an inter-communal level. In this ecosystem of Cappadocia (and elsewhere in the Empire), the borders between "us" (Self) and "them" (Other) were determined by religion, and the Anatolian Orthodox did not want to lose members to either the dominant religion of Islam, or any other Christian denomination like Protestantism. The Orthodox Community was already small and was shrinking due to emigration in the nineteenth century, so border maintenance was particularly important. However, although Muslims were both numerically and culturally dominant in Cappadocia, non-Muslims did not necessarily close themselves off from them. Despite the prevailing competition at the inter-communal level, there was also proximity and intimacy at an inter-personal level.

Like the non-Muslims of other regions of the Empire, the Cappadocian Orthodox entered a process of nationalization in the late nineteenth century. I analyze their Hellenization and show the relation between pre-existing cohabitation practices and nationalism. Three main factors helped in the creation of broader community consciousness and proto-national bonds among the Cappadocian Orthodox: first, the increasing male emigration to foreign lands due to economic opportunities that emerged with the arrival of European capital in major port cities of the Empire, and construction of railroad networks that facilitated the connection between homeland and foreign lands; second, the foundation of the Greek Kingdom and its irredentist policies over the Asia Minor Orthodox, initially through cultural means like education and propagation through the *syllogoi* (societies) and press; and third, the importance attributed to education by the Church as a response to missionaries and as an outcome of Ottoman reforms that facilitated the entrance of lay people to administrative bodies of *millet*. Consequently, the Anatolian Orthodox became aware of their kinship ties with the Orthodox of other regions for the first time, and began to realize the presence of a broader Community that included other communities as well as their own local community (koinotis).

Until the nationalist aggressiveness of CUP policies particularly targeted foreign investments and non-Muslims, Orthodox folk were still relatively indifferent to nationalism, and regarded it as an attack on their religious identity. On the other side of the coin, among the intellectual circles of the Orthodox there were Greek nationalists who received their educations at the important institutions of Athens, Istanbul and elsewhere, there were Ottomanists who were also educated at major schools but believed in the integrity of the Empire, and there were proto-nationalists who received education from local community schools and were taught by nationalist teachers. As for the remaining people, seeds of Greek nationalism could only bear fruit after the Young Turk Revolution, and only then did nationalism begin to forge the social identity of the great amount of people. During this process, the germ of nationalism settled on the pre-existing Self–Other dichotomy that had long been based on religious differences. In the end, both Turkish and Greek nationalisms were religious nationalisms that chose their prospective members according to their religion. As a general rule, the relatively peaceful atmosphere created by antagonistic tolerance dissolved in times of crisis, and mostly ended in internecine wars and massacre, which is what happened in the Balkans, for example. In Cappadocia, however, even during times of crisis, we don't see big clashes or conflicts but instead the rise of communal borders and an adoption of national identity of a deeper intensity than previously. Accordingly, I argue that the nationalization of the Cappadocian Orthodox could only be completed after their expulsion and their direct exposure to the ideological apparatus of the Greek state.

Returning to the tolerance debate, there were occasions when the Anatolian Orthodox were in the position of tolerators. In their relations with the Greek Protestants, who had changed their denomination under missionary influence, the Orthodox were either intolerant or, due to kinship with the converts, they remained indifferent and negatively tolerant. I analyze the curious case of the Greek Protestants who remained invisible in the historiography of the non-Muslims of the Ottoman Empire, and portray their lives especially in their relations with the Orthodox with whom they had blood ties.

Notes

1 "I am moving around Keçi (Gesi) vineyards; I have lost my beloved and I am looking for him". A well-known folksong in Turkey and, apparently, in Greece. The song was sung by Nikos Papazoglou in September 2009 in Neokaisaria, Ioannina, Greece. His parents were refugees from Kayseri and his mother tongue was Turkish.
2 Early Turkish novels can give us some perspective on the Turkish point of view towards the Greek or Orthodox element in the Ottoman Empire. However, having been written in the strife-filled first two decades of the 1900s and mostly by intellectuals who had been deeply affected by the political circumstances, I do not think that these novels portray a lay point of view. For Cappadocia in particular, it seems that the only novel that was written about the Orthodox of the region was Mahmut Yesari's first novel "Bir Namus Meselesi" (*A Matter of Honor*) which was serialized in the magazine *Kelebek* in 1923. This was a novel about Orthodox Christians from Kayseri who continued their lives in Istanbul. For more information about this novel see, S. T. Anestidis, Yunan ve Türk Edebiyatında Erken Karamanlı Tiplemeleri. In short, due to a lack of sources the Turkish point of view about their Christian compatriots is unfortunately absent from this study.
3 See E. Hobsbawm, *Nations and Nationalism since 1780: Programme, Myth, Reality*.
4 See R. M. Hayden, (Ed.), *Antagonistic Tolerance: Competitive Sharing of Religious Sites and Spaces*; P. Van der Veer, *Religious Nationalism*.
5 Aslı Iğsız devotes a title for the discussion of Neo-Ottomanism in her new book and labels it as an anachronistic vision of history. According to Iğsız, the Neo-Ottomanism talk is all about marketing Turkey as a brand. See A. Iğsız, *Humanism in Ruins*, pp. 199–203. See also A. Iğsız, Documenting the Past and Publicizing Personal Stories: Sensescapes and the 1923 Greco-Turkish Population Exchange in Contemporary Turkey.
6 For a typical example of this scholarship, see Y. Yıldırım & K. H. Karpat, (Eds.), *Osmanlı Hoşgörüsü*. In the introduction to the book, the authors explain that their purpose for studying Ottoman tolerance is to present this historical model as an inspiration to find ways to develop peaceful co-habitation for the peoples of the Middle East. For another example, see J. McCarthy, *The Ottoman Peoples and the End of Empire*, pp. 2–9.
7 See F. Benlisoy & S. Benlisoy, Türkdilli Anadolu Ortodokslarında Kimlik Algısı.
8 See E. Balta, Gerçi Rum isek de Rumca Bilmez Türkçe Söyleriz: The Adventure of an Identity in the Triptych: Vatan, Religion and Language; R. Clogg, Some Karamanlidika Inscriptions from the Monastery of the Zoodokhos Pigi, Balıklı, Istanbul; F. Benlisoy & S. Benlisoy, Türkdilli Anadolu Ortodokslarında Kimlik Algısı.
9 R. Clogg, Some Karamanlidika Inscriptions from the Monastery of the Zoodokhos Pigi, Balıklı, Istanbul, p. 56.
10 In addition to Evangelia Balta, Richard Clogg, Elif Renk Özdemir, Merih Erol, Şehnaz Şişmanoğlu Şimşek and Robert Anhegger preferred to use various versions of the term *Karamanlı*, like *Karamanlides* (plural Greek form), *Karamanlis* (an anglicized form), and *Karamanlılar* (plural Turkish form). See E. Balta, Gerçi Rum isek de Rumca Bilmez Türkçe Söyleriz: The Adventure of Identity in the Triptych: Vatan, Religion and Language; R. Clogg, A Millet Within a Millet: Karamanlides; E. R. Özdemir, Borders of Belonging in the "Exchanged Generations of Karamanlis"; M. Erol, Cultural Manifestations of a Symbiosis: Karamanlidika Epitaphs of the Nineteenth Century; Ş. Ş.

Şimşek, The Anatoli Newspaper and the Heyday of the Karamanlı Press; R. Anhegger, Evangelinos Misailidis ve Türkçe Konuşan Dindaşları.
11 For a critical article about the use of the term *Karamanli*, see F. Benlisoy & S. Benlisoy, Türkdilli Anadolu Ortodokslarında Kimlik Algısı.
12 According to the Greek census of 1928, there were 103,642 Turcophone Christians in Greece. 50,000 of them were from Cappadocia and the others were from Pontus and other regions of Asia Minor. M. Harakopoulos, *Ρωμιοί της Καππαδοκίας: από τα Βάθη της Ανατολής στο Θεσσαλικό Κάμπο. Η Τραυματική Ενσωμάτωση στη Μητέρα Πατρίδα*, p. 34.
13 S. A. Manousaki, *Μνήμες Καππαδοκίας*, pp. 43–44.
14 In this book the names "Pontus" and "Black Sea Region" are used interchangeably.
15 When I write Community with a capital "C", I mean the Greek Orthodox Community as a whole rather than a local community.
16 It does not seem proper to call the Orthodox Community in the nineteenth century an ethnic group, since they were simply a faith group, most of whose members had primitive to no ethnic consciousness that time. Here, I use the term "ethnic" from a contemporary perspective.
17 R. Dawkins, *Modern Greek in Asia Minor: a Study of the Dialects of Silli, Cappadocia and Pharasa with Grammer, Texts, Translations and Glossary.*
18 CAMS, Cappadocia, Gelveri, Symeon Kosmidis.
19 S. Anagnostopoulou, *Μικρά Ασία: 19^{ος} Αιώνας -1919: Οι Ελληνορθόδοξες Κοινότητες. Από το μιλλέτ των Ρωμιών στο Ελληνικό Έθνος*, pp. 161–163; E. Balta, "Gerçi Rum isek de Rumca Bilmez Türkçe söyleriz" The Adventure of an Identity in the Triptych: Vatan, Religion and Language, p. 26.
20 M. L. Merlie, Οι Ελληνικές Κοινότητες στη Σύγχρονη Καππαδοκία, pp. 42–43.
21 M. L. Merlie, Οι Ελληνικές Κοινότητες στη Σύγχρονη Καππαδοκία, p. 57. According to *Xenophanes,* a periodical of the "Society of Anatolians, The East," the number of Orthodox in Gelveri was three thousand five hundred by 1905. For statistics about the inhabitants of Cappadocian settlements, and for information about Orthodox schools, see Στατιστική της Επαρχίας Ικονίου, *Xenophanes (3)*, pp. 44–47; Στατιστική της Επαρχίας Καισαρείας (Στατιστικός Πίνακας), *Xenophanes (3)*, pp. 230–233.
22 See P. Papailias, *Genres of Recollection: Archival Poetics and Modern Greece Anthropology, History, and the Critical Imagination*; E. Kapoli, Archive of Oral Tradition of the Centre for Asia Minor Studies: Its Formation and its Contribution to Research.
23 E. Kapoli, Archive of Oral Tradition of the Centre for Asia Minor Studies: Its Formation and its Contribution to Research, p. 19.
24 M. N. Layoun, *Wedded to the Land? Gender, Boundaries and Nationalism in Crisis*, p. 38.
25 P. Thompson, *The Voice of the Past*, p. 128.
26 CAMS, Cappadocia, Niğde.
27 A. Portelli, What Makes Oral History Different? p. 69.
28 CAMS, Cappadocia, Endürlük (Androniki), Evanthia Ikenderoglou.
29 CAMS, Cappadocia, Misti, Mak. Damianoglou.
30 D. Walder, *Post-colonial Nostalgia: Writing, Representation, Memory*, p. 4.
31 S. Caunce, *Sözlü Tarih ve Yerel Tarihçi*, p. 26
32 T. Philipp, Bilād Al-šām in the Modern Period: Integration into the Ottoman Empire and New Relations with Europe, p. 401.
33 S. Tarinas, *Ο Ελληνικός Τύπος της Πόλης*, pp. 143–144.
34 N. T. Soullidis. (11 December 1890). Hemşerilerimize. Anatoli, 4271; N. T. Soullidis. (5 December 1895). Anatoli Gazetesi Ser Muharriri Rıfatlı Ioannis Kalfaoglou Efendi'ye. Anatoli, 5173.

1 Ottoman tolerance reconsidered

We are surrounded by nostalgic sentiments, triggered by personal archeology, investigating our individual past in the identity-oriented world of the post-Cold War era. The nostalgia for ancestral lands that no longer exist, that never existed, or longing for some phantasmagoric past, is closely associated with the reinvention of identity. Nowadays, we frequently ask ourselves who we are. Why is it that modern individuals are so preoccupied with inventing or discovering new identities for themselves? With the dissolution of the Soviet Union in 1991, identity politics replaced the ideological politics of the Cold War era. Identity politics did not, of course, appear suddenly as a result of the weakening of ideological politics. They have actually existed for a long time. Scholars date the beginning of identity politics to the civil rights movement of Martin Luther King Jr., the Black Power movement and global anti-colonial movements, where activists called for a new collective identity to counterbalance White imperialism. When the Cold War ended, identity politics became much more popular than in the past. Interestingly, not only those of lower status but also other individuals invented new ways to show their particular identity: they established foundations and societies in their ancestral hometowns, celebrated with feasts, opened museums, performed arts focusing on specific identity traits and initiated a new form tourism that essentially amounted to nostalgic pilgrimages to places of origin.[1]

The activities of the associations (σύλλογοι) of the Cappadocian Greeks in Greece such as *Gavoustima* (see introduction) all came about in the post-Cold War era. The contemporary story of the Cappadocian Greeks is not the concern of this book. I focus primarily on the historical community of the Cappadocian Christians in the last decades of the Ottoman Empire – and I only give the above example to show that talk of "origins" and "identity" still prevails, not only in immigrant countries like the U.S. and Canada but also in nation-states like Greece. The only distinction is that Cappadocians do not make any political demand of the Greek government other than freely celebrating their identity. For many identity groups,[2] this is not the case. They are mostly preoccupied with demands for recognition and representation, which in turn create a huge debate concerning the dilemma between balancing the liberal ideal of individual liberty and group autonomy.

In the last twenty years or so, scholars in Western liberal societies have produced ideas to reconcile group demands and group autonomy with individual liberty and individual autonomy in an effort to attain justice. This dilemma opened to discussion liberalism's flaws and shortcomings when it comes to dealing with diversity, and introduced different theories of justice to Western politics. In this process, scholars from various schools rediscovered forms of living together in remote geographies and in the histories of faraway countries and revived debates about possible ways of cohabitation in nations in turmoil. The Ottoman "*millet* system" is one of those historical examples of group autonomy and religious tolerance rediscovered in the West.[3]

"Ottoman romanticism" is, however, a relatively new phenomenon in Turkey. Until recently, the official historiography had a nonsensical tendency to underestimate anything that belonged to the Ottoman past. Today, the river flows in the opposite direction, and this situation generates ahistoric studies and discussions and non-scientific perspectives both toward the past and the present. In parallel with Western scholarship references to the Ottoman experience of pluralism, some scholars and politicians in Turkey are driving a discourse about contemporary Ottoman tolerance. In other words, these scholars and politicians support their theses of Ottoman tolerance with the studies in the West and regard the Ottoman way of dealing with pluralism as a remedy to Turkey's current minority problems, including the political demands of Kurds, the religious accommodation of Alawites and Assyrians, the violation of the minority rights of Greeks, the Armenians, the Jews and the stigmatizing language used against all minorities, including the Roma. There are two problems with this: first, they use "tolerance" as a free-floating concept without any analysis of what it implies in both pre-modern and modern times; second, they offer an imitation of historical cases as a means of solving the identity claims of today.

I claimed previously that if we were to talk about peaceful living together and tolerance in the Ottoman context, Cappadocia would be the best-suited example compared to other regions of the Ottoman Empire. For example, in Lebanon there was sectarian warfare between Maronite Christians and Druzes in 1860; in the Balkans, peasant revolts turned into nationalist movements of Serbs, Greeks, Bulgarians and Albanians; in Crete, despite the presence of kinship ties, Christians and Muslims were at each other's throats; on the Western shores of Anatolia, Cretan refugees were in conflict with local Greeks; there are many other examples. In Cappadocia, there was no turmoil or visible clash between different religious groups until the very last decades of the Empire, and so it presents a great example of religious diversity because of its inclusion of Sunni and Alawite Muslims, Orthodox Christians, Armenians, Protestants and foreign missionaries. As such, it is a perfect example to study tolerance and cohabitation in the Ottoman context and consequently offers an ideal case study to open for debate the practicality of "Ottoman tolerance" in today's Turkey.

To employ modern concepts like tolerance and multiculturalism might not seem appropriate for a book that is occupied with a historical community and I completely agree with the criticism that argues that it is often futile and anachronistic to evaluate historical situations and events using modern concepts. In contemporary evaluations, however, tolerance is repeatedly used in the Ottoman context, referring to the "peaceful co-existence" of different religious groups, where it is portrayed as an ideal world to be emulated in today. However, a detailed discussion of the term has not been attempted until recently. I therefore argue that in order to address tolerance, this notion must be discussed both in terms of religious tolerance and as a modern liberal concept, taken from a study that aims to respond to and challenge an understanding of a historical model purporting to provide solutions to today's minority issues.

This is not an easy task for two reasons. First of all, except for notions of pre-modern religious tolerance, tolerance discussions are conducted in the context of liberal democratic societies. These debates take liberal democracies as givens and envisage a kind of ideal world which is usually inadequate in the face of the complex poly-cultural realities of life, as well as in terms of diversity of identity/affinity groups, inner heterodoxies, permeability of group boundaries and irremediable characteristics of identities. Additionally, critical theories of tolerance are occupied with the replacement of this system altogether and with attempting to make fundamental transformations to society and in its norms in a range, from its constituting principles to its basic codes of relationship between diverse human beings. Therefore, the pre-modern Ottoman world remains totally alien to contemporary tolerance debates for a very basic reason: it was not a liberal democratic country; rather, it was a pre-modern monarchy.

Second, and leaving aside the critiques of a liberal capitalist system, in contemporary liberal states justice is an end, an objective to be reached by setting fundamental rights of freedom and equality for every citizen. But for the Ottoman Empire, justice was a tool, a means to preserve the hegemony of the dynasty over its subjects. Therefore, we are again talking about two completely different systems. The only resemblance is that in both systems tolerance is required as a means to minimize conflict and ensure continuity, even though the scope of the concept is different. In the Ottoman context, tolerance is a form of "religious tolerance" (in a non-Lockean sense). Only religious diversity was tolerated and even this type of tolerance was limited to "the peoples of the book" in line with Islamic rule. In the Ottoman tradition, there was no room for heresies and heretics of any religion. People could exist as long as they belonged to a religious community. For contemporary liberal societies, however, we can talk about super-diversity and accordingly, tolerance has been discussed in a broader context and some scholars even think of replacing tolerance with the idea of recognition or respect.

Considering these pitfalls, how can one possibly apply contemporary tolerance debates to benefit a historical study? In the first place, contemporary tolerance disputes strengthen my position that romanticizing the Ottoman experience as an example for contemporary minority problems is pointless because Ottoman tolerance was totally irrelevant to contemporary needs. Second, such debates help us to unsettle our general point of view about the concept of tolerance, which is often employed arbitrarily and regarded positively. Accordingly, we need to analyze and understand the Ottoman interpretation of tolerance from a more sophisticated perspective. Last, this will provide a basis to build a comparative perspective between past and present without committing the error of anachronistically judging the past with present ideals, and imitating past practices for current problems of diversity.

Tolerance

Tolerance[4] is a thick concept with different layers each evoking different meanings that can be considered either positive or negative depending on one's political stance. One can either take it as a core of liberalism or as that of fascism. While in Western scholarship it is mostly seen as a liberal value and a civilizational virtue that each liberal individual should carry, it is regarded as the dominance of the powerful over the weak by critical theory. By its nature, tolerance does not have a unified meaning across nations and cultures. It is attached to different objects in different national contexts[5] including groups with various identity or interest demands like religion, race, ethnicity, sexual tendency, patriarchy, environmental concerns and so on.

Tolerance is complicated by the dichotomy between tolerance in public versus private spheres; we can call the former positive tolerance and the latter negative tolerance. The question here is to what extent we can tolerate differences. Do we tolerate them as long as they remain in the private sphere (negative tolerance), or are there any mechanisms to appreciate diversity in the public sphere (positive tolerance)? I believe asking a few questions might be helpful in attempting to develop a perspective for the term tolerance:

1. Who are the objects of tolerance?
2. Do people need to tolerate those whom they appreciate and like?
3. What are the different levels of tolerance?
4. Is it inherently a power relationship?
5. Is tolerance a middle way between rejection and assimilation?
6. Do two equally powerful people/groups tolerate each other?[6]

Toleration, as a term, was first coined by Locke as "religious tolerance" in his 1689 *A Letter Concerning Toleration* to his friend Philipp van Limborch. In the letter, Locke described the Christian virtues of charity and love and criticized the insistence of penalizing these beliefs, which he considered to be against Christianity. For him, no one who follows Christ and his teachings is a heretic, and tolerating those who have different religious views is compatible with the Gospel. Corresponding with this view, he offered to distinguish between religious and political matters and to define the boundary between religion and commonwealth, which for him was an association of people constituted solely for the purpose of preserving and promoting civil goods like life, liberty, physical integrity, freedom from pain, external possessions (including money) and the necessities of life. The ruler is solely responsible for civil goods, and the care of souls cannot belong to him. Locke states that neither persons, nor churches, nor even commonwealths can have any right to attack another's civil goods or steal another's worldly assets on the pretext of religion. And the ruler, who plays the most important part in toleration, cannot use sanctions of civil law to enforce any ecclesiastical rites or ceremonies in the worship of God, nor can he prohibit any ritual performed by any church. Basically, Locke's "religious toleration" refers to the separation of church and state. Later in the nineteenth century, John Stuart Mill questioned the limits of the authority of society over the individual:

> Individuality has its proper field of action. In the conduct of human beings towards one another, it is necessary that general rules should for the most part be observed, in order that people may know what they have to expect; but in each person's own concerns, his individual spontaneity is entitled to free exercise.[7]

Certainly we have the right to act upon our unfavorable opinion of anyone but not where it amounts to the oppression of his individuality. Therefore, straying from Locke's "religious toleration," Mill determines the necessary conditions for the tolerable intervention of society on individuals. These are the harmful activities and the inconveniences which are inseparable from the unfavorable judgment of others.

Monk describes the practice of toleration as the voluntary acceptance of attitudes and/or actions, which are severely disapproved of since they are judged to be wrong, and which could be prevented or restrained if the dominant force chose to do so.[8] Similarly, Miller regards toleration as more of a negative toleration of indifference. A policy of toleration, he claims, involves leaving groups free to assert their identity and express their cultural values in private or through associations of their members. The state's role in this form of toleration is negative, since it neither forces minority groups to conform to the dominant culture, nor erects artificial barriers that make it harder for minority cultures to flourish. Adding to that, it does not shoulder a positive responsibility to protect minority cultures.[9] Walzer, though, broadens its content and lists various forms of tolerance. In his view, standing up for those whom you think have fallacies, solely for the sake of peace, can be a form of toleration. Moreover, disregarding the Others or accepting firmly that they also have rights might in effect be different levels of toleration. We can also be curious or even enthusiastic about the Others. Does that imply tolerance? Walzer queries this last point and wonders if it is possible to be tolerant toward someone about whom we feel supportive. The important point is that if you are tolerating someone then you think that (s)he is different than you because they have different values and beliefs, and you are inclined to stay away from her/him. However, if you want Others to live with you in a society or you are enthusiastic about them, this means that you are not tolerating but supporting them. After all, people do not tolerate the things or people they appreciate; they instead are happy to live with them. Loved ones are never the objects of toleration because they are not aliens who break into our comfort zone. For Walzer, whatever your motive to be tolerant, you are ultimately virtuous because you do not have to like and appreciate a certain Other but one way or another you cohabit. From the perspective of states, there will always be some groups who have peculiar characteristics that do not correspond to the general norms of the society.

The scope of tolerance might either be allowing the Other to enjoy her peculiar identity in public, or expecting her to keep it in her private life. So the public–private dichotomy is still prevalent. For Phillips, a prescription of mutual disinterest and indifference can only work in societies where power is relatively evenly distributed. By that, she means an understanding where an attitude of "you leave me alone to do what you disapprove of and I will leave you alone in turn" is adopted. However, for her, toleration is often called on to regulate a relationship between minority and majority groups where this kind of mutuality is rare. Quoting her example, those who happily tolerate their unassuming gay neighbor may still object violently to the high-profile activist who "flaunts" his sexuality in public. She calls this type of toleration "hands-off" toleration, which confines diversity to the private sphere and assimilates a plurality of ethnic groups into a unified citizenship.[10] This form of tolerance is negative tolerance, since the majority is either totally indifferent to minority culture or consciously confines it to the private sphere. Similarly, but in a stricter sense, Brown defines tolerance as a power relationship. For her, tolerance usually comes into existence when there is an asymmetry of power. According to Brown, almost all objects of tolerance are marked as deviant, marginal or undesirable – something one would prefer did not exist – by virtue of being tolerated, and this creates a hierarchical relationship based on subordination of the tolerated.[11]

To put it another way, if X is tolerating Y:

a. There is a power relationship between the two.
b. X is more powerful than Y.
c. X is tolerating; Y is tolerated.
d. X is issuing power on Y.
e. X is the norm holder; Y is the deviant.

Like Phillips, Brown criticizes the individualizing aspect of tolerance in liberalism that maintains a separation between politics and culture and permits individuals only private enjoyment of their identities. For this reason, she rightly sees tolerance as a middle road between rejection and assimilation.

What has to be done then? What would be other mechanisms to provide peaceful living together without one dominating the other? Brown can expand our horizons on this point. She neither positions herself against tolerance, nor does she support intolerance. She is basically against the liberal notion that sees tolerance as a virtue:

The pronouncement of "I am tolerant man" conjures seemliness, propriety, forbearance, magnanimity, cosmopolitanism, universality and the large view, while for those for whom tolerance is required to take their shape as improper, indecorous, urgent, narrow, particular, and often ungenerous or at least lacking in perspective [...] [T]he tolerating and tolerated are simultaneously radically distinguished from each other and hierarchically ordered according to a table of virtue.[12]

To put it more simply, she does not see tolerance as useless, and accepts that it ended some violence in human history. Instead, she calls on us to remove the scales from our eyes regarding the innocence of tolerance in relation to power, and warns that tolerance is more a historically protean element of liberal governance than a virtue. Her solution is to deploy alternative political speech and practices. Phillips' solution, on the other hand, is to use the difference to enter into politics a dynamic process of deliberation, contestation and change. Walzer, though not critical of the nature of tolerance as a virtue, seeks a value beyond tolerance, such as mutual respect. For him, the better solution would be to encourage individuals to participate in a deliberative process by joining groups, because individuals are the products of community life and they cannot reproduce by themselves without the relations that make their power realizable. Thus, he advocates a positive form of tolerance which allows individuals to enter a deliberative process as members of groups and permits their culture to flourish.

For Brown, present-day liberal political culture and legal doctrine situate culture as its Other, antagonistic to its principles unless it is subordinated or liberalized. This is a valuable criticism, but we cannot simply trash tolerance discourse because it reifies identities or invents new ones. Some scholars suggest evaluating tolerance in accordance with the motive behind it. Monk, who discusses the issue from a moral will perspective, argues that a crucial feature of toleration is that we can only name acts as tolerant in terms of the motive from which they were performed:

> We can only correctly even identify cases of tolerance if we know that an individual or authority failed to interfere with a disapproved of action not because he/she/it judged themselves incapable of affecting it, but because they regarded it as right and proper to so refrain.[13]

However, for Monk, detecting the motivation behind indifference to some minority behavior helps only to identify toleration, not appraise it. So he encourages us to think about the morality behind tolerance in order to identify and evaluate it. In a similar vein, King explores what it really means to be tolerant, and concludes that one can only be accepted as tolerant if she/he chooses to be tolerant in disregard of any benefit, fear, incapability or other type of motive. It is tolerance when one has the power or is not stopped by any other motive from persecuting but in fact chooses not to do so. If one is prevented from persecuting by some motive like religion, fear, incapability or interest, then she/he is not being tolerant but acquiescing or exercising expediency. So, tolerance means objection and acceptance but only where the acceptor is free to reject it.[14]

Without a doubt tolerance is better than intolerance and we need it to cope with the troublesome outcomes of intolerance. Tolerance is not a virtue in itself, but it may be a necessity or a strategy. I contend that tolerance is interwoven with expediency so it cannot be regarded as a virtue. Even if we do not have a reason to be tolerant, we have the tendency to act with tolerance to minimize any sort of conflict. This is expedient behavior, too. So I argue that the most important reason to behave tolerantly is expediency.

Correctly for some, toleration is needed because the alternative to toleration is war; war is too costly – in all sorts of ways – as a method for negotiating disputes and disagreements. Correspondingly, toleration is a practical strategy to be adopted by reasonable people who realize that the attempt to convert all others to their cause can never be successful.[15] Such rationality behind tolerance basically refers to the principle of prudence. And for some, it is also the reason why tolerance should be seen as a virtue.

Can tolerance be accommodated?

The whole discussion above takes tolerance as a relationship between the tolerating power holders and the tolerated minority members. Carter, however, questions if toleration is always a power relationship and if respect and toleration are compatible. He first states that the toleration discourse is mostly disliked by minorities since it implies inferiority. So, he prefers to talk about respect rather than toleration. Respect, for him, means assigning persons a set of rights through which to exercise their political agency. And where the relationship of two mutually powerful groups is concerned, it is more a matter of recognition and acting mindful of the Other's equal rights for the public good. Carter differentiates between two forms of respect: the recognition respect and the appraisal respect. The former requires treating people as opaque, whereas the latter requires a positive evaluation. He explains it further with an example:

> We might show respect for a judge in virtue of her status by recognizing her legal authority and avoiding any kind of behavior that would amount to contempt of court. We might at the same time think her a very bad judge, and in this alternative sense have 'little or no respect' for her as a judge. These two attitudes are compatible, for the first is one of recognition respect while the second is one of appraisal disrespect.[16]

For him, toleration might be – if not always – compatible with recognition respect but not with appraisal respect since the latter implies affirmation and support rather than any sort of objection or power-based relationship. So what he implies is that toleration always requires a power condition and for this very reason, when two equally powerful groups are concerned, their relation would not be toleration but respect.

Arendt described respect as

> a kind of "friendship" without intimacy and without closeness; it is a regard for the person from the distance which the space of the world puts between us, and this regard is independent of the qualities which we may admire or of the achievements which we may highly esteem.[17]

To the extent that we depersonalize public and social life, we lose respect. Her opinion takes us back to the distinction between public and private space. If we follow Arendt, people should be represented in the public space with their values, beliefs, differences, that is, by the Self; they should not be enclosed in their private space. Only under these conditions can we exchange tolerance for respect. In a system of inequality respect is unachievable. Sennett avers that the inequalities of class and race obviously make it difficult for people to treat one another with respect. His definition of respect is different from Arendt's: it is rather expressive, where treating others with respect does not just happen, even with the best will in the world; to convey respect means finding the words and gestures which make it genuine and convincing. He rightly wonders how, in a world of inequality, where people feel themselves in a disadvantaged position in terms of their class, race, ethnicity, sexual orientation and so on, or to put it differently, when they struggle with a loss of confidence, can people be aware of others?[18]

Since other formulations still remain weak, it seems that we cannot simply ignore "tolerance" in the modern era. What should be done is to change the perceptions about tolerance and re-design the term justice. In this regard, I agree with Tyler's position:

> A peaceable global society – coexistence – renders necessary a cross-cultural, interreligious conceptualization of tolerance. An understanding of tolerance must be developed (or restored!) that is not divorced from the comprehensive doctrines out of which moral clarity and societal consensus must ultimately find succor. Common, overlapping foundations are imperative, but they must first be found within the ultimate concerns of the individual and his community – not simply under the moral shadow of political liberalism.[19]

In other words, we can deliberate on the motivations and principles of tolerance (and respect as an ultimate outcome) as human beings who have the capacity to act freely in the public sphere to create fairer, more attainable conditions both for groups and for individuals without being deprived of Self in the public realm and without domination of one group over another.

Contemporary diversity issues are complicated because today individuals are in search of new possible identities for themselves, and identity attachments are much more fluid and numerous compared to previous times when people's horizons were limited by their motherland, occupation and religion. Additionally, today's immigration patterns are very diverse and unsystematic. Despite the incomparable difference between past and present, all these contemporary debates provide an insight into the concerned historical context. These normative discussions will prevent me from arbitrarily employing terms like tolerance and multiculturalism; they will also prevent me from an anachronistic attitude of judging the past with present ideals, and imitating the past for present minority issues. Lastly, these discussions are relevant to refute the Pax-Ottomana perspective within which Ottoman plurality is offered to address the contemporary minority demands.

Ottoman tolerance and the *millet* system myth

In the Turkish context, multiculturalism debates are blended with romanticism toward Ottoman plurality and the pundits of multiculturalism started to demonstrate the Ottoman way of handling diversity as the pre-modern model of multiculturalism. One of the problems with this Pax-Ottomana nostalgia is not that Ottomans were intolerant of diversity; they, in fact, were tolerant. The problem is that the Pax-Ottomana equates Ottoman tolerance with "peaceful living together," which is totally erroneous. Another problem to be addressed is the unquestioned belief in the so-called *millet* system, labeling it as an Eastern multiculturalism mostly in reference to Western scholarship, including Thornberry, who described the *millet* system as a beneficial autochthonous system, not imposed by treaty, in comparison with the Christian world where the treatment of religious (and later national) minorities was set out by treaties.[20] Last, although viewed mostly as a liberal virtue in contemporary studies, tolerance is not a virtue but a power relationship. Therefore, when we are concerned with Ottoman tolerance, we have to consider this and temper our perspective of the Ottoman way of managing diversity. To put it differently, we cannot simply conclude that tolerance is a positive, humanistic phenomenon and define it within the context of "peaceful living together."

Without a doubt the concept of tolerance is not a contemporary phenomenon. Walzer differentiated between five different regimes of toleration, one of which is multinational empires. In this regime, as long as they received their taxes and there was peace, the state administrators would not interfere in the internal affairs of the communities. They also would not care about how the members of communities treated one another. The individuals, on the other hand, were confined to their communities, to a particular ethnic or religious identity. Thus, given the fact that the administrators and the group leaders were often cruel to heretics who broke the rules of the group that they were a part of, we can only talk about group autonomy rather than individual autonomy. Walzer gave the Ottoman *millet* system as an example of this regime. In the *millet* system, the Greek Orthodox, Armenian and Jewish religious communities were permitted to establish group autonomy to regulate the internal restrictions of their group and to control their members. In this system, everyone belonged to a religious community and individual liberty was unknown.[21] Kymlicka also touches upon the *millet* system and defines it as a federation of theocracies in which Muslims did not try to suppress the non-Muslims and granted them a substantial measure of self-government. He also points out that heretics were always punished and apostasy was banned; in this way, he emphasizes the lack of individual liberty and the *millet* system's insufficiency for the modern era.[22] Similarly, Tyler points out that despite the anachronistic misinterpretations of Ottoman intercommunal co-existence as equality, tolerance of individual liberties within and across the various *millets* remained historically unwarranted and theoretically inconceivable.[23] Parekh also notes the subordinate status of minority communities in pre-modern societies, including the Ottoman Empire and minorities' extensive cultural but few political rights.[24] Walzer, Kymlicka, Tyler and Parekh are all political philosophers who have an understandably shallow knowledge of Ottoman history. Hence, their views have to be clarified through an in-depth analysis. First, there was no *millet* system!

Where the Ottoman treatment of non-Muslim communities is concerned, it is inevitable to talk about the Kur'anic texts and the Sunna of the Prophet Muhammad. The Prophet's attitude toward Jewish groups in Medina and in other parts of Arabia after the expansion of his authority across Arabia, "his edict to all Christians" and then "to all mankind," and the so-called "Covenant of Umar," the first formal, institutional arrangement of tolerance between Muslims and the "People of the Book," were recognized as the basis for the treatment of non-Muslims.[25] The articles of the Covenant, which limited non-Muslim behaviors from restrictions on clothing to church repair, from respect toward Muslims to a prohibition on carrying arms,[26] demonstrate the negative tolerance wielded by the Muslims and the acknowledgment and obedience of them by the Christians of Syria. Additionally, the essential Kur'anic text IX, 24: "Fight those who do not believe [...] until they pay the *djizya* [...]" implies that if they are paying the *djizya* tax (cizye), there is no reason to fight the non-Muslims. This was the case in the Ottoman Empire as well; as long as they received their taxes, they remained indifferent to the internal affairs of the non-Muslims. However, not every community enjoyed this regime of tolerance. In Islam, only the *dhimmis* (zımmi) are granted the right to receive hospitality from Islamic society and, of course, the flexibility of these rules was dependent upon changing local circumstances and popular attitudes.

> The *dhimmi* is defined as against the Muslim and the idolater (with reference to Arabia, but this is scarcely more than a memory); also as against the *harbi* who is of the same faith but lives in territories not yet under Islam; and finally as against the *musta'min*, the foreigner who is granted the right of living in an Islamic territory for a short time (one year at most). Originally only the Jews and Christians were involved; soon, however, it became necessary to consider the Zoroastrians, and later, especially in Central Asia, other minorities not mentioned in the Kur'an.[27]

30 Ottoman tolerance reconsidered

In the case of the Ottomans, the Greek Orthodox people, the Armenians and the Jews were recognized as *Ahl al-kitab* (i.e., People of the Book) and were considered to be *dhimmi*s; on the other hand, the *zındık*s (i.e., heretics, Ar. zindiq) were not beneficiaries of tolerance in Islamic law. According to the *Encyclopedia of Islam* published by the Directorate of Religious Affairs in Turkey, *zındık* would originally mean Manichean but in time it was also used for atheists and those who did not believe in a judgment day – the hypocrites (münafık) and those who behaved irresponsibly in religious matters; likewise, for the *Encyclopedia of Islam*, the Abbasid caliphs, who were intolerant of religious diversity, carried out a systematic purge of individuals suspected of *zandaqa* (abstract/collective noun for the *zındık* behavior) and their repression was directed against Manichean tendencies in Islam and, more generally, against nominal Muslims suspected of holding Persianizing, dualistic, syncretistic, subversive, free-thinking and atheistic ideas.[28] The people who renounced Islam were not considered *zındık* but instead *mürted* (i.e., apostate, Ar. murtadd) and they were executed. All in all, both heretics and apostates were regarded as Islam's dissidents and subject to intolerance.

The *dhimmis*, traditionally, were given autonomy of their internal law, and, if they wished, they were able to apply to a Muslim judge. However, they could not marry a Muslim woman, even though the reverse was possible; they could not own a Muslim slave, although the converse was possible; they were distinguished in dress; they paid additional taxes like *kharadj* (haraç) and djizya (cizye); they were also forbidden from constructing new buildings or to possess ones higher than those of Muslims; and they were excluded from government offices. However, all these regulations had never been respected for any length of time in Islamic states and the Ottoman Empire was no exception.

The Ottomans followed Islamic tradition in their treatment of non-Muslims. In addition to this, they introduced an independent body of practical rules and regulations based on a ruler's judgment, and these were not always in line with the *shari'a*. In the halls of academe, the Ottoman regime was regarded as unique, and the *millet* system myth was created and adopted by early Ottomanists, including Halil İnalcık, who in his 1991 work argued that the *millet* system was part of the Ottoman state system from the beginning. Like İnalcık, Stanford Shaw back in 1976 affirmed that the Ottomans added few details to the system and institutionalized it by making it part of the structure of the state as well as society. Similarly, Bernard Lewis argued that there were organized and legally recognized religious communities in the Ottoman Empire. The *millet* system myth originates from the contention of the Greeks, the Jews and the Armenians that Mehmed II had close relations with their respective community heads.[29] In the Greek case, the *millet* myth was based on a lost *berat* (charter) given to Gennadius by Mehmed II in 1453 after the conquest of Constantinople, wherein extensive privileges were believed to be devoted to the Patriarch and the Greek Orthodox Community.[30] The charter is lost; all we know is that Mehmed the Conqueror, in appointing Gennadius to the Patriarchate, made it clear that he would have no less power and authority than that enjoyed under the Byzantine Emperors.[31] No charter survives for the Armenian Patriarchate, either. According to eighteenth-century historian Mikayel Camcean (1738–1823), after Mehmed II conquered Constantinople, he brought Bishop Yovakim from Bursa with a number of eminent Armenian families and made the Prelate the patriarch; however, Camcean did not identify his sources and this information remained unsupported. For Bardakjian, during the reign of Mehmed II, there were at least four bishops under Ottoman rule with uncertain jurisdiction, and this strongly suggests that the Ottomans recognized the Armenian communities separately. For him, there is some evidence to show that the transformation of the seat of Constantinople from a vicariate into a universal Patriarchate was an evolutionary process rather than a conscious or explicit Ottoman policy.[32] A similar story applies to the Jews as well. When Constantinople was captured by the Ottomans, Rabbi Moses Capsali, the head of the Jewish community under the Byzantines, emerged as the political and spiritual head of the community but the scope of his jurisdiction at the time is unknown[33] and there was no Jewish institutional entity.

According to İnalcık, the reason why the Ottomans maintained the churches, including the Armenian and Jewish religious structures, originated from the peculiar social system of previous Islamic empires, in which the authority of the state was often directed to the individual. In medieval empires, individuals were not citizens in the modern sense of the term, and they were perceived as members of a community. The charter given to the heads of these communities would grant them a sort of autonomy to look after their communal affairs, but it was not a total autonomy and the heads of the *millet*s were not regarded as state officials by the Ottomans.[34]

An examination of Greek Orthodox "ecclesiastical" documents shows that it was not until the end of the seventeenth century that the term *millet* was used to refer to non-Muslim religious communities, and it came into common use only from the beginning of the nineteenth century. During the first period of Ottoman rule, the word *ta'ife* (pl. teva'if, in Greek sources taifas) was used to refer to non-Muslim communities. In respect of the Greek Orthodox, throughout the first three centuries of the Empire, in ecclesiastical *berat*s or firmans, the Greek Orthodox Patriarch was never called as *ethnarches* or *milletbaşı*.[35] It was as late as the eighteenth century that the term "Patriarch of the *Romioi*" (Romans) was first used, and it coincides with the concession of increased power to the Patriarchate as well as to the leaderships of other religious communities.[36] Orthodox Christians and other non-Muslim communities never possessed legal corporate status and the establishment of *millet*s was a latter-day phenomenon in the Ottoman Empire and even that did not change their legal status. For the Greek Orthodox communes, the later day regulations regarding recognition of legal corporate status seemed to tie their hands more than it allowed them certain rights in relation to their legal identity such as property ownership.[37]

For Braude, it was with the reforming decrees of Mahmud II and Abdülmecid in the nineteenth century that the European understanding of "*millet*" was applied to

Figure 1.1 A depiction showing Mehmed II presenting his "lost" *berat* to Patriarch Gennadius II. The Greek Orthodox Patriarchate, Istanbul.
Photograph: Gülen Göktürk

Ottoman legal documents.[38] For example, the rank of *Hahambaşı* was created with an imperial decree in 1835, showing that it wasn't until then that the Ottomans recognized the Jews as a unified whole.[39] So, the historians pursuing a *millet* system view are very much mistaken on two counts. First, *millet* as a term was commonly employed only in the nineteenth century and, second, no legal corporate status was ever granted either to the communities themselves or to the heads of the communities throughout Ottoman history, including the nineteenth century. For instance, when we look at the communal structure of the Greek Orthodox *millet*, what we observe is a very loose structure changing from one place to another.[40] Ozil claims that from the perspective of the Ottoman authorities, there were Greek leaders, Christian metropolitans and the people themselves, but never institutions. In a similar vein, the Jewish community was not institutional and was rarely hierarchical; the congregational organizations were jealously opposed to any superstructure of authority; and the Ottomans felt little institutional need for a Jewish community head.[41] They were only concerned with whether the communities effectively administered themselves, relieving the Ottoman administration from that task, as well as in the taxes they received.

In the eighteenth and nineteenth centuries, intense political struggles to strengthen their hegemony over the masses led by the Greek Orthodox and Armenian Apostolic elites in Istanbul ended in a definitive establishment of the *millet*s acknowledged by the Sultan's writ during the *Tanzimat* era (1839–1876). However, in the final analysis, this, rather than creating a peaceful atmosphere, instead centralized the administration of the non-Muslims into one single authority, the patriarch, and paved the way for nationalism.[42] Augustinos agreed with this argument in consideration of Greek nationalism in the nineteenth century. He claimed that the Ottoman reforms legitimizing the *millet*s solidified the ethnic character of the different churches with the other developments including the new economic opportunities created by the imperial European powers, increasing missionary activities and the establishment of the Greek Kingdom.[43] Interestingly enough, contrary to the assumptions of the scholars following the *millet* system myth, when the *millet*s were officially recognized in the nineteenth century, the cohabitation practices began to dissolve since the churches started to adopt a national character and the pace of nationalism intensified.

The arguments I have illustrated above were not meant to claim that there was no Ottoman tolerance. In fact, there was Ottoman tolerance, giving certain autonomy to recognized ethno-religious communities, but it was not a well-structured system, but rather a loose composition based on Islamic doctrine and Sultanic *firmans*, and for the authorities it helped collect taxes and prevent conflicts. This was religious tolerance, but not in the Lockean sense, since the state was highly involved in religious matters. The basis of tolerance was religion and the Ottomans ruled the country with Islamic law. They never allowed heretics of any religion; apostasy was prohibited and conversion to any religion other than Islam was not permitted. Therefore, there was no separation between state and religion. The Ottomans were at the same time intolerant with persecution, imprisonment, banishment, exile, corporal punishment, boycott, prohibition and exclusion practiced against its minorities, including non-Muslims and heretics. The level and degree of (in)tolerance changed from time to time depending on the conditions of time and space. Therefore, Ottoman tolerance was based on political pragmatism rather than a well-structured system.[44]

The reason for crediting Ottoman tolerance stems from its comparison with its predecessors like the Roman Empire and the Byzantine Empire and its contemporaries like the Spanish Empire, the Habsburgs and the Russians. The

Roman Empire persecuted the Christians; the Byzantines tried to convert Jews and Muslims; the Spanish Empire expelled the Jews; and in the Habsburg Empire there was a policy of "confessional absolutism." Among all these examples, the Russian Empire most resembled the Ottomans in handling diversity with its state pragmatism, flexibility and tolerance. Despite the existence of episodes of forced conversion, assimilation and persecution, it also granted protection and privileges to some groups like the Muslims, especially during the reign of Catherine the Great.[45] We can also add to this list the persecutions during the Reformation of Europe. Barkey rightly points out that empires did not have direct goals of tolerance and persecution. Rather, they tried to preserve their dominions, conquer and maintain their power. The relatively good position of the *dhimmis* in the Ottoman Empire compared to the position of religious minorities in its contemporaries was an outcome of pragmatic policy (based on Islamic law and principles) and expediency to receive consent, minimize conflict, collect taxes and preserve the continuity of domination.

So, what was the limit of Ottoman tolerance for non-Muslims? As we have seen, in Islamic societies, there were things that non-Muslims were not permitted to do: *dhimmis* were not allowed to wear clothes in certain colors and fabrics; they could not ride a horse, carry weapons or own Muslim slaves; their buildings could not be higher than those of Muslims; they were prevented from living close to a mosque; and there were even restrictions if they wanted to construct, or even restore, buildings or temples. Additionally, before the court, non-Muslims were treated like second class subjects. As an example, a Muslim would be sentenced to less punishment if he killed a non-Muslim than those who killed a Muslim. A non-Muslim was not accepted as a witness in Muslim cases. And the language of the laws, *fetwas* (ruling by Ottoman judges) and legal records was humiliating for non-Muslims. Humiliation in terminology includes that the non-Muslim women were not addressed with the title of respect *hatun* added after the name, and that the dead body of a non-Muslim would be called *leş* (carrion) which had a pejorative meaning.[46] In another example, the language used in the rulings of Ebu Suud Efendi (1490–1574), *Şeyhülislam* (the chief religious official) of the Empire, reinforced the public opinion that the second class *dhimmi* communities should be separated from the Muslim community. He also preferred to use the term *kafir* (unbeliever) to label non-Muslims, rather than the valued natural term, *dhimmi*.[47]

As for the clothing prohibitions, they were to differentiate Muslims from non-Muslims, as well as to demonstrate the different social status of the peoples. Certainly, the regulations concerning non-Muslims were intended to show their inferior position in society. For example, from the beginning of the seventeenth century, Jews were required to wear purple and dark blue. Sometimes they were also restricted from wearing expensive jewelry and gorgeous clothes. There were also restrictions concerning the shape and length of their turbans and caftans.[48] The clothing regulations provided a sort of social discipline and segregation for the different religious communities, emanating from Mahmud II's clothing regulations that replaced occupational signs of differentiation with a homogenizing status marker, the fez;[49] these restrictions disappeared during the *Tanzimat* era but differences in clothing continued, especially in port cities among the upper-class people since non-Muslims more readily adopted European dress.[50]

In the Ottoman Empire different religious communities mostly lived in separated neighborhoods. (Certainly, there were exceptions. As we will see in the upcoming chapter, in Cappadocia, there were also mixed villages.) For example, in Istanbul, the non-Muslim communities were mostly pushed toward the fringes and periphery of the city – Greeks along the Golden Horn and Marmara shores, Armenians in Yenikapı, Samatya and Topkapı and Jews on both sides of the Golden Horn but more specifically in the facing quarters of Balat and Hasköy. The sole exceptions to this ethno-religious segregation were the districts with a financial and economic function.[51] In Izmir, different religious communities lived in homogeneous ghettos built around mosques, churches and synagogues.[52] In this way, potential frictions that might result from excessive contact and intermingling were avoided. The constitution of physical ghettos provided non-Muslims with a relative freedom in the management of their internal affairs and an indirect assignment of collective responsibility and the Ottoman administrators were reluctant – and very often, unable – to impose any unifying concept of identity different from the vague notion of being a tax-paying subject of the Empire. The Ottoman state was attempting to preserve and strengthen all other forms of identity and solidarity, thus creating an illusion of freedom and autonomy for the *dhimmis*. Ultimately, what was nostalgically perceived as pluralism or even cosmopolitanism, today is in fact a diversity that could not possibly develop into any real integrative process.[53] Interestingly, the relations of minority religious communities were not very easy. For example, Greeks and Jews did not get along well due to economic rivalry and blood libel accusations against the Jews.[54] Additionally, conversion from one religion to another was prohibited until the *Tanzimat* period (1839–1876). A Christian or a Jew could only become Muslim. A Christian could not convert to Judaism, nor was the inverse possible. I think spatial segregation, impervious concrete boundaries and rivalries between religious communities played a prominent role in the nationalization that occurred later in the nineteenth and early twentieth centuries.

All the restrictions set for non-Muslims intended to differentiate them from the rest of society, providing group solidarity and preventing integration. The restrictions were not always very strict; there were certainly exceptions. For example, Jewish doctors of the palace were permitted to ride horses and wear kalpak. And there were times when the Ottomans behaved more or less tolerantly to their non-Muslim subjects. For Ben-Naeh, to receive the support of the Muslim public and the religious authorities, and to mediate their inconvenience in crisis times, the Ottomans behaved more strictly and less tolerantly to non-Muslims.[55] The religious authorities also influenced the administrative authorities to restrict *dhimmi* behavior. For example, a group of zealot Sunni preachers called *Kadızadelis* (1630–1680), who were against any non-Muslim groups and

Sufi orders, put the Sultans under pressure. Hence, Ottoman history was not totally free of persecution and intolerance, and all the above-mentioned diversities and exceptions directed at the *dhimmis* were related to Ottoman political pragmatism in addition to Islamic principles. The *dhimmis* were tolerated as long as they did not disturb or go against Islamic order as secondary subjects.[56] We should also note that during the formation years of the Empire tolerance was deemed necessary to legitimize their domination in the eyes of their mostly non-Muslim subjects. As Campos rightly observes:

> The Ottoman state throughout much of its existence looked upon ethnic and religious diversity among its subject population and state officials in an altogether pragmatic fashion; it did not care about their "identity" per se [...] This political pragmatism, to a certain extent, was born of demographic realities. For the first centuries of its existence, the Ottoman Empire had a majority non-Muslim population, and the dynasty was careful not forge favorable alliances with adjoining Christian principalities.[57]

In addition to early demographic concerns, this policy later brought other benefits. First of all, the state maintained a sort of inter-communal order; it accommodated religious diversities, and in a way pursued its interests legitimately in the eyes of its subjects. Community leaders settled agreements with the Ottoman authorities because they wanted to preserve their community's existence and religious autonomy.[58] In this way, religious communities maintained their distinctiveness and control in their competitive relations with the Other, be it other minority religious communities or the dominant majority of the Muslims. Thus, the results were multiple, and such political pragmatism – or, as I call it, negative tolerance – bore fruit in the form of "minimum conflict" until the age of nationalism. In this system of dealing with a minority, one with whom you could not eat, marry or enter into political or military alliance, both parties could concentrate on a rational cost-benefit analysis of the actual specific deal in question, and expect, on the whole, to get what had been bargained for.[59] What was exercised in this transaction by the hegemonic power was tolerance; for the minorities, however, it was simply consent.

King called the Ottoman version of handling diversity expedience rather than tolerance, since it pursued such policies for two reasons: Islamic law and tradition and the benefits it received from this order. As I mentioned previously, in his theory, if something restricts one and forces her/him not to act or not to persecute, then that is not tolerance but expediency. Were the Ottomans expedients, rather than tolerators? My answer would be that they were expedient tolerators; because there were also times when they persecuted people. This means that their motive was pragmatism in line with the circumstances of that time. While crediting King's differentiation between tolerance and expediency, I find it problematic on two points: first, I think that expedient behavior is also tolerant behavior; second, if we follow his approach, we would inevitably accept that tolerance is a virtue, since in his theorization one can only be seen as tolerant where the disliked person is borne irrespective of any interests, moral codes, fear and so on.

Although there were times when the Ottoman Sultans were zealous enough to pressurize groups of people to convert (like the curious case of Rabbi Shabbatai Tzevi and his followers in 1665),[60] there was no strategy of forced conversion and there was a solid economic reason behind this policy; the "head tax" (cizye) was one of the major sources for the treasury.[61] This also meant a lack of religious persecution and homogenization, but there was a limit to such religious tolerance; the apostates and the heretics, including believers of some forms of Sufi, heterodox order (zındık), unbelievers (kafir) and those who were critical of the doctrine of Islam and the Prophet (mülhid), were never tolerated. Only during the period of Tanzimat (1839–1876) were the Ottoman authorities relatively indifferent to cases of apostasy and capital punishment rarely employed. However, they were unwilling to officially demonstrate their indifference – or let's say tolerance – to apostasy.[62] As for the heretics, most were adherents of mystical orders (tarikat) and were persecuted despite the fact that some of these orders, like the Mevlevis, Bektaşis and the Nakşibendis, served as the architects of the rise of the Ottomans. The reason was that heterodox orders did not fit in with any organizational pattern of the Empire; although their ideology and doctrines were familiar to the Sultans and even adopted by some of them, the continued fluidity of movement, the covert activities and alternative assemblies and ceremonies were seen as threats since they remained outside the purview and organization of the state.[63]

There are four points to differentiate between the Ottoman practice of tolerance and contemporary debates about tolerance: a) the Ottoman Empire was pre-modern and not democratic; inequality was the norm and nobody questioned it; b) justice was a means to preserve the domination of the ruler over his subjects; whereas in modern liberal societies it is the objective to be reached through promotion of freedom and equality; c) in the Ottoman world, the only acceptable diversity was religious diversity, and with the exception of the heretics of any religion, people were confined to their religious communities and prevented from disrupting them with any sort of individual opposition as there was no individual freedom or authority; in modern societies, diversity is varied, much more complicated and multi-faceted, and people demand both group-specific rights and individual freedom; d) in the Ottoman context we can only discuss the scope of tolerance in its historical setting; any debate about respect or recognition cannot possibly be made whereas in our modern societies we can discuss ways and motives to be tolerant but we can also be concerned with replacing tolerance with respect and recognition. In consideration of these differences, one could feel tempted to ask why modern normative theories of justice and tolerance are being discussed here. First of all, without a thorough understanding of these discussions I would not be able to assert that Ottoman plurality and plurality in modern liberal democratic societies are incompatible with one another. Second, they provide a thorough knowledge about the term tolerance. Considering the fact that many studies and scholars randomly employ the term with a lay point of view, attributing virtue to it, in the absence of an analysis of modern debates I would fall into expressing the same attitude. Third, after examining modern concerns, I showed that Ottoman tolerance cannot be a remedy to our modern diversity concerns in Turkey. It is historical and should be evaluated in line with the conditions of its time. Therefore, I showed that the modern debates *de facto* refute the Ottoman romanticism that prevails nowadays.

Notes

1 For a discussion about how memory and nostalgia generate new market opportunities, see E. Özyürek, *The Politics of Public Memory in Turkey*; and A. S. Alpan, But the Memory Remains: History, Memory and the 1923 Greco-Turkish Population Exchange.
2 Amy Gutmann differentiates between four different types of identity groups: cultural groups, voluntary associations, ascriptive groups and religious groups. These are neither good nor bad in and of themselves, and they should be evaluated in accordance with their affirmation of democracy and justice. See A. Gutmann, *Identity in Democracy*.
3 For studies that discuss and appreciate the so called "*millet* system", see J. A. Sigler, *Minority Rights: A Comparative Analysis*; V. V. Dyke, *Human Rights, Ethnicity, and Discrimination*; P. Thornberry, *International Law and the Rights of Minorities*. For two studies that critically discuss Ottoman tolerance see W. Kymlicka, Two Models of Pluralism and Tolerance; M. Walzer, *On Toleration*.
4 There is confusion about either employing "tolerance" or "toleration". For Walzer, "tolerance" is an attitude or virtue; on the other hand "toleration" is a practice. In a similar way, Tyler states that "toleration" is principally a sociopolitical sanction or concession by which the majority/strong "tolerate" the weak/minority, whereas "tolerance" is an attitude and it has no relation to the power holders. For Tyler, "toleration" and "tolerance" can be employed as strategies by individuals, communities, or regimes but "toleration" is more restrictive than "tolerance" because of its limited application. Cohen, on the other hand, after conducting a detailed debate on the semantics of these two words, portrays the ambiguity of "tolerance" and "toleration" and claims that we do better if we reserve "toleration" for the activity, using endurance and "tolerance" for the attitude (or virtue). See M. Walzer, *On Toleration*, p. xi; A.Tyler, *Islam, the West, and Tolerance: Conceiving Co-existence*, p. 6; A. J. Cohen, What toleration is, pp. 68–95, pp. 76–77. My argument at this point is that anyone can exercise "tolerance" because it is a behavior, but not everyone is capable of "toleration" since it is an action or sanction. Since I am referring to both government policies of tolerating minorities and behavior of tolerating the Other in relation to co-existence, I use the term "tolerance" unless scholars I have quoted here use "toleration".
5 W. Brown, *Regulating Aversion: Tolerance in the Age of Identity and Empire*, p. 3.
6 I am particularly inspired by Michael Walzer in questions 2 and 6; and by Wendy Brown in questions 4 and 5.
7 J. S. Mill, *On Liberty*, p. 129.
8 I. H. Monk, Toleration and Moral Will, p. 18.
9 D. Miller, Group Identities, National Identities and Democratic Politics, p. 104.
10 A. Phillips, The Politisation of Difference: Does This Make for a More Intolerant Society? pp. 127–128.
11 W. Brown, *Regulating Aversion*, p. 14; p. 25.
12 W. Brown, *Regulating Aversion*, pp. 178–187.
13 I. H. Monk, Toleration and Moral Will, p. 24.
14 P. King, *Toleration*, pp. 22–23; p. 60.

15 C. McKinnon, *Toleration: a Critical Introduction*, p. 15.
16 I. Carter, Are Toleration and Respect Compatible? p. 198.
17 H. Arendt, *Human Condition*, p. 243.
18 R. Sennet, *Respect: The Formation of Character in an Age of Inequality*, p. 23; p. 47; p. 207.
19 A. Tyler, *Islam, the West and Tolerance: Conceiving Coexistence*, p. 82.
20 P. Thornberry, *International Law and the Rights of Minorities*, p. 29.
21 See M. Walzer, *On Toleration*.
22 W. Kymlicka, Two Models of Pluralism and Tolerance, p. 82.
23 A. Tyler, *Islam, the West and Tolerance: Conceiving Coexistence*, p. 123.
24 B. Parekh, *Rethinking Multiculturalism: Cultural Diversity and Political Theory*, p. 7.
25 See C. Cahen, Dhimma; C. E. Bosworth, the Concept of Dhimma in Early Islam; A. Tyler, *Islam, the West and Tolerance: Conceiving Coexistence*.
26 See P. Halsall, Pact of Umar, 7th Century: The Status of Non-Muslims under Muslim Rule.
27 C. Cahen, Dhimma, p. 227.
28 E. L. Daniel, Manicheanism, p. 429.
29 See H. İnalcık, The Status of the Greek Orthodox Patriarch under the Ottomans, p. 196; S. Shaw, *History of the Ottoman Empire and Modern Turkey: Empire of the Gazis: The Rise and Decline of the Ottoman Empire, 1280–1808* (Vol. I), p. 151; B. Lewis, *The Emergence of Modern Turkey*, p. 335; B. Braude, Foundation Myths of the Millet System, p. 75.
30 See H. İnalcık, The Status of the Greek Orthodox Patriarch under the Ottomans, p. 204.
31 Kritovulos, *İstanbul'un Fethi: Tarih-i Sultan Mehmet Han-ı Sani*, p. 82.
32 K. B. Bardakjian, The Rise of the Armenian Patriarchate of Constantinople, p. 89; p. 91; pp. 96–97.
33 A. M. Epstein, The Leadership of the Ottoman Jews in the Fifteenth and Sixteenth Centuries, p. 103.
34 H. İnalcık, The Status of the Greek Orthodox Patriarch under the Ottomans, p. 207.
35 P. Konortas, From Ta'ife to Millet, pp. 171–172.
36 D. Stamatopoulos, From *Millets* to Minorities in the nineteenth Century Ottoman Empire: An Ambiguous Modernization, p. 254.
37 See A. Ozil, *Orthodox Christians in the Late Ottoman Empire: A Study of Communal Relations in Anatolia*, Chapter 3.
38 B. Braude, Foundation Myths of the Millet System, p. 73.
39 D. Stamatopoulos, From *Millets* to Minorities in the nineteenth Century Ottoman Empire: An Ambiguous Modernization, pp. 258–259.
40 Ozil makes a detailed analysis of Greek Orthodox communities in Northwestern Asia Minor and shows that structures of the *koinotis* (or koinotita) differed greatly from one town to another in a variety of matters, including legal, financial, material, and administrative issues. In her study, Ozil also indicates that "commune" and "community" denoted different meanings for the Greek Orthodox people: commune consisted of community leaders rather than the whole society, and it was not an institution since it lacked legal status and changed from one settlement to another; community or *Rum millet* meant a loose belongingness for people of the same faith. See A. Ozil, *Orthodox Christians in the Late Ottoman Empire*.
41 B. Braude, Foundation Myths of the Millet System, p. 75.
42 B. Masters, *Christians and Jews in the Ottoman Arab World: the Roots of Sectarianism*, pp. 273–274.
43 G. Augustinos, *The Greeks of Asia Minor: Confession, Community, and Ethnicity in the Nineteenth Century*, pp. 188–190.
44 Ottoman tolerance can also be interpreted as governmentality in Foucaultian sense, since it is a technique or an art of the state to maintain order. According to one of

its definitions, governmentality is the mentality behind three forms of power which are "sovereignty-discipline-government". See M. Foucault, Governmentality; M. Dean, *Governmentality: Power and Rule in Modern Society.*
45 K. Barkey, *Empire of Difference: The Ottomans in Comparative Perspective*, pp. 111–112.
46 Y. Ben-Naeh, *Sultanlar Diyarında Yahudiler: 17. yüzyılda Osmanlı Yahudi Toplumu*, p. 105; pp. 108–109.
47 A. Tyler, *Islam, the West, and Tolerance: Conceiving Co-existence*, p. 121.
48 Y. Ben-Naeh, *Sultanlar Diyarında Yahudiler: 17. yüzyılda Osmanlı Yahudi Toplumu*, p. 112.
49 For Mahmud II's clothing regulations, see D. Quataert, Clothing Laws, State, Society in the Ottoman Empire 1770–1829.
50 R. Davison, The Millets as Agents of Change in the Nineteenth-century Ottoman Empire, pp. 321–322.
51 E. Eldem, Istanbul: from Imperial to Peripheralized Capital, p. 152.
52 D. Goffman, Izmir: from Village to Colonial Port City, p. 103.
53 E. Eldem, Istanbul: from Imperial to Peripheralized Capital, p. 154.
54 K. Barkey, *Empire of Difference: the Ottomans in Comparative Perspective*, p. 117.
55 Y. Ben-Naeh, *Sultanlar Diyarında Yahudiler: 17. yüzyılda Osmanlı Yahudi Toplumu*, p. 112; p. 118.
56 K. Barkey, *Empire of Difference: The Ottomans in Comparative Perspective*, p. 110; p. 113.
57 M. Campos, *Ottoman Brothers: Muslims, Christians, and Jews in Early Twentieth-Century Palestine*, p. 9.
58 K. Barkey, *Empire of Difference: The Ottomans in Comparative Perspective*, p. 114.
59 E. Gellner, *Nations and Nationalism*, p. 104.
60 For the cases of Sultans' zealotry, see M. D. Baer, *Honored by the Glory of Islam: Conversion and Conquest in Ottoman Europe.*
61 S. Deringil, *Conversion and Apostasy in the Late Ottoman Empire*, p. 17.
62 İ. Ortaylı, *Osmanlı'da Milletler ve Diplomasi*, p. 66.
63 K. Barkey, *Empire of Difference: The Ottomans in Comparative Perspective*, pp. 161–163.

2 Maintaining boundaries
Faith and co-existence in late Ottoman Cappadocia

In some circles, both in Turkey and Greece, there remains the romantic belief that throughout Ottoman history Muslims and non-Muslims lived peacefully within the "*millet* system" until the Great Powers intervened in the domestic affairs of the Ottoman Empire arousing the nationalistic sentiments of non-Muslims, leading to the promotion of national consciousness in collaboration with Western powers and eventually to the destabilization of the peaceful cohabitation of previous years.[1] I contend that for a scholar engaged in nationalism studies, one of the most crucial and debatable issues is how and under what circumstances nationalism coalesced and was adopted by the people. Over what conditions was nationalism placed, and did these conditions inadvertently provide the necessary infrastructure for it, one less visible or less meaningful during previous centuries? Prominent scholars of nationalism studies have been preoccupied with such questions for a very long time. For instance, Anderson wondered why the advent of nationalism seemed so attractive to humble people. Likewise, Hobsbawm inquired why and how the concept of "national patriotism" so remote from the real experience of most human beings, could so quickly become a political force of such magnitude.[2]

Asking questions similar to those I listed above, Anthony Smith tried to understand national identities and ideologies by analyzing them within the long-lasting perspective of group identities and attitudes. He named long-prevailing group identities *ethnie*. According to this perspective, "many nations and nationalisms spring up on the basis of pre-existing *ethnie* and their ethnocentrisms, but in order to forge a 'nation' today, it is vital to create and crystallize ethnic components."[3] Thus, a social identity that had no relation with nationalism for centuries could evolve into a national identity under specific conditions brought about by modernity. I partly agree with Smith in that previous relations offered a foundation for the nationalist ideal to settle, but I don't accept his conceptualization of *ethnie*, since common characteristics believed to be shared by a group people before the era of nationalism were mostly random, and humble rural populations had no way of seeing themselves as a part of a larger whole. Take languages as an example. As a component of *ethnie*, language exchange had many variations depending on geography and the flexibility of communal boundaries, in relation to Others in a locality. Further to that, the socio-economic, regional differences and diverse customs of people were highly dependent on their locality. Lastly, a community in one settlement had little to no information about communities in other regions who, in the age of nationalism, were claimed to be their kin. For instance, the *Pontiaka* (Greek dialect of Pontus region) speaking Greek Orthodox Community of Pontus had few similarities with the *Kritika* (Greek dialect of Crete) speaking Greek Orthodox population of Crete before the age of nationalism. They most likely – at least as a majority – were unaware that they could form a Community together. Previous boundaries certainly worked well for the articulation of a local community into a nation, but in the end this process favored not the similarities of distantly located kin groups, but the differences with the Other sharing the same locality. Therefore, I would rather adopt Tilly's approach, according to which relationships hold the master key to understanding social processes, as it was the intercommunal dynamics within a settlement that offered a suitable basis for the seeds of nationalism.[4]

In this chapter, I will discuss tolerance at a societal level and analyze the practices of living together. The theoretical concepts that shape my thinking here are the "antagonistic tolerance" of Robert Hayden, the "religious nationalism" of Peter Van der Veer, and the "proto-nationalism" of Eric Hobsbawm. Antagonistic tolerance prevails when there is competition between groups who share the same space, and "tolerance" is a pragmatic adaptation to a situation in which repression of the other group's practices may not be possible. For Hayden, this competition produces syncretism, which has commonly been seen as the proof of peaceful living together.[5] In a similar vein, "religious nationalism" refers to a type of nationalism in which pre-existing religious antagonisms determine the constituting Other of nationalism and members of different religious groups automatically become members of different nations. "Religious nationalism" was put forward by Peter Van der Veer following his studies on the co-existence of different religious groups in India. For him, nationalism in India has fed upon religious identifications since its beginnings in the nineteenth century, and the Hindu-Muslim, Hindu-Sikh and Hindu-Buddhist antagonisms directly affected nation-building.[6] Robert Hayden was influenced by Van der Veer's "religious nationalism" in developing his concept of "antagonistic tolerance," and William Hasluck's writings on religions and denominations under Ottoman rule contributed to his perspective. For competitive living together, where antagonistic tolerance triumphs, religiously separated groups define themselves and one another respectively as Self and Other. Such groups, while frequently intermingling, rarely inter-marry. For Hayden, "antagonistic tolerance" refers to "tolerance" in the passive sense of permitting the subordinated group to follow their religion and its practices (permitted co-existence), and only occurs when dominance is clear. The dominated groups, on the other hand, simply consent in order to protect their religion and keep their group intact.

In my case, I believe that competitive relations between different religious groups kept the group members together, preserved boundaries and provided the necessary infrastructure to proto-nationalism first and, later, to a nationalism that aimed to mobilize feelings of collective belonging. By proto-nationalism, I am referring to a pre-national feeling of collective belonging, a transitory phase toward nationalism, which is eminently possible in modern states and nations. For Hobsbawm, features like language and religion could be constituents of proto-nationalism, though the concept is vague and can easily be confused with Smith's *ethnie*. The main difference between the two is that proto-nationalism is not essential like the concept of *ethnie* that is that proto-national bonds are constructs, whereas the attributes that form *ethnie* are regarded as objective characteristics in Smith's understanding. It is extremely difficult to detect proto-national bonds because traditional, proto-national and national identities can exist at the same time within a community. In the case of the development of a national Greek identity in Cappadocia, for instance, there were nationalistic teachers who had already adopted a Greek identity during their education in Athens or elsewhere, there were proto-nationalist students who acquired a broader Community consciousness through education, along with traditional, mostly illiterate, people whose main constituents of identity were still religion and soil.

For proto-nationalism, Hobsbawm maintained that it is the consciousness of belonging or having belonged to a lasting political entity that is the strongest cement, and that the existence of proto-national bonds does not necessarily mean that the outcome will be nations or nationalities.[7] In applying Hobsbawm's theory here, I have concentrated on co-existence practices and means of maintaining communal borders for the religious groups in Orthodox settlements in Cappadocia. During the age of nationalism through schooling, these local communal bonds transformed into proto-national bonds. Later during the long war, these proto-national bonds started to transform into national bonds due to a complete rupture from the past. Tolerance was replaced with intolerance and nationalism served as a security blanket for people to bear their resentment.

As I claimed previously when discussing Smith's *ethnie*, it is the dichotomization of others as strangers rather than the similarities of a group that distinguishes a community. I tend to follow Barth's perspective about discrete/ethnic groups: "Ethnic groups are not merely based on the occupation of separate territories. They only persist as significant units if they imply an obvious difference in behavior."[8] Hence, for me, it is not the similarities that hold groups together but the specific difference(s) that separate the group from the Other. In our case, it was a religious difference that shaped the inter-communal relations and served later as a national bond. Put simply, it was not religion itself but structural opposition or competitive cohabitation based on a religious distinction that eased the embracement of nationalism in a time of discontinuity from the past, despite the existence of shared characteristics, even including language in some localities of Cappadocia.

Studying the co-existence practices of Muslims and Orthodox Christians in Greater Cappadocia will inform us about the borders of belonging, social or communal identities and the reasons why nationalism found a space in a region without any visible conflict.

Disrupting illusion, normalizing Ottoman plurality

There are two major perspectives on Ottoman history: the nationalist anti-Ottoman perspective in ex-Ottoman territories, seeing the Ottoman administration as a "yoke," and the recent romanticist perspective that is overtly nostalgic for Ottoman plurality. Both views are misleading. We are familiar with the rhetoric of the former. For advocates of the latter perspective, people were totally innocent and the politicians and Great Powers provoked the atrocities,[9] a trend that portrays the Ottoman Empire as "a world without national borders" and a multicultural empire, memories of which were silenced by the nationalisms of the Balkan states. An example of this view is the "A Balkan Tale" project. Put into action in 2012 and 2013, it was a European-Union-sponsored project led by historians from Balkan countries and pioneered by the Greek historian Christina Koulouri. The project included photographic exhibitions, historical excursions, education programs and documentaries with the goal of providing some historical awareness to both adults and children about the Ottoman Empire as a response to official nationalistic history narratives of the Balkan countries.[10] For Hayden and Naumovic, this initiative presented an ideal Ottoman co-existence – a fantastical world in which people of different faiths lived together, cultivated together, shopped from each other and enjoyed each other's company in coffee shops and market places – and it was all about "imagining commonalities."[11] Interestingly enough, despite any mention of it, most of the places mentioned in this project were still heterogeneous both in royal and socialist Yugoslavia. For the authors, this project was more of a contemporary political agenda that emphasized multiculturalism as opposed to nationalism. This is what I want to stress in this book: Ottoman romanticism is an ahistoric perspective with the present-day intention of replacing the nation-state with a form of multiculturalism, which has particularly Islamic references in Turkey. If it was not the case, the followers of this view would have already found proper answers to these questions: why the so-called "harmony" was disturbed suddenly with nationalism in the Ottoman Empire; how politicians, nationalist intellectuals or the Great Powers stirred up conflicts if people were enjoying peaceful cohabitation; and what made people believe in them?

Most of the time, it is the people themselves who produce enmity. Certainly, I am not talking about rigid or continuous feelings of negativity from one group to the Other. Time influences the practices of living together and can generate various feelings like intimacy, expediency, competition and aggression. In times of aggression, community boundaries become less flexible and much more rigid. To put it differently, even in the absence of mobilization of the nationalist elites, communities can be unfriendly to each other. Some case studies, especially those from Bulgarian and Greek revolts, show that the nationalist elites benefited from existing conflicts and mobilized them for nationalistic purposes. In short, communities can be at each other's throat for reasons other than ethnic conflict – it might be because of religious or economic reasons, or it might be an uprising against the existing power structure – so we cannot blame nationalism alone for separating people. Rather, nationalism is the last straw which leads to the drawing of the irrevocable border in such examples. Communities that are not in direct conflict with each other are not necessarily living together peacefully. There might be intimate interpersonal relations but at an inter-communal level they might be in competition due to other reasons. In this chapter, I discuss and defend the need to consider cosmopolitanism, identity formation, borders of belonging, practices of living together and the flexibility or relativity of all these parameters before nationalist ferment was introduced to people's life in Cappadocia, because explaining hostilities with nationalism is an oversimplification. Furthermore, Eurocentric explanations of the emergence of nationalism like industrialization, modernity and reformation remain inadequate to understand the nationalisms of Ottoman communities. Accordingly, to conduct a better analysis I make a distinction between inter-communal relations of the public sphere, which are competitive in nature, and inter-personal relations of the private sphere, which are better able to accommodate differences. At this point, I have to admit that I follow the agonal public that Arendt employed for the ancient Greek model with Benhabib's interpretation, according to which a morally homogeneous and politically exclusive community behaves in an egalitarian way to its members but antagonistically to those it sees as Others.[12] In the end, where the Ottoman Empire is concerned, we are still talking about a pre-modern society where private and public spaces were shaped by faith. The faith groups were egalitarian within themselves, but antagonistic at the inter-communal level; they did not intermingle as in modern societies. I believe that this perspective will prevent me from being trapped by romanticism. As another measure to cope with romanticism, I open to discussion the meanings of some free-floating terms employed in romanticist reading of Ottoman plurality like cosmopolitanism, inter-communality, tolerance, peaceful cohabitation and religious syncretism.

The study that inspires this chapter is a book by Nicholas Doumanis: *Before the Nation: Muslim and Christian Co-Existence and its Destruction in Late-Ottoman Anatolia*, in which the author analyzes inter-communality on the basis of relationships, religious traditions and routines before nationalism separated the communities in Asia Minor. The framework of the book is mainly constructed on the Oral Tradition Archives of the Centre for Asia Minor Studies (CAMS), as with this book. There are two fundamental ideas in the book: Doumanis, first, argues that before the Young Turk Revolution (1908) and the succeeding Balkan Wars (1912–1913), people in Anatolia enjoyed what is called inter-communality, which refers to the accommodation of differences between religious communities that happened to live in the same neighborhood, until it was destroyed by nationalism. Second, he argues that the testimonies of refugees are a veiled criticism of nationalism since they also experienced the good old days before nationalism penetrated the Ottoman lands. Their vision of a "Turk" was in fact a good person and a neighbor, which completely clashes with the vision of the "educated" (μορφωμένος) nationalist Greek who is required to see the "Turk" as an eternal enemy.

Doumanis portrays a very romantic vision of Anatolia before the Balkan Wars and blames nationalism for being solely responsible for terminating the inter-communal life of communities as well as *inter-faith cohabitation, religious transculturation* and *popular ecumenism* (the *italics* are mine) they enjoyed. In a similar vein, several other scholars emphasized the *harmonious co-existence* of religious groups in Asia Minor on the basis of their interviews with the refugee origin people.[13] Unquestionably, we can talk about relative harmony at certain periods and in certain localities in Asia Minor, or specifically in Cappadocia, but it was often competitive. Scholars make such statements on the basis of the narratives of neighborly relations between individuals. We must understand that inter-personal relations cannot be summed up and portrayed as inter-communal relations. Friendship between members of different communities cannot infer a lack of competition or conflict at an inter-communal level. And friendship or religious syncretism does not mean that people were confused about their religious identity. Despite the presence of friendly inter-personal relations, the boundaries between communities were sharp and people were well aware of their religious identities. For example, they were totally against inter-marriages between group members.

Therefore, we have to be very cautious not to be seized either by romanticism or by a "clash of civilizations" thesis. For me, a careful reading of CAMS oral tradition accounts paints a realistic picture of co-existence in Cappadocia. What I sought to find in oral testimonies were not facts, but meanings and symbols. It must be remembered that the interviews with refugees conducted by CAMS researchers took place many years later, and memories were highly affected by disappointment in Greece owing to severe hardships. When they were interviewed, beginning in the 1940s, a lot of water had flowed under the bridge and their days in Asia Minor were like a distant dream. However, despite the nostalgia in oral testimonies, the refugee narrations overtly demonstrate the borders of belonging and the scope of co-existence. On the one hand, these interviews portray relations of neighborliness, openness, sympathy and intimacy; on the other, in almost all testimonies, the "Turk" is specified as the Other, a stranger who is outside the community borders. The refugee narration is full of dichotomies like past and present, good neighbor Turk and bad outsider Turk, Christianity and Islam, Greece and Turkey, before and after the Young Turk Revolution, and so on. All these dichotomies help to detect the meanings and symbols that I seek to find in oral history accounts.

Doumanis defines inter-communality as simply the accommodation of differences between cultural, ethnic or religious communities that happened to occupy the same street, neighborhood, village or rural environs. For him, these practices of co-existence were conducted in a manner of neighborliness, and highlighted by everyday practices, social bonds and shared values. In his eyes, inter-communality is the reason many former Ottoman Greeks and Turks recall the years before the Balkan Wars as a *belle époque*. In contrast, I distinguish between inter-personal and inter-communal relations. Neighborly relations do not necessarily denote a lack of competition or conflict at an inter-communal level. As for his argument about the years prior to and following the Balkan Wars, it is true that testimonies emphasize "the good old days" before the Balkan Wars (1912–1913) or *Hürriyet* (Liberty, the Young Turk Revolution of

1908). However, I believe such accounts should be analyzed more carefully since each of them implies a different meaning in their use of the phrase "good old days." The following testimonies reveal various narratives referring to dissimilarity in refugee lives before and after the Young Turk Revolution:

> We got on well with the Turks. We were like brothers until Hürriyet. Things spoiled afterwards (χαλάσανε τα πράγματα). The Turks became wild (αγρίεψαν οι Τούρκοι).[14]

> Until the Balkan Wars, we got along well. We traded with each other. We did not have social relations (κοινωνικές σχέσεις δεν είχαμε). They did not interfere in our affairs. They left us free in our religion; we sang our national anthem among us. Their ministry of education did not get involved because we had privileges. Everything spoiled afterwards.[15]

> We did not have complaints about the Turks. In older times our relations were better. After Hürriyet, in our last years, before the Exchange, during the time of Kemal, they got wild. Not all of them. There were always good Turks. They were good friends and they would sacrifice themselves for us.[16]

> Until 1908, we and the Armenians were responsible for the trade in Bor. The Turks were sleeping. The Young Turks awakened them; they encouraged the Turks to enter the Christian (fields of) trading.[17]

In all these testimonies, Doumanis alleges a shared opinion: things were relatively good before the Young Turk Revolution of 1908 and the Balkan Wars (1912–1913). However, unlike Doumanis, it strikes me that the perceptions of "good old days" and "good Turk" differ from interviewee to interviewee since they were from different localities, their relations were shaped by distinct socio-economic situations and their experiences of co-existence and the frequency of their encounters with Turks varied greatly from person to person. For some, before the *Hürriyet*, things were better since they enjoyed relative freedom in trade and in their internal affairs, including religion and education, and the Turks were fine because they were indifferent to non-Muslims. However, for others, the old days were better because their relations with Turks were friendly and harmonious. Some of their good neighbors became wild after the Young Turk Revolution, and for this reason things worsened in their last decades in Cappadocia. Therefore, the only thing that we can generalize from the CAMS testimonies is that the lives of Christians were better before 1908 in Cappadocia. We cannot, however, claim that the years before the Young Turk Revolution were a *belle époque* in which people enjoyed a completely harmonious inter-communality. It may have been so for some regions but, as we have seen in the above-stated testimonies, some Christians did have minimum relations with the Turks.

Doumanis's romantic perspective should also be evaluated from the aspect of the Ottoman state's Islamist policies of censorship and forced conversions, and its general attitude toward non-Muslims during the reign of Abdülhamit II. For example, Orthodox Christians were worried about their situation when their Armenian neighbors were killed during the massacres of 1894–1895:

> The Armenians of our village were saved and were not harmed thanks to the intervention of Yosifaki Tatsoglou, the son of Makariou. Yosifakis was in Caesarea when the persecution and slaughter broke out in 1895. He happened to find the hodja of the village there. He commanded him not let the Turks to do what happened in Caesarea. After paying him, he asked him not to touch in general any Christian so he wanted to protect the Armenians. The hodja rode his horse to village, found the Turks, gathered them, talked to them and persuaded them.[18]

> During the Hamidian years, some problems arose with the Armenians. The Turkish army came to Nevşehir to massacre Armenians. They did not touch the Christians. A rich Turkish man Hatzigoura (Hacımurat?) saved them.[19]

All in all, the Hamidian years may have been relatively more peaceful than the continuously anxious years of the long war (1912–1922) for Orthodox Christians in terms of inter-communal relations and the attitude of authorities toward non-Muslims, but it was certainly not a *belle époque*.

Some scholars also refer to the concept of cosmopolitanism[20] in their studies of inter-faith cohabitation in the Ottoman Empire, but they mainly refer to major port cities, especially after the influx of Europeans into the Ottoman Empire for economic reasons. For this reason, cosmopolitanism is regarded as "quasi-colonialism" by sociologist Georg Simmel. In my case, I prefer Lessersohn's *"provincial cosmopolitanism,"* meaning

> a local cosmopolitanism, a lived disposition, affinity, and identity of individual persons and of collective groups that was the direct result of living in a demographically concentrated provincial urban environment in which individuals and groups of diverse and differentiated ethnic, linguistic, religious and cultural composition engaged in an ecosystem of interaction.[21]

Provincial cosmopolitanism, as its name suggests, applies to provinces where diversity prevailed. For Cappadocia, things were too complicated to apply the term, as Cappadocian provinces were predominantly Turkish in character and generally the non-Muslims were either ghettoized in villages or in separate neighborhoods (mahalles). For this reason, I also like Georgelin's interpretation that cosmopolitanism is not an anarchic social process, and that not all components of a multiple society have the same role in the resulting balance.[22] Generally speaking, for Ottoman cosmopolitanism there were various levels: imperial, urban governance, neighborhood, professional association and so on.[23] At each of these levels there were two parameters: the general structure of the Ottoman society in which non-Muslims were secondary citizens, and the provincial dynamics, which were more diverse and based on demographics, socio-economic differences and linguistic predominance. For example, in Izmir, until 1922, the shops belonged overwhelmingly to non-Muslims, but Turkish remained the main language spoken in markets and bazaars. There was cultural dominance of Greeks over the native Christian populations, including the Armenians.[24] For Cappadocia, cosmopolitanism was dominated by Turkish-Muslim culture to the extent that, according to foreign observers, some Greek-speaking villages adopted Turkish in the last decades of the nineteenth century. Demographics were also in favor of Muslims, with Christian communities continuously losing population as a result of immigration.[25]

Another important point to be stressed in eschewing Ottoman romanticism is that people of different faiths rarely shared the same spaces; in cities they lived in different neighborhoods, and their villages were mostly separated; if they lived in a mixed village, their neighborhoods were separated.[26] Separation meant protecting the comfort zone. When faith groups lived close to each other in mixed spaces, they were rarely comfortable with the presence of one another.[27] This included Cappadocia:

> There were no Turks in our village. We did not let them stay. Once a shepherd wanted to live, he was not permitted because in Telmison (a nearby village) there were only Christians once upon a time. A shepherd went there and got married. Later, they (the Turks) became more than the Christians (in number).[28]

> All the residents of our village were Christians. There were only a Turkish bath keeper and a Turkish baker. The bath keeper with his family was living in our village. The baker would come in the morning and leave in the evening.[29]

> Kayabaşı (Christian neighborhood of Niğde) was ten minutes away from Niğde. There were around seven hundred Greek families,[30] a number of Armenians and no Turks.[31]

> Listen how they founded our village! Fifteen Greek, fifteen Turkish families left Tsouhour (Çuhur – a village in Kayseri) after the revolution (επανάσταση, Greek Revolution of 1821). Do you know why? Because they had suffered much from the Turks. The Turks wanted to come with them [...] They said: "we leave Tsouhour to stay away from the Turks; why to stay with the Turks again?" [...] So they left the Turks and built a village near Sivas.[32]

> In Andaval, we were always scared of getting massacred. There were only Christians and no Turks [in our village]. In mixed villages they [the Christians] were not afraid of [massacres] because the Turks would fend off the bandits.[33]

Turkish neighborhood with its dirty roads and short houses was separated from our neighborhood which had beautiful houses and clean and good roads. We got on well with the Turks as they were always the best of us (γιατί αυτοί ήταν πάντα καλύτεροί μας). They would reap our fields.[34]

There were four hundred fifty Turkish and fifty Greek families in our village. We had good relations. We lived like brothers (ζούσαμε σαν αδέλφια). They were honest in trading. They were respectful to our religion and to our women. They would go to foreign lands (gurbet, ξενιτιά) with our people.[35]

As we see in these testimonies, Turks and Christians rarely shared the same space, and if they did, the scope of co-existence did not always show signs of inter-communality as they usually remained socially separated. Furthermore, the fear of losing community members and being suppressed under the demographic dominance of the Turks indicates competitive living together, where communities tried to protect their communal borders and to keep their members intact. There was also a gender difference in terms of their communication with the Turks. For example, in Tsarikli (Çarıklı-Niğde), women did not speak Turkish and were familiar with few Turkish words because they had almost no communication with Turks. Their husbands, on the other hand, were mostly quilt makers and moved around Anatolia for their work so they had relations with the Turks and knew Turkish.[36] Unquestionably, there were places where different religious communities enjoyed inter-communality, as seen in the last two testimonies, but it was not a paradigm of society and we should not over-generalize the aspects of practices of living together. Additionally, we should be cautious when labeling relationships as inter-communal. Inter-personal relations generally denote neighborliness and intimate relationships between individuals at a private level. Inter-communal relations, on the other hand, indicate group behaviors or behaviors that affect the other group members. For example, an economic transaction between a Muslim and a non-Muslim may not symbolize an inter-communal relationship,[37] but the Muslim community (not just a few individuals) attending Christian weddings might be a sign of inter-communality.

The source of romanticism in some studies about Ottoman plurality comes from the contention that tolerance equals peaceful living together. Such a perspective has two major problems. First, tolerance and peaceful living together do not always mean the same thing; as I previously stated, tolerance is exercised when there is a power relationship, so we should be careful not to dress a wolf in sheep's clothing. Second, the lack of visible conflict between communities does not prove that there is peaceful cohabitation; there might also be competition between the communities. Cohabitation, in fact, might be experienced in two ways: people might be unbiased toward each other, in exchange of goods and values, and in full communication with one another, or they might just not be at each other's throats. The former version is peaceful cohabitation. The latter is antagonistic cohabitation but

Figure 2.1 Kayabaşı: An Orthodox Christian neighborhood in nineteenth-century Niğde.
Photograph: Gülen Göktürk

this does not mean that in the second version they are not tolerating one another, since we can still talk about the negative tolerance of not persecuting the undesired. Certainly, these are superficial categorizations and in real life things are always much more complicated and interwoven and the practices of living together might change in scope from time to time depending on the situation in the locality. At this point, what I try to emphasize is that co-existence is not always evidence of the positive valorization of pluralism. It can also be a matter of competition between members of different groups manifesting the negative definition of tolerance as passive non-interference.

Tolerance means voluntary acceptance of the people or the attitudes that we disapprove of. Hence, it requires some form of self-restraint by the tolerator. Appreciating people, liking them and wanting to live with them, is not practicing tolerance. Tolerance is something you perform when you can wield power but choose not to do so. Therefore, only the powerful can exercise tolerance. For the Ottoman Empire, only the Muslims could be tolerant of the Others. The non-Muslim subjects, regardless of how wealthy or powerful they were, were considered to be second class citizens by the Ottoman authorities, so the position of non-Muslims in contrast to Muslims cannot be called tolerance, but rather expediency or consent.

52 *Maintaining boundaries*

Concerning the structure of the Ottoman Empire, non-Muslims, as secondary subjects, were simply too powerless to exercise tolerance. Certainly, in interpersonal relations we can talk about tolerance but as for inter-communal relations, only the Muslims were given the power to be tolerant. No matter if a non-Muslim was wealthy and prestigious in his relation to Muslims, in the end; Islamic law designated the Muslim subject superior to him. Therefore, in inter-communal relations, the tolerant side could only be the Muslims; the non-Muslims, since they were powerless, could only be in compliance with the disapproved Other, or they could wield expediency or consent to facilitate their lives. As for Muslim tolerance, it extended from non-persecution to peaceful living together from time to time, changed from one locality to another and, after 1908, in many places it became intolerance.

Although non-Muslim subjects were incapable of being tolerant, they were definitely not passive at all levels of human interaction. They would continuously rebuild their social identity and determine their position in accordance with the changing Muslim attitude of tolerance, governmental policies and other developments that affected them. Additionally, they had the power to be (in)tolerant of people whom they themselves considered heretics: the Protestants.

Communal identity and border maintenance

We first come across the concept of the Other in the Hegelian Master–Slave dialectic according to which man's humanity "came into light" as he satisfies his Desire through recognition by the Other and that it is the Desire which generates his Self-Consciousness. In a fight for recognition to satisfy the Desire, both parties should be alive since death is the complete negation of Consciousness. Hence, each party inevitably has to assume the role of either Master or Slave. The Slave is the one who accepted life given to him by the Master and thus he depends on another. The Master, on the other hand, is objectified and "mediated" by the Slave.[38] In short, Hegelian philosophy necessitates the existence and the recognition of the Other for a person to realize and enjoy his/her Self-Consciousness and so be a complete human agent.

The Hegelian Master–Slave dialectic involves a tension between two parties "othering" each other. Taylor, though, focuses on the dialogical character of human life and claims that through our acquisition of rich human languages of expression we become full human agents capable of understanding ourselves and hence of defining our identity. For him, discovering my own identity does not mean that I work it out in isolation, but that I negotiate it through dialog with others, partly overt, partly internal. However, for both perspectives, to define and realize ourselves we need the Other. Tilly also comments that identities reside in relations with others: you-me and us-them and Barth argued that what closed community borders was a particular difference from the Other, not the similarities shared within the Self.[39]

Here, I am not particularly concerned with individual identity, since it is a modern concern, although we cannot simply dismiss individual identities, since refugee testimonies reveal not only communal matters but also personal feelings and belongingness. Certainly, the identity question in this part will not be a Post-Cold War concern of individual identity, but this does not mean that individual feelings and inter-personal relations are ignored. I rather make a differentiation between inter-personal and inter-communal encounters in order not to mix apples and pears.

For the Muslim–Christian co-existence in Cappadocia, many studies refer to the commonalities that people of different faiths share in the region, including the language. First of all, we have to note that for people sharing the same geography, it is almost impossible not to have many things in common. Can anyone claim that different religious communities did not share common characteristics in areas like Trabzon, Aleppo, Salonika and Diyarbakir? Additionally, not only in Cappadocia but in many other places in Asia Minor and Pontus, where Muslim Turks dominate non-Muslims in number, the Anatolian Christians were mostly monolingual Turcophones and they had a multitude of relations with the Turks either at minimum or maximum level of proximity. Bearing this in mind, Cappadocia cannot be considered a unique case. Therefore, as Tilly and Barth argue, commonalities and interaction with the Other are not obstacles to establishing borders. One distinctive feature is enough to encircle a social group, and in our case it was religion.

In the pre-modern world, the most important constituent of one's identity was a person's religion. Historical surveys show that this was so both for the Muslims and Christians of Cappadocia. For Anagnostopoulou, Cappadocia, with its mountainous landscape, its lack of resources and its abandonment by the state, harbored feelings of religiosity in the hearts of both Christians and Muslims. Religion was so important that, unlike the coastal areas like Smyrna, in Cappadocia, it was the priests who wielded absolute power in communal organizations during the Ottoman epoch.[40] Adding to that, many studies built upon the testimonies of Asia Minor refugees or *Karamanlidika* publications show the value given to religion by the Cappadocians.[41]

Similarly, Hirschon observed in her field study of Asia Minor refugees in Piraeus that "the sense of identity of the Asia Minor refugees was rooted in a shared heritage which centered on their religious affiliation."[42] For her, Ottoman Greeks had a tendency to ignore regional and socio-economic divisions among their community and it was their religious identity that bonded them. The CAMS Oral Tradition Archives also demonstrates that religion was the constituent element of the Christians' identity and boundary maintenance in relation to the Muslim Turks in Cappadocia. First, the refugees would often use the word "Christian" when they were talking about themselves, their possessions and their characteristics in relation to their Other: the Turks. We can list them as such: Christian women/men, Christian neighborhoods, Christian families, Christian population, Christian settlers, Christian labor, Christian houses and so on. They rarely employed the word "Greek," and we are not sure if they labeled themselves as Greek

54 *Maintaining boundaries*

(Έλληνας, Yunan) or *Rum* (Ρωμηός, Roman, Greek Orthodox Christian), since most of the interviewees coming from Cappadocia were Turcophone and we do not know if the CAMS interviewers preferred to translate *Rum* as Greek or if the interviewees actually used the word *Yunan* (Greek) when they were referring to themselves. This differentiation is particularly important because Greek refers to ethnic whereas *Rum* refers to religious identity. Second, in *Karamanlica* (Turkish in the Greek alphabet) publications, the publishers would address their readers with the words "Christians," "Orthodox Christians," "Christians of Anatolia" and "Orthodox Christians of Anatolia." Balta, in her analysis of forewords of the *Karamanlıca* publications, classified these terms and determined the turning points in the lives of Greek Orthodox people. According to her study, the readers were simply called "Christians" or "Christians of Anatolia" in the early years of *Karamanlıca* publications. When the activity of Protestant missionaries began, they added the designator "Orthodox" to emphasize their denomination.[43] In my own observations, including *Anatoli*, *Terakki* and several other *Karamanlıca* publications, I often came across the terms "Orthodox Christians," "Anatolians," "Anatolian Orthodox Christians" and "Anatolian *Rums*" (Anatol Rumları).[44] This identification was again based on religion since religion was the main constituent of the Self. It was so important that when a person converted to Islam, she/he would automatically become a Turk in the eyes of Christians:

> My brother Dimitris Prodromos' sister in law was Turkified (τούρκεψε) [...] She stayed in Limna (Gölcük). There are 25–30 women who were Turkified and stayed in our fatherland and they have relatives here [in Greece].[45]

> Eighty years ago, a Christian of our village got Turkified because she married to a Turk. Her grandchildren became the worst of all Turks. Once they stoned the Ai Giorgi (Άη Γιώργη) Church which was neighboring with Turkish neighborhood (mahalle).[46]

In these testimonies, they use the term "Turk" not in ethnic but in religious terms. A person who changes his/her religion would inevitably be considered a member of the Other in the eyes of group members. No matter a convert's origins, he/she would already be seen as the Other. Barth affirms that "ethnic boundary defines the group, not the cultural stuff that encloses."[47] I exchange "ethnic boundary" in Barth's wording with "communal boundary" because this concept makes more sense for our case, as, for the time span we focus on, the conditions were not ripe enough to designate the religious communities in Cappadocia as ethnic communities. I also agree with his conclusion that when one passes the dividing line that defines and encircles a social group, despite whatever shared commonalities may exist, one remains outside the group.

Reading co-existence from another angle

In this book, I intentionally hesitate to use the term "inter-communality" when referring to Muslim–Christian co-existence in Cappadocia. The reason for this is the arbitrary treatment of tolerance and inter-communality as coequal. For instance, this testimony refers to peaceful living together since attendance at one another's weddings can indicate inter-communality:

> We were sweethearts (with the Turks) (Ἡμασταν αγαπημένοι).They would come to take us as agricultural laborers (εργάτες) to reap their fields. They would invite us to their weddings and come to ours.[48]

There is no expediency in attending one another's wedding. In this example, the communal borders are not closed and the boundary between "us" and "them" is permeable. However, a solely economic relationship or a transaction between religious communities cannot be regarded as peacefully living together since there is no intimacy but expediency or necessity.

I very often came across lines such as *"we were sweethearts," "we lived like brothers,"* or *"we got on well"* in refugee testimonies in folders about the "relationships with the Turks." Doumanis claims that the accounts in the Oral Tradition Archives of CAMS have the potential to refute the official nationalist discourse in Greece. The following testimony openly exemplifies the dichotomy between official historiography and refugee narration. I have to confess that such testimonies are not exceptions:

> I wish everyone was like the Turks. They were very good and respectful to women. Nowadays a lot is said about them (she means in a negative way). We never met such people. Those had to be the other Turks.[49]

Such testimonies referring to peaceful and intimate aspects of living together cannot and should not be disregarded. However, we should be careful in the analysis of such testimonies to verify that they narrate inter-personal relations of neighborliness or inter-communal relations. The personal practices of living together and the border maintenance of community should not be mixed since while the former refers to intimacy, the latter might refer to competition. In other words, the relations of Ayşe and Eleni might be very friendly and sympathetic, but the relations of Muslims and Christians in their village may be competitive in terms of maintaining the borders and keeping the group intact against the potential interference of the Other. To say that identities are "fluid" and changeable does not mean that distinctions between groups can easily be removed.[50] Bringa outlines the conditions in a Catholic-Muslim mixed village in Bosnia that equate with mine in Cappadocia:

> The neighborhood (komšiluk) was an important sociopolitical unit within the village [...] Hospitality and related social exchange (such as women's coffee visiting and men's work parties) was the basis for neighborliness between

56 *Maintaining boundaries*

them. These activities involved the two communities and in emphasizing a shared (and therefore nonreligious) identity acknowledged the existence of a village community beyond the ethno-religious one. Socializing between villagers, Muslim and Catholic, provided an opportunity for identifying with one's ethno-religious community and expressing this belonging to nonmembers [...] Symbolic boundaries of separateness were initially established by referring to "our customs" or "among us" Muslims or Catholics respectively, or "ours" and "theirs," "we" and "they" [...] The separate identities of the Muslim and Catholic communities are ultimately maintained by the disapproval of intermarriage between members of the two communities.[51]

Figure 2.2 A Greek-speaking Orthodox family from Ürgüp (Prokopi) in the late nineteenth century.
Source: Photography Archive of Centre for Asia Minor Studies

Religious syncretism

Competitive cohabitation is mostly evinced in two seemingly minor but important issues: religious syncretism and inter-marriage. It is my contention that the case of Cappadocia involved competitive cohabitation originating from the motive to protect community borders and community members. Although it eventually offered a foundation for national identities to emerge, in the initial phases of nationalization it served paradoxically as a fulcrum for people to resist the primacy of nation as the main constituent of their social identity. That is to say, religious identity was so important for people that they resisted any identity that had the potential to replace their religious identity. Accordingly, national identity was initially regarded as irrelevant and uninteresting for ordinary people. For some it was even a threat to their religious identity. As long as nationalism kept its distance from religion, laypeople remained indifferent to it. For this reason, Greek and Turkish nationalisms integrated religion into other components of national identity. The end result was religious nationalism, which does not really accord with modernist explanations of nationalism since nothing else but religion designated the ethnic categories of "Greek" and "Turk."

In the case at hand, nationalism set itself on the pre-existing religious segregation. This does not indicate that Huntington was right in his "Clash of Civilizations" theory. As mentioned above, it is in fact the interaction between religious groups that preserves the group boundaries and it does not have to be antagonistic at all times, as Huntington claimed. It could be either competitive or peaceful. Ottoman Cappadocia was not an ideal world of freedom and equality both at an individual and a communal level but even in pre-modern Cappadocia people managed to live together without any visible conflict until the age of nationalism. This proves Huntington to be wrong: we see in our case that inter-faith cohabitation is not inherently violent although it had competitive and even antagonistic aspects.

Both "religious nationalism" and "antagonistic tolerance" theories argue that the pre-existing faith groups of an area – be it South Asia, the Balkans, or Cappadocia – were disturbed when a new religion arrived via trade, conquest or indigenous development and challenged them. For example, in India it is thought that Hinduism is the natural religion of the land, while Islam is seen as coming from the outside to convert Hindus.[52] This was the case in Anatolia as well. When its inhabitants were predominantly Orthodox Christian during Byzantine times, with the Turkish raids and conquests masses gradually became Muslim. For Ménage and Vryonis, the Islamization of Asia Minor was effectively completed by 1500, and the Christian majority gradually became a minority.[53] Since the adherents of a religion often see the adherents of other religions as rivals with the desire to convert or persecute them, they develop and enclose their social identity on the basis of religion and feel themselves in contestation with the Other. Hayden calls it structural opposition; an opposition based on long-lasting religious rivalry.

58 *Maintaining boundaries*

The romanticist vision opposes this view by referring to common religious rituals or shared religious shrines, and calls it religious syncretism by attributing a solely positive value to the term. Syncretism means borrowing, affirmation or integration of concepts, symbols or practices of one religious tradition into another through a process of selection and reconciliation. It is not an anomaly, it happens everywhere and it is definitely not the same as tolerance. Syncretism is regarded positively by some as a sign of tolerance, but negatively by others as a decline of pure faith and loss of identity.[54] Syncretic behaviors are also held up as proof of claims about a community's origins and nature. Based on syncretism and crypto-Christianity, some Serbian scholars, for example, argue about the real religion and Serbness of Muslim or Catholic populations of their neighborhood.[55] Others like Hayden regard syncretism more as pragmatism; I lean toward this perspective rather than the essentialist arguments about communities' origins.

The romanticist scholarship focusing on Ottoman plurality agrees with the former view and makes references to the common religious practices, supernatural beliefs and people's way of bypassing Orthodoxy. For example, Doumanis reserved two chapters for the popular understanding of religion and adopted a particular nomenclature such as popular ecumenism, religious transculturation and inter-faith intimacy. Ottoman subjects, he claimed, were prepared to stray beyond the boundaries of their own religion, limited by high religious authorities, and appealed to the same saints, shrines and shared the same superficial beliefs. To Doumanis, this was intense religious transculturation and inter-faith intimacy. Additionally, for him, the most intimate forms of Ottoman inter-communal engagement, which he observed in CAMS testimonies, where Muslims and non-Muslims could recognize most clearly each other's humanity without consciously crossing the line of apostasy, would imply popular ecumenism.[56] Doumanis' argument is not totally wrong but it is misleading since he did not consider the competitive nature and restricting aspects of "intimacy" or, as I like to call it, "flirting" between different faiths. A careless reading of the CAMS Oral Tradition accounts, in fact, could easily lead a researcher to a romanticist vision since it is full of testimonies narrating common religious and superstitious practices:

> One day a Turk from Eskigümüş came and said "Muhtar Efendi (Mister Headman), I love a woman from our village; would you go to Priest Nikolaos for me to ask if he writes an amulet to make this woman love me?" Priest Nikolaos wrote some nonsense on a piece of paper in Greek, folded it and gave it to me. I brought it to the Turk and said him to put the paper on the way of this woman so she could step on it. They got married. The Turk sent me four hundred walnuts; I gave half of it to Priest Nikolaos.[57]

The Turks would not come to our churches. Neither would they interfere in our religion. Only once we saw a Turkish woman in our Church Ioannis Prodromos [...] There was food in her bag. She stayed silently and watched carefully what we were doing. When we were crossing ourselves, she was doing the thing that they do [when praying]. She told the Christian women she knew that she would come to church every year. The priest blessed the food she brought from home for her to have everything well at home.[58]

In addition to such unique stories, one can frequently find stories narrating how Muslim Turks would become mentally or physically healed after sleeping in a churchyard or when a priest prayed for them. Valensi, in her article about Ottoman Syria, claims it was proximity that facilitated reciprocal borrowing of social practices and sharing of customs and values among Muslims and non-Muslims, but at the same time the passage from one church to another through marriage was frowned upon by the communities of origin which sought to defend themselves by every available means.[59] Hence, we can conclude that cultural borrowing does not mean that there were no communal borders or conflict between the two groups; neighborliness, personal feelings of friendship and individual demands of help from the Other do not mean that people were confused about their religion. Additionally, we should note that syncretic behaviors are often pragmatic behaviors for two simple reasons. One is that individuals have the desire to seek help through whatever means will bring about the end they need in their lives. They ask for supernatural intervention and miracles and they hope to receive good no matter if the way to good is through another religion. For example, people who faced special dangers often displayed ecumenical piety, such that, for example, sailors of all faiths – especially pirates and corsairs – respected icons of the Virgin Mary. Specific saints were believed to protect some cities, and their ability to prevent danger was recognized by Muslims and Christians alike in the Balkans.[60] In the end, they believed that if some people believed and benefited from miracles of a saint or a ritual, they could as well. Second, in an ecosystem of antagonistic tolerance, the tolerated group inevitably follows the dominant group's traditions, since their own traditions are suppressed by the Other. At this point, I again want to warn the reader that inter-personal relations do not correspond to inter-communal relations. It is much like having a gay friend but simultaneously feeling uncomfortable about gay marriage; one can be against something while still maintaining good personal relations with people who exemplify the thing to which one is opposed. In our historical case, personal relations and the pragmatic behavior of syncretism do not refute the fact that there was competitive cohabitation between religious groups and the contestation was fundamentally religious. For Hayden, it is in fact the syncretic behaviors that prove that there is antagonistic tolerance in an ecosystem of co-existence. In the following testimonies, note the pragmatic behavior of Christians in benefiting from the healing capability of the Muslim practitioners. In Cappadocia, both priests and *hodjas* were considered medicine men:

> When we would run a temperature, we would go to the house of hodja. He would take a cotton yarn, bless it, make knots and tie it to our hand. It sounds strange but we would become well.[61]

> When I was nine, I had a terrible toothache [...] My grandmother took me to the nearby mosque. We had heard that it was once the church of St. Nicholas. The hodja of the mosque was called Tap Tap Hodja. He was a respectable old man [...] He asked me to put my finger over the aching tooth; I did. He wrote something in Turkish letters on a paper and put the paper on a piece of wood. Every time I told him that my tooth was still aching, he banged a nail on each letter he wrote on the paper until my tooth stop aching.[62]

In Asia Minor, there were many cases of worshiping at the same shrines, and Cappadocia was no exception. One of many such examples was the shrine of the Christian Saint Mammas, known as Şammas Baba by the Turks, which was famous for a series of miraculous incidents in an entirely Turkish village of *Mamasun* (Gökçe) in Aksaray, Cappadocia. The sanctuary was called *Ziyaret Kilise* (Pilgrimage Church) and east of it there used to stand a Holy Table with an icon of St. Mammas for the Christians, while in the south wall there was a niche (mihrab) for the Muslims. The skull and other bones of the saint, discovered on the site, would be shown in a box and worked miracles for Christians and Muslims alike. The sanctuary would be tended by a dervish and itinerant Christian priests would officiate at the Holy Table.[63] I came across testimonies about Saint Mamas in the Aksaray folder of the CAMS oral tradition testimonies:

> A Turkish woman used to come to our house to make pastry for us [...] She told us a miracle of St. Mammas: "my son was in the army and I did not even receive a letter from him. I thought of lighting a candle of St. Mammas and begging to him to show me my son [...] I took the key of the church, opened its door and asked for a miracle. I saw my son even before I arrived at home. He showed his miracle."[64]

Certainly, the shrine of St. Mamas was not unique. Many other shrines served Muslims and Christians alike:

> The patients from Turkish and Greek villages would come to Agioi Anargyroi Church (Ο Ναός των Αγίων Αναργύρων) to sleep and get well. Turks called it a tekke (dervish lodge).[65]

For Hasluck, the reverse concept of Christians visiting Muslim shrines also happened, though less frequently. *Hacı Bektaş tekkesi* (dervish lodge) near Kırşehir was the most important Muslim shrine in Cappadocia. The *tekke* was not only frequented by Muslims of the *Bektaşi* order but also by the Christians. For some local authorities of the time, Hasluck cites, it was believed by Christians that in the place of the *tekke* there had been a monastery that was the site of Saint Haralambos; in this example, while the same holy site was indeed shared, the identity of the saint is contested. As Hayden refers to a similar example in India, transformation of the shrine and the identity of the saint seem to be an expedient case of pure power and oppression. Since the dominant religious community was the Muslim community, the shrine was attributed to their own saint. The Christians, on the other hand, privately continued to name it for their own saint. In this particular case, Hasluck argued about the competition between Islamic sects and Christianity and the non-violent triumph of the former over the latter. For him, Bektashism gained ground at the expense of Christianity through acceptance of the new God by the old one or through the identification of the two personalities. In his words:

> A religion carried by a conquering race or by a missionary priesthood to alien lands super-imposes itself, by force or persuasion, on an indigenous cult; the process is expressed in mythological terms under the figure of a personal combat between rival gods or of the "reception" of the new god by the old. Eventually either one god or the other succumbs and disappears or is relegated to an inferior position; or, again, the two may be more or less completely identified and fused.[66]

Mazower regarded Bektashism as an Islamic mysticism that was counterposed to the formal hierarchies of Sunni Islam and that united Christianity and Islam with the claim that "a saint belongs to the whole world."[67] The ecumenical character of Bektashism might be a source of syncretism for Cappadocia. In the eyes of the Orthodox, the followers of Bektashism were the Turkmens (Turcomans) – they were not called Turks in order to emphasize their denominational difference – to whom the Orthodox felt closer than to Turks since they drank wine.[68] The heterodox practices of the Bekthashi order do not change my argument about religious syncretism. In the end, there were borders between all religions and denominations and, despite the existence of shared practices, the members of communities never wanted to lose members to another religion or denomination.

Coming back to shrine sharing, Hayden strictly regards it as a pragmatic attitude and stresses the competitive nature of syncretism. He claims that whoever is acknowledged as a community in a region, it is likely that the practice of the believers will continue to incorporate that community's religious elements in the worship of the saint. Bowman finds Hayden's point of view to be an over-generalization:

> Identities at syncretistic shrines can function with relative unfixity, only being forced towards aggressive articulation, closure and mobilization by the perception of another setting itself against the inchoate identity it focuses and brings to expression. That perception can be propagated by political and/or religious elites, or can result from antagonistic activities by another community of people.[69]

Bowman criticizes Hayden for regarding identities as fixed, but I do not read his "antagonistic tolerance" in the same way. First of all, he clearly states that syncretism is a practical behavior. To behave in accordance with interest implicitly means that individual identities were unfixed and had the tendency to adapt to conditions. Additionally, it is true that people practiced rituals in contrast with the doctrines of their religions in plural Ottoman society. However, despite the presence of gray areas between religious communities, they were at variance since they wanted to keep their groups intact. As an example, a Muslim woman might go to a priest to ask for help to cure her illness, but this does not indicate that she questions her own religion. If asked if she wanted to be converted, she would refuse and most probably would not want to listen any further. On an individual level, people were cognizant of their religions, and at a community level none wanted to lose its members to the Other.

Religious syncretism in Cappadocia was not restricted to visiting the same shrines or sanctuaries or believing in the healing capability of other religions. Kostas Tsolakidis narrates in his memoir that her grandmother and the other Christians of their village Zincidere (Flaviana) did not eat pork, rationalizing that the animal was dirty. For the author, they must have been affected by their Muslim neighbors. This probably began as a desire not to provoke their neighbors, and this respect gradually turned into a belief.[70] Not eating pork is a syncretic behavior, but again there is expediency and a power relationship behind the idea: not to provoke Muslims so as not to engage in conflict with them. There is contestation in this example too. Had the Christians been greater in number, it's likely they would not have cared what their Muslim neighbors thought: there were Muslims in the Peloponnese but the Christians outnumbered them and did not give up eating pork.

As another example of syncretism, Erol's article on *Karamanlıca* epitaphs of the nineteenth century demonstrates the linguistic manifestation of syncretism since she detected Islamic terms like *Amin* (Arabic invocation said after a prayer meaning "so be it"), *Allah* (Arabic name for the God) and *hadji* (used for pilgrims to Jerusalem, derived from the Arabic *hajj* meaning to make the pilgrimage to Mecca). Utilization of Islamic terms is also observed in *Karamanlıca* publications.[71] I have myself observed the display of Islamic concepts like *Mashallah* (May God preserve him/her from evil) in fountain and door epigraphs. Concerning the fact that Christians were very few in number among a Muslim majority, and some had lost their vernacular Greek over time, it is fairly understandable that they adopted Islamic terms. Again, we do not see such examples in the particularly Christian territories where Muslims were the minority. These were the outcomes of the demographic dominance of the Muslim Turks in the region.

When discussing religious syncretism, one should not forget the fact that some Muslim populations of Asia Minor were local converts. As previously mentioned, the Islamization of Anatolia was almost complete by the sixteenth century and was followed by individual conversions thereafter. Accordingly,

Figure 2.3 An inscribed stone panel of a house door from Cappadocia: "the house of Tylkiar Anastas, Masallah, 1871."
Photograph: Gülen Göktürk

some Christian rituals might have lasted past conversion due to their perceived effectiveness over the ages. As we saw in the observations of Busbecq about the Muslims on the island of Lemnos:

> If you ask them why they do this, they reply that many customs have survived from antiquity the utility of which has been proved by long experience; the ancients, they say, knew and could see more than we can and custom which they approved ought not to be wantonly disturbed.[72]

All in all, religious syncretism or "flirting" between believers of different faiths in Cappadocia was based on pragmatic logic and its existence does not refute the competitive side of the story. The first volume of Hasluck's *Christianity and Islam under the Sultans* records in detail the transference of Christian sanctuaries and shrines to Muslims, including converted churches

64   Maintaining boundaries

and secularized sanctuaries, when the dominance of Islam was established in Anatolia. Testimonies about transferences also exist in oral accounts:

> There [in Eskigümüş] was a church called St. Haralambos. We would go there to light candles. Turks converted it to a larder. It was carved into a rock and there were icons. Turks would say that it was once a monastery. Eskigümüş was a Christian village, then came the Turks.[73]

For Hayden, transference and conversion of sanctuaries from one religion to another are symbols of dominance, and one would be hard-pressed to find a clearer instance of a contest between believers. In Anatolia, and particularly in Cappadocia, the Christian element gradually declined[74] and religious manifestations followed the dominant polity of the Muslims. Parallel to this, Van der Veer's evaluation of Islamization in India is also applicable to Anatolia:

> The evidence of a gradual process of Islamization should not make us forget that identity formation works by a dialectics of inclusion and exclusion. It is often observed that Sufism has open boundaries, that its beliefs and practices are syncretistic, allowing room for local customs. While this is true, it should not be exaggerated. There have always been mechanisms for boundary maintenance within Sufism that stress Islamic exclusivity.[75]

The dominance of Muslims over Christians and the threat of Islamization in the eyes of the Christian population were the main reasons behind the competitive nature of relations between communities. By the eighteenth century, the Greek Orthodox Church was already becoming interested in the Turcophone Christians of the Anatolian interior and how to protect them from conversion to Islam and from the religious propaganda of other Christian denominations.[76]

From another angle, contestation between religious groups is also observable in refugee testimonies about religion. The Orthodox believed that their religion was better than that of the Muslims:

> Turks would admire and respect the Christian religion. We would invite Turkish couples to our wedding ceremonies at church. They would watch the ceremony with admiration [...] They would say to each other that the Rums had good traditions.[77]

> They [Turks] would say that our religion was better than their religion but the sword had the power and they would handle it so we were not able to select our administrators.[78]

Such testimonies show that the Christians were proud of their religion and placed it at a higher level among monotheistic beliefs, a view that is echoed by Hirschon. In her fieldwork in Piraeus, her informants often told her that the Turks were envious of them since their religion was beautiful (οι

Τούρκοι μας ζηλεύανε, η θρησκεία μας είναι ωραία).[79] The Muslims, on the other hand, called the Christians *gavur* (infidel) to show that they did not rate their religion.

To sum up, in Cappadocia, people enjoyed religious syncretism in numerous activities and attitudes, including visiting the same shrines, employing the same religious concepts and adapting the Other's religious behavior to the Self, and in the end what mattered most for them was the benefit obtained from practice rather than the dogma. However, even while experiencing these overlapping features, people maintained their borders and believed in the superiority of their religion over the Other, especially as the political domination of the Muslims overtly established itself in the sharing of religious sites. These two seemingly contradictory behaviors actually complemented one another. For Hayden, syncretism exists as long as the dominance of one over the Other continues. When dominance is challenged, it is likely that the interaction between the self-differentiating groups will turn to violence until dominance is restored.[80] That is essentially why Christians found themselves more intensely on the path of nationalization, if not violence, when the dominance of the Ottoman Empire was challenged during and after the Balkan Wars.

Inter-marriages

I now turn to the scholarly view that mixed marriages were a sign of inter-communality. I discussed above that we cannot simply call Muslim–Christian co-existence inter-communality, since it was inherently competitive and that inter-personal intimacy and the fluid nature of individual identities could not eliminate the borders between religious communities. Certainly, in times of crisis, the borders were more concrete, and in times of peace they were more permeable. However, one way or another, there were always borders, and the issue of inter-marriage clearly indicated their presence since it was frowned on by community members and leaders, including religious authorities. Here I should stress that I look at the issue of inter-marriages as a part of the issue of conversion. In the end, mixed marriage meant either conversion of the woman, or an acceptance on her part to raise her children as Muslims. This is a clear infringement of border maintenance for Christians since it meant the loss of both current and prospective members.

Contrarily, Layoun regards the visual image of a Greek woman becoming Turkish through marriage as a powerful sign of inter-communality.[81] She was wrong in this because the oral testimonies reveal that marriage with a Turk meant crossing the border and Turkification, and it was not approved of by the Christian Community. Interestingly, the Ottoman authorities were also very concerned about forced marriages and conversions, and when such cases were brought to the *kadis* they often stood in favor of the families of the forced person. For example, the *Anatoli* newspaper reported the case of a young Greek Orthodox girl who went to a *hodja*'s house in order to become Muslim.

66 *Maintaining boundaries*

According to the newspaper her mother was suspicious of the situation, so she went to a clerk of local pasha to complain. As a result, the girl was interrogated to see if she really wanted to convert. After seeing her hesitation, she was returned to her mother.[82] Inter-marriages, if they happened how CAMS informants stated, were usually impeded by members of the community who then tended to find excuses to legitimize this unapproved behavior:

> In 1890, a widow got Turkified. A hodja took her by force. It was said by force but she was eager [to get married] too. The council of elders (δημογεροντία) wanted to prevent her but she did not listen [to them].[83]

> In our village, women would not migrate; they would rather stay at home and do the agricultural labor. They were so poor that they would work in nearby villages. Because of poverty, some of them got married to Turks and got Turkified.[84]

In the rest of the testimony, the interviewee listed the names of fourteen women who married Turks. Except for one of them, who married for love, all of them wed because of their impoverishment. Interestingly, five were widows and had children from their deceased husbands. Some became second wives in polygamous marriages, and some wanted to leave their Turkish husbands and depart for Greece with their relatives during the exchange. According to the refugee narration, these women were excused because they were desperate. Indeed, some of them wanted to leave their Turkish husbands so their behavior could be forgiven. Be it direct or as an outcome of inter-marriage, conversion was a sensitive issue. As Bojan Aleksov indicates, conversion is among the most unsettling and destabilizing events in a society, since it necessitates a change of balance between members of different faith communities.[85] This instability relates to inter-marriage as well. In the example below, we see a mixed marriage that resulted in unrest between Muslim and Christian communities:

> The Turkish (man) Hayrullah who got married to Lavrentia murdered four men in our village because they went to his wife and said that it was not good to marry a Turk. She told this to her husband and he killed them.[86]

In his memoir, Kostas Tsolakidis devotes a chapter to the story of Lavrentia and Hayrullah. He recounts that the Council of Elders convened after they had heard that Lavrentia had married a Turk and asked the bishop to resolve this inappropriateness in accordance with the old traditions; those who had asked for a motion to dissolve the marriage were the ones who were subsequently murdered. As seen in the testimonies, inter-marriages were not approved of by Christians, even in cases of marriages with Christians of other denominations. In the only case I encountered in the oral testimonies, the father of a Greek Orthodox woman accepted his daughter's marriage to an Armenian man only

Maintaining boundaries 67

after the man was baptized as an Orthodox Christian.[87] In earlier centuries, conversion reduced the number of non-Muslims and demoralized communities; in the nineteenth century, however, conversion and the abandonment of a religious community were approached as *denationalization* and particularly dangerous because the apostates/converts were seen as potential *unravellers* who could reveal "national" secrets. Deringil describes *denationalization* as "the loss of a soul and a body from an increasingly 'nationally imagined' community. This loss is like a symbolic rape of the community's honor if the convert/apostate was a woman or a child." As we will see later, religion, as a pre-modern person's fundamental denominator of identity, was to be the main constituent of national identity for the peoples of the Ottoman Empire in the age of nationalism. Given the role of religion in nation-building, loss of community members, either through conversion or inter-marriage, meant exclusion from the prospective nation and becoming a member of the Other, and thus being seen as a potential traitor, especially if the conversion/apostasy was voluntary.[88]

Up to this point, we have discussed the practical dimension of mixed marriages. What about the dogma? How would Islam and Christianity approach the idea of inter-marriage? Mixed marriages are allowed in Islam; conversely, Christianity and particularly Orthodox Christianity are stricter and do not permit inter-marriages. According to Islamic law, Muslims are allowed to take non-Muslim (Christian or Jew) wives if there is a lack of Muslim women. It was not recommended, but it was tolerated. Mixed marriages were in line with Prophet Muhammad's order, which deeply permeated the religious consciousness of most Muslims who from the beginning married non-Muslim women, but the women were required to join them in Islam. In terms of Islamic law, it was unacceptable for a Muslim woman to marry a non-Muslim man as it resulted in an incongruity between the superiority that the women should enjoy by virtue of being Muslim, and her unavoidable wifely subservience to her infidel husband. Such a marriage involved an extreme lack of *kaf'a*, that is, compatibility between husband and wife, which required that a woman not marry a man lower in status than herself.[89] The inter-faith marriage between Muslims and Christians was according to Islamic law like the marriages between Muslims, with one main difference: children resulting from inter-marriages always belonged to the Muslim parent. Even if it was a valid marriage according to Islamic law, a mixed marriage was often regarded as defective in the consciousness of the Muslim public.[90]

In Christian canon law, mixed marriages are only allowed if they occur after the conversion of the non-Christian spouse. However, numerous councils of the church urged Christians of both genders not to enter into wedlock with any non-Christian and some of them imposed stiff penalties for breaking this rule.[91]

As for the Orthodox denomination, since the end of the nineteenth-century interchurch marriages involving Orthodox and non-Orthodox Christians within the Orthodox Church were allowed with the official authorization of the Church, but such marriages were subject to certain conditions:

68 Maintaining boundaries

1. the marriage had to be performed by an Orthodox priest;
2. children born must be baptized and brought up in the Orthodox faith;
3. marital problems must be arbitrated by the Orthodox.[92]

The two religions were very contradictory regarding the topic of mixed marriages. While Islam permitted it only for Muslim men and required the conversion of the non-Muslim woman to Islam, Christianity completely prohibited marriages with people of different religions both for women and men and required conversion of the non-Christian party prior to marriage. In our case, all the marriages were contracted within the Islamic religion despite the strictness of Christian law. As seen in the above testimonies, the Orthodox Community was uncomfortable with inter-faith marriages. Unfortunately, we do not have any testimony from the Muslim point of view. However, despite this, I can confidently claim that it was the dominant position of the Muslims over the Christians that Islam prevailed when a Christian woman wanted to wed a Turk. If a Muslim man and Christian woman agreed to get married, the Christian community had no other option than to consent. As stated in a testimony, "the sword had the power"[93] and it was the Muslims who held it. However, the power of the sword was generally compassionate. Marriage and conversion did not happen when the non-Muslim party was reluctant or a minor in such cases, family and community members had the right to intervene and ask for adjudication before the *kadi* courts. Such cases were often resolved in favor of non-Muslims.[94]

Inter-marriages, therefore, in contrast to the view of Layoun who regarded them as a clear sign of inter-communality, were in fact an overt symbol of competition, since the subordinate Christians tried to prevent apostasy and preserve their population. Inter-faith marriages were prohibited by Christian canon law; thus, the Christian communes constantly attempted to discourage and warn Christian women against marrying Turks. However, such attempts were generally volatile since Muslims were dominant and Christians were only able to wield consent. There was too much imbalance in society – as Muslim women could not be wives to non-Muslims – to categorize inter-marriages as a sign of inter-communality. Interestingly enough, in cases of inter-faith marriages or direct conversion, converts were automatically regarded as Turks, demonstrating religion's role in boundary maintenance. As Deringil points out, "beliefs, syncretic as they may be, are still beliefs, and even the most 'syncretic' of Christians could violently object to any forced Islamization."[95]

In conclusion, I could add that for the case of Cappadocia, inter-communal differences did not restrict inter-personal affection; however, the presence of inter-personal intimacy between members of different denominational communities, religious syncretism and inter-marriages did not indicate balanced cosmopolitanism. In fact, the inter-communal relationship in Cappadocia was imbalanced in favor of Muslims; for this reason, Christians of the

Figure 2.4 The wedding ceremony of Rahil Loukopoulou in Nevşehir.
Source: Photography Archive of Centre for Asia Minor Studies

region came to see religion as the only remaining disparity that separated them from the Other, and it became the strongest component of their social identity. Therefore, Christians tried to protect their community borders and demonstrate that they were a firm and intact group through whatever means necessary, in part by building giant churches in their villages – despite the decreasing population due to immigration – during the *Tanzimat* era, when permits to church construction was given relatively more easily than in subsequent years.[96] These churches were very much the symbols of competition between Muslims and the Orthodox in Cappadocia. All in all, what I seek to emphasize is that despite the various forms of cultural "flirting," the boundaries of religious communities were always preserved and religion was at all times a domain of contestation.

70 *Maintaining boundaries*

Figure 2.5 St.Vasilis Church of Misti (Çarıklı) Niğde. The construction of the church was completed in 1922. The Orthodox Community of the village could only use it for two years (Karalidis, 2005, p. 99). It is enormous for the size of the village community at the time.
Photograph: Gülen Göktürk

Notes

1 For a response to such views, see A. Aktar, Debating the Armenian Massacres in the Last Ottoman Parliament, November–December 1918; S. Anagnostopoulou, *Μικρά Ασία: 19ος Αιώνας -1919: Οι Ελληνορθόδοξες Κοινότητες. Από το μιλλέτ των Ρωμιών στο Ελληνικό Έθνος.*
2 B. Anderson, *Imagined Communities: Reflections on the Origin and Spread of Nationalism*, p. 80; E. Hobsbawm, *Nations and Nationalism since 1780: Programme, Myth, Reality*, p. 45.
3 A. D. Smith, *The Ethnic Origins of Nations*, p. 17.
4 C. Tilly, *Identities, Boundaries & Social Ties*, p. xiii.
5 R. M. Hayden, Antagonistic Tolerance: Competitive Sharing of Religious Sites in South Asia and the Balkans, p. 219.
6 P. Van der Veer, *Religious Nationalism*, p. 2. The term "religious nationalism" was first coined by the Serbian scholar M. Ekmečić in his *Stvaranje Jugoslavije 1790–1818* in 1989.
7 E. Hobsbawm, *Nations and Nationalism since 1780: Programme, Myth, Reality*, pp. 45–77
8 F. Barth, Introduction, pp. 9–15.

9 For responses to the romantic view of co-existence in the Ottoman Empire, see A. Aktar, Debating the Armenian Massacres in the Last Ottoman Parliament, November–December 1918; S. Anagnostopoulou, Μικρά Ασία: 19ος Αιώνας -1919: Οι Ελληνορθόδοξες Κοινότητες. Από το μιλλέτ των Ρωμιών στο Ελληνικό Έθνος; E. Kirtsoglou & L. Sistani, The Other *Then*, the Other *Now*, the Other *Within*: Stereotypical Images and Narrative Captions of the Turk in Northern and Central Greece; R. Hirschon, Knowledge of Diversity: Towards a More Differentiated Set of "Greek" Perceptions of "Turks."
10 For more information, see www.balkantale.com/
11 R. M. Hayden & S. Naumovic, Imagined Commonalities: The Invention of a Late Ottoman "Tradition" of Coexistence, p. 32.
12 S. Benhabib, The Embattled Public Sphere: Hannah Arendt, Juergen Habermas and Beyond, p. 5.
13 See R. Hirschon, Knowledge of Diversity: Towards a More Differentiated Set of "Greek" Perceptions of "Turks"; R. Hirschon, *Heirs of the Greek Catastrophe: The Social Life of Asia Minor Refugees in Piraeus*; B. Tanc, Where Local Trumps National: Christian Orthodox and Muslim Refugees since Lausanne.
14 CAMS, Cappadocia, Niğde, Konstantinos Haleplidis, Elisavet Hasirtzoglou.
15 CAMS, Cappadocia, Talas, Iordanis Giabroglou.
16 CAMS, Cappadocia, Bor, Grigorios Azariadis.
17 CAMS, Cappadocia, Bor, Sofoklis Fakidis, Dim. Haralampidis.
18 CAMS, Cappadocia, Erhilet (Erkilet), Anastasios Isaakidis.
19 CAMS, Cappadocia, Neapoli (Nevşehir), Triggidou Euf.
20 For a detailed overview of "cosmopolitanism" literature, see W. Hanley, Grieving Cosmopolitanism in Middle East Studies.
21 N. Lessersohn, "Provincial Cosmopolitanism" in Late Ottoman Anatolia: An Armenian Shoemaker's Memoir, p. 552.
22 H. Georgelin, Armenian Inter-Community Relations in Late Ottoman Smyrna, p. 184.
23 N. Lafi, The Ottoman Cosmopolitan Hypothesis in the Light of Pheng Cheah's Critical Explorations of Cosmopolitanism.
24 H. Georgelin, Armenian Inter-Community Relations in Late Ottoman Smyrna, pp. 179–181.
25 According to demographical statistics, before the Balkan Wars (1912–1913) in the vilayet of Konya the total population was 1,101,549. The number of Greek Orthodox was 87,021, the Turks were 988,723 and the other groups were 25,805. M. Harakopoulos, Ρωμιοί της Καππαδοκίας: από τα Βάθη της Ανατολής στο Θεσσαλικό Κάμπο. Η Τραυματική Ενσωμάτωση στη Μητέρα Πατρίδα, p. 34.
26 See E. Eldem, Istanbul: from Imperial to Peripheralized Capital; D. Goffman, Izmir: from Village to Colonial Port City; K. Barkey, *Empire of Difference: The Ottomans in Comparative Perspective*.
27 K. Barkey, *Empire of Difference: The Ottomans in Comparative Perspective*, pp. 116–117.
28 CAMS, Cappadocia, Aravan, Lioudaki?.
29 CAMS, Cappadocia, Tenei, Stefanos Yazitzoglou.
30 In oral testimony, it is written as "Greek" families (Ελληνικές οικογένειες). We do not know if the interviewee named her people as *Yunan* (Greek, Έλληνες) or *Rum* (Greek Orthodox Christians or Romans, Ρώμηοι). This difference is important since the former refers to ethnic identity and the latter refers to religious identity. We can never know what she called her people, only that the interviewer noted it as "Greek" families.
31 CAMS, Cappadocia, Fertek, Pipina Arapoglou.
32 CAMS, Cappadocia, Rumkavak, Iosif Parlakoglou.
33 CAMS, Cappadocia, Andaval, Anas. Athanasoglou.

72 Maintaining boundaries

34 CAMS, Cappadocia, Agirnas, Alexis Sevdinoglou.
35 CAMS, Cappadocia, Zile (Kayseri), Eleutherios Iosifidis.
36 K. I. Karalidis, *Τσαρικλί Νίγδης Καππαδοκίας*, p. 112.
37 A. Ozil, *Orthodox Christians in the Late Ottoman Empire: a Study of Communal Relations in Anatolia*, p. 18.
38 A. Kojève, In Place of an Introduction, pp. 3–30.
39 C. Taylor, The Politics of Recognition, pp. 32–34; C. Tilly, Identities, Boundaries & Social Ties, pp. 8–9; F. Barth, Introduction, pp. 9–15.
40 S. Anagnostopoulou, *Μικρά Ασία: 19^{ος} Αιώνας -1919: Οι Ελληνορθόδοξες Κοινότητες. Από το μιλλέτ των Ρωμιών στο Ελληνικό Έθνος*, pp. 361–362.
41 See R. Hirschon, *Heirs of the Greek Catastrophe*; E. Balta, Karamanlıca Kitapların Önsözleri; E. Balta, The Adventure of an Identity in the Triptych: Vatan, Religion, Language; F. Benlisoy, S. Benlisoy, "Karamanlılar," "Anadolu Ahalisi" ve "Aşağı Tabakalar": Türkdilli Anadolu Ortodokslarında Kimlik Algısı.
42 R. Hirschon, *Heirs of the Greek Catastrophe*, p. 17.
43 E. Balta, Gerçi Rum isek de Rumca Bilmez Türkçe Söyleriz: The Adventure of an Identity in the Triptych: Vatan, Religion and Language, pp. 40–41.
44 See *Anatoli*, 1891: 4280, 4287, 4288, 4295, 4297, 5440; also see I. H. Kalfoglou, *Ημερολόγιον: η Ανατολή*.
45 CAMS, Cappadocia, Limna, Anastasia Prodromou.
46 CAMS, Cappadocia, Zincidere, Iraklis Papazoglou.
47 F. Barth, Introduction, pp. 9–15.
48 CAMS, Cappadocia, Andaval, Paraskevas Ignatiadis.
49 CAMS, Cappadocia, Endürlük, Evanthia Ikenteroglou.
50 R. M. Hayden, Antagonistic Tolerance: Competitive Sharing of Religious Sites in South Asia and the Balkans, p. 207.
51 T. Bringa, *Being a Muslim the Bosnian Way: Identity and Community in a Central Bosnian Village*, pp. 65–79.
52 R. M. Hayden, H. Sözer, T. Tanyeri-Erdemir, A. Erdemir, The Byzantine Mosque at Trilye: a Processual Analysis of Dominance, Sharing, Transformation and Tolerance, p. 3; P. Van der Veer, *Religious Nationalism*, p. 28.
53 See V. L. Ménage, The Islamization of Anatolia; S. Vryonis Jr. Religious Change and Continuity in the Balkans and Anatolia from the Fourteenth through the Sixteenth Century.
54 Berlin quoted in P. Van der Veer, Syncretism, Multiculturalism si Discursul Tolerantei, pp. 198–199; P. Van der Veer, *Religious Nationalism*, pp. 185–186.
55 See B. Aleksov, Perception of Islamization in the Serbian National Discourse, p. 120.
56 See N. Doumanis, *Before the Nation: Muslim-Christian Co-Existence and its Destruction in Late Ottoman Anatolia*.
57 CAMS, Cappadocia, Andaval, Paraskevas Ignatiadis.
58 CAMS, Cappadocia, Gölcük, Eleftheria Alexiadi.
59 L. Valensi, Inter-Communal Relations and Changes in Religious Affiliation in the Middle East (Seventeenth to Nineteenth Centuries), pp. 256–257.
60 M. Mazower, *The Balkans*, p. 55.
61 CAMS, Cappadocia, Tsouhour, Ioakeim Papadapoulou.
62 CAMS, Cappadocia, Zile-Kayseri, Eleftherios Iosifidis.
63 W. F. Hasluck, *Christianity and Islam under the Sultans*, pp. 43–44.
64 CAMS, Cappadocia, Gelveri, Evdoxia?.
65 CAMS, Cappadocia, Gelveri, Makrina Loukidou.
66 W. F. Hasluck, *Christianity and Islam under the Sultans*, pp. 564–565.
67 M. Mazower, *The Balkans*, p. 63.
68 CAMS, Cappadocia, Gelveri, Symeon Kosmidis.

69 G. Bowman, Comment on R. Hayden, Antagonistic Tolerance: Competitive Sharing of Religious Sites in South Asia and the Balkans, p. 220.
70 K. Tsolakidis, *Belki Bir Gün Dönerim*, p. 355.
71 M. Erol, Cultural Manifestations of a Symbiosis: Karamanlidika Epitaphs of the Nineteenth Century, p. 92.
72 Busbecq quoted in M. Mazower, *The Balkans*, p. 59.
73 CAMS, Cappadocia, Andaval, Paraskevas Ignatiadis.
74 For more on the Islamization of Anatolia, see S. Vryonis Jr., *The Decline of Medieval Hellenism in Asia Minor and the Process of Islamization from the Eleventh through the Fifteenth Century*; S. Anagnostopoulou, Μικρά Ασία: 19^{ος} Αιώνας -1919: Οι Ελληνορθόδοξες Κοινότητες. Από το μιλλέτ των Ρωμιών στο Ελληνικό Έθνος.
75 P. Van der Veer, *Religious Nationalism*, p. 43.
76 E. Balta, Gerçi Rum isek de Rumca Bilmez Türkçe Söyleriz: The Adventure of an Identity in the Triptych: Vatan, Religion and Language, p. 29.
77 CAMS, Cappadocia, Zile-Kayseri, Eleftherios Iosifidis.
78 CAMS, Cappadocia, Tsouhour, Ioakeim Papadopoulou.
79 R. Hirschon, *Heirs of the Greek Catastrophe: the Social Life of Asia Minor Refugees in Piraeus*, p. 21.
80 R. M. Hayden, H. Sözer, T. Tanyeri-Erdemir & A. Erdemir, The Byzantine Mosque at Trilye: a Processual Analysis of Dominance, Sharing, Transformation and Tolerance, p. 3.
81 M. N. Layoun, *Wedded to the Land? Gender, Boundaries and Nationalism in Crisis*, p. 42.
82 *Anatoli*, October 16, 1851, 39.
83 CAMS, Cappadocia, Zile, Kayseri, Eleftherios Iosifidis.
84 CAMS, Cappadocia, Limna, Anastasia Prodromou.
85 B. Aleksov, Perception of Islamization in the Serbian National Discourse, p. 113.
86 CAMS, Cappadocia, Zincidere, Maria?.
87 CAMS, Cappadocia, Tsouhour, Sofia Koutlidou.
88 S. Deringil, *Conversion and Apostasy in the Late Ottoman Empire*, p. 3; p .4.
89 Y. Friedmann, *Tolerance and Coercion in Islam: Interfaith Relations in the Muslim Tradition*, p. 161.
90 A. P. D. Pashalidou, Η Λύση του Γάμου στο Μουσουλμανικό Δίκαιο: με Ειδική Αναφορά στα Προβλήματα των Μεικτών Γάμων, p. 191; p. 192; p. 221.
91 10 and 31 of Laodicea, 21 of Carthage [419], 14 of Chalcedon and 72 of Trullo address the issue of "interchurch marriage," or marriage with a non-Orthodox Christian. Characteristically, the normative canon 72 of Trullo states: "An Orthodox man is not permitted to marry a heretical woman, nor an Orthodox woman to be joined to a heretical man." Marriage with a non-Christian or non-believer is not mentioned at all, except in the case of pre-existing marriage, where either one of the spouses had subsequently espoused the Orthodox faith. The continuation of such marriage is permissible, according to the teaching of St. Paul (I Cor 7, 12–14), if so willed by the adherent spouse. See, L. J. Patsavos, C. J. Joanides, Interchurch Marriages: An Orthodox Perspective.
92 L. J. Patsavos, C. J. Joanides, Interchurch Marriages: An Orthodox Perspective, pp. 434–435.
93 CAMS, Cappadocia, Tsouhour, Ioakeim Papadopoulou.
94 For a detailed study about conversion, see S. Deringil, Conversion and Apostasy in the Late Ottoman Empire; S. Deringil, "There is No Compulsion in Religion": Conversion and Apostasy in the Late Ottoman Empire 1839–1856.
95 S. Deringil, *Conversion and Apostasy in the Late Ottoman Empire*, p. 18.
96 During the *Tanzimat* era, non-Muslims could receive permits to build churches, schools and charity organizations relatively easily in comparison to previous years. However, there was not total freedom on this issue; they had to continue to ask for permission in the old way. See İ. Ortaylı, *Osmanlı'da Milletler ve Diplomasi*, p. 63.

3 The path toward nationalism

Scholars have long been trying to explain and understand the emergence and success of nationalism. They do not commonly agree upon the "date of birth" of nationalism. The political explanations of nationalism place it either around the time of the English Civil War or the American or French Revolution; economic explanations, on the other hand, put the emphasis on the capitalist mode of production and industrialization. It is always difficult to pinpoint a particular period for the emergence of a historical phenomenon since timing changes from place to place. For this reason, it is difficult to apply modernist theories to explain the nationalisms that emerged from Ottoman territories. Concerning the non-Muslim Balkan populations, who had their own kingdoms at different points in history, as well as separate churches and literary languages, the second defeat of Ottoman Empire in Vienna (1683) created suitable conditions for them to foster secessionist ideals as a result of the loss of Ottoman authority both inside and outside its territories.[1] This seems too early a date for developing national awareness from a modernist perspective. It is most likely though to have come out from millenarian ideology prevailing among Orthodox Christian clerics and intellectuals since the conquest of Constantinople (1453). According to millenarian belief, Ottoman rule was a punishment for the sins of Christians and their "liberation" was predicted to occur simultaneously with the Second Coming.[2] Millenarianism was not nationalism; it was a religious belief, separate from nationalism, designed as a secular ideology. It could be that it was not the defeat in Vienna but the commercial activities of non-Muslims in Europe and their encounter with the ideals of the Enlightenment in the eighteenth century that fostered nationalistic ideals among the non-Muslim intellectuals and elites. A student of nationalism has to be cautious not to confuse nationalism with millenarianism.

The question of the genesis of nationalism is certainly a concern of modernists since in their understanding neither nations and nationalism were givens, already existing in nature as the primordialists claim, nor ancient or immemorial, as the perennialists suppose. Modernists approach nationalism as a manifestation of a particular *zeitgeist* and regard it within a specifically modern and European time and space.[3] In other words, the modernists refer to some "discontinuity" from which nationalism was generated. For Gellner, this discontinuity was the transformation of societies from agricultural to industrial. For Anderson, the deep-seated transformation in societies as an outcome of the Age of Enlightenment, Reformation and geographical discoveries, including the declining authority of the monarchs and religions and the birth of administrative vernaculars and print capitalism, paved the way of nationalism. Similarly, some scholars refer to the progressive collapse of a cultural value system derived from the predominance of religion and its substitution by the principle of the nation-state. Hobsbawm, on the other hand, uses the term "nationalism" in the sense defined by Gellner, to mean "primarily a principle which holds that the political and national unit should be congruent" as a necessity of the capitalist mode of production.[4] All these modernist explanations contributed to the explanation of the date of birth of nationalism; however, they explain the nationalisms of some countries more than others. There is a major problem in these approaches, which is that "nationalism is narrowed down to the dichotomy between traditional and modern."[5] What about the in-between situations like that of the still-traditional societies which imported nationalist ideals from the industrialist ones? For modernists, tradition is what societies had when they were still under the influence of religion, before they experienced the great transformation of capitalism. For example, Anderson claims that nations could only be "imagined" within the ruins of the traditional world. Is that really so? I believe that we need a broader perspective to explain and understand the nationalisms of traditional or quasi-industrial societies.

In my view, what makes the modernist explanation reliable is this magic word: "discontinuity." There are some points or epochs in human history that transform societies and the pre-existing belongingness of people and lead to new forms of attachments. I place myself close to the modernist school of thought, but at the same time maintain a certain distance from it. With a strong emphasis on elite activism and circumstances of modernity and with a strong belief in the idea that nations are the children of nationalism, my perspective differs from the modernity school of thought on two main points: first, I find the modernist school very Eurocentric, as it remains inadequate to explain nationalisms of traditional or quasi-industrial societies; second, I acknowledge and even emphasize the previous structures of inter-faith relations, particularly religion and its symbols, which were well suited to the needs of nationalism. This is not to say that nations are givens or have historical roots. Neither do I claim that pre-modern *ethnies* turned out to be nations in times of discontinuity, since I do not accept the ethno-symbolist theorization of nationalism which totalizes accidental belongingness or arbitrary common characteristics of people as *ethnies*. Rather, I assert that we should take into consideration the previous relations of different communities, most of whom were divided on the basis of their religion, denomination, local belongingness or power relations.

For the case at hand, it was the religious factor that shaped the collective identity of people. In Cappadocia, the borders of belonging were determined by religion and the relations of religious groups were fundamentally competitive since no minority community wanted to lose a member to the dominant Other, that is, the Muslim Turks. The reverse was not possible. Under such conditions, the dominant religious group would exercise negative tolerance of indifference and received consent in return. The existing system of relations had the tendency to evaporate only in times of crisis or discontinuity – be it modernity, industrialization, violence or structural inequalities – depending on the degree of resentment of the minority communities and certainly on other factors, like how their resentment was mobilized by able elite and intellectual hands through nationalist propaganda. So, it is my contention that nationalism owes its presence to discontinuity; and to be able means for the intelligentsia, as Smith argues, is to rediscover an entire ethnic heritage, ancestry and history that furnish vital memories, values, symbols and myths.

Therefore, to achieve success, the nationalist presumption must be able to sustain itself in the face of historical inquiry and criticism. The search for the past, the invention of tradition and the rediscovery of symbols that are supposed to unite people is certainly the job of intellectuals, but without an existing mechanism of self-differentiation *vis-à-vis* the already present Other, nationalism would remain ineffective.[6] In line with this argument, I follow Hobsbawm's proto-nationalism, except in contrast I take the view that proto-national bonds are set more by inter-communal relations and structural opposition between groups rather than shared intra-group characteristics like religion, language and customs.

In traditional societies, religion was the main determinant of inter-communal relations. Interestingly, in the era of nationalism, people's adherence to religion has two contradictory outcomes: on the one hand, people resist any propagated national identity with an emphasis on their religious identity, and on the other hand, nation formation itself utilizes religious identity as an ingredient of national identity in determining the Other, through which nationalism is built. In our case, this dichotomy is quite clear since Cappadocian Christians resisted accepting any self-definition other than Christian for a long time, despite the endeavor of Greek nationalism to incorporate them into the Greek national identity. One's religion was the primary component of his/her identity, and it was religious identity that fundamentally shaped one's life, not only in religious terms but also in aspects ranging from taxation to selection of a spouse. Regardless of one's religiosity, if he belonged to the Orthodox Christian Community, he had to pay higher taxes than Muslims and he had no option to marry outside his religious community. Boundaries were clear and based solely on one's religion.

Nationalism has been viewed among social scientists as a secular ideology that replaced the religious systems found in pre-modern, traditional societies. In this context, "religion" refers to tradition and "nationalism" refers to modernity; the former is replaced unavoidably by the latter in an evolutionary process.[7] I think that for some societies this might have been the case, but for Turkish and Greek nationalism, religion was not switched to nationalism. Certainly, we can talk about a discontinuity since the two peoples became the inimical Other of one another at certain times, but rather than a replacement between religion and nationalism, we can talk about a coalescence between the two, which we can call "religious nationalism." Religious nationalism comes into being when religion constitutes the main aspect of national identity and when nationalism settles into existing religious identifications and antagonisms.[8] The term "religious nationalism" may be incongruent with the modernist view since it regards nationalism as a secular entity in which religion is out of context. However, as we will see, despite the elite endeavor to place it in secular denominators like ancient past, territory and common language, both the Turkish and Greek nationalisms were carved in opposition to religious rivals of the faith groups, and laypeople rationalized it within the framework of their existing relations. Further to this, we should consider that in the age of nationalism the Ottoman Empire was still agrarian to a great extent and nationalism entered its territories not as a natural outcome of industrialism or capitalism but as a fruit of intellectual endeavor. Nationalism was so unknown to the Ottoman language that nationalist vocabulary first entered the vernacular through the letters of ambassadors in European capitals in the early nineteenth century and later through the translated manuscripts of leading nationalist intellectuals of the Greek Revolution.[9] Nationalism became a matter for the Ottomans during the Serbian (1804) and the Greek (1820s) revolts as for the first time in its history, the Ottomans faced secessionist movements. These happened without any relation to any substantial transformation from traditional to industrial society. Therefore, it is more appropriate to consider elite and intellectual power in nationalizing communities in the Ottoman Empire.

There were five factors for the transformation of identity of the Ottoman Orthodox in the nineteenth century: 1) the foundation of the Greek Kingdom and its irredentist policies; 2) an urban class of merchants, as the carriers of the idea of nationalism, who were mostly educated in Europe; 3) the Ottoman reform edicts; 4) immigration of all sorts; 5) missionary activities. All of these had direct and indirect effects on the *Hellenization* of the Orthodox.

Greek nationalism

By the middle of the eighteenth century, German, French and English scholars provided in printed form the entire extant corpus of the Greek classics. In the last quarter of the century, this "past" became increasingly accessible to a small number of Greek ex-pats living in Italy (especially Venice), the Romanian lands, the Habsburg territories (especially Vienna and Trieste), the Russian Empire (Black Sea) and elsewhere. They not only became familiar with philhellenism but also expanded their experience, their imaginative and intellectual horizons, explored a wider world, learned the ways of foreign peoples (thereby learning about themselves as a people) and extended their social, economic, political and intellectual possibilities. The outcome of this encounter with European civilization was the desire to make a radical break with the past and embrace Western modernity with a renewed interest in the heritage of Classical Greece.[10] They began to see the presence of Greeks under Ottoman rule as an

78 The path toward nationalism

interval period throughout which the Greeks suffered from unjust administration, superstition and ignorance of their glorious past and ancestral origins.

Early in the eighteenth century, the only alternative to tolerating the Ottoman dominance was to expect and pray for "salvation" by Russia, which would have meant being ruled by an Orthodox Christian Empire instead of a Muslim one. Catherine the Great in fact made Russia the protector of the Orthodox populations of the Ottoman Empire and gave the opportunity for enormous economic development to the bourgeois elements of the Greek peninsula.[11] The Russian Expectation, in Kitromilides's phrase, was abandoned after the signing of a peace between the Russian and Ottoman Empires in 1792,[12] since the Greeks regarded it as a betrayal by their Russian Orthodox co-religionists; they stopped placing their hopes in the prophecies, according to which the Orthodox populations would be saved by fair-haired Christian saviors. When they gave up their hopes about "the blonde race (ξανθό γένος)," the Greeks felt the necessity to achieve independence on their own.[13]

In refutation of Gellner's point of view, which rejects the power of the intelligentsia in nationalization, Greek nationalism was created and propagated by intellectuals and elites. At first sight, Modern Greek nationalism is indebted to the revival of ancient Hellenism.[14] Adamantios Korais, for example, aimed at reviving in the minds of his compatriots the cultural and intellectual primacy of Classical Greece.[15] His writings aimed to fill his compatriots with pride; for him, the modern Greeks were ultimately the grandchildren of a glorious ancient civilization that enlightened the contemporary Europeans: the Greeks, he would preach, [being] "proud of their origins, far from shutting their eyes to European enlightenment, never considered the Europeans as other than debtors who were repaying with substantial interest the capital which they had received from their own ancestors."[16] For Rhigas Pheraios (Velestinlis), on the other hand, the main pillar of Greek nationalism was the common heritage of Byzantium.[17] For this reason, he addressed his message not only to the Hellenic nation or to Orthodox Christians, but also to all religious communities of the Ottoman Empire. Highly influenced by the French Revolution, "he called for the overthrow of the despots by the coordinated action of all Balkan peoples." Sharing similar views with Rhigas, the Friendly Society (Φιλική Εταιρεία), a nationalist conspiratorial organization founded in Odessa in 1814 by three merchants (Emmanuil Ksanthos, Nikolaos Skoufas, Athanasios Tsakalof), aimed to replace the Patriarchate's religious and the Porte's political authority with a new secular, liberal authority inspired by the French Revolution. The Society succeeded in building a coalition among different Balkan communities and organized an Orthodox Balkan uprising in 1821.[18]

Thus, we can claim that Greek nationalism in the beginning had a secular character highly influenced by the French Revolution and the Enlightenment. However, religion could not be underestimated in the long run. Even Korais himself realized later, at the time of the Greek Revolution, that the accommodation of Orthodoxy in a Modern Greek nationalist project was needed, perhaps because it was inevitable. The Orthodox Church was in fact still influential in rural societies so they could neither ignore Orthodoxy nor Byzantium.[19] Greek nationalism inevitably played the religion card for its national propaganda on "unredeemed Greeks" in Ottoman territories, especially on those who spoke foreign languages. As Grigoriadis put it, only religion could unite Orthodox Christians with such diverse vernaculars. Early in the nineteenth century, Greek nationalism turned out to be "religious nationalism" since, in the end, the official narrative excluded all non-Christians and kept a certain distance from those of different denominations, like the Protestants, Catholics and Eastern Rites Catholics (the Eastern Rite Churches). Adding to that, the Exchange of Populations was based on religious criteria, and the Greek-speaking Muslims of Crete, Macedonia and Epirus were exchanged with mostly Turkish speaking Orthodox Christians of Cappadocia and Pontus (the Greeks of Western Anatolia and Thrace were already expelled from Turkey during and after the Turco-Greek War (1919–1922)).

Grigoriadis gives two other examples that demonstrate Greek nationalism as "a sacred synthesis" of nation and religion. These set March 25 as Greece's Independence Day and invented the myth of the "Clandestine School (κρυφό σχολειό)." According to the national narrative, the revolution officially began on March 25 when the Bishop of Old Patras, Germanos, summoned all the leading revolutionaries to the monastery of Agia Lavra and swore them to the revolution under a banner. However, there is no official indication that any such meeting actually occurred. Interestingly, this is the very same date when, according to the Christian calendar, the Archangel Gabriel visited the Virgin Mary and announced that she would conceive a son (the Annunciation of Virgin Mary). The Greek national narrative thus built a myth of "national annunciation" and allotted a religious meaning to a national day. The "Clandestine School" contention, on the other hand, is a legend of secret schools run by priests and monks to keep alive the national identity of Greeks throughout the Ottoman domination. These two myths portray the role of the church as "an ark of national values"[20] and prove my argument of "religious nationalism" at an intellectual level. Religion was assigned to secular nationalist ideas by intellectuals. The reason was simple. For laypeople, religion was the determinant of identity and it was the basis that separated communities from one another. There were already borders between "us" of religion A and "them" of religion B. Nationalism simply settled into the existing circumstance and transformed and even closed the borders. At times of crisis, like war, economic rivalries and so on, the task was easier since people were more prone to manipulation.

Almost a century after intellectuals began to develop nationalist ideals, in significant parts of the Southern tip of the Balkans, the populations, many of whom were Greek-speaking Christians, grew dissatisfied with the corruption of Ottoman administrators. The unrest of the people was utilized by nationalist intellectuals to reshape and portray protests as a nationalist revival. The *topos* (place) and the inhabitants of Hellas were rediscovered; social malaise and unrest fused with a political and intellectual movement inspired by European Romanticism. "Culturally superior" Greeks were now rising against the "backward" and "oriental" Ottomans.[21] The upheaval achieved by skillful hands, blended with nationalist romanticism, generated "discontinuity" from the past led to the replacement of "traditional" with "modern." Interestingly, it was an overlap of religious millennialism with secular nationalism. We are, in fact, not sure what the motivation of the Peloponnesians was when they were fighting against their religious Others and, at the same time, their rulers. It's likely that millennialism was still dominant over nationalism. Consequently, the Greek Kingdom was established in 1832, and it was time to reunite the Greeks who had once been a heterogeneous group of people under the administration of the Greek Orthodox Patriarchate, including Orthodox Christians of various cultures as well as Grecophone or Hellenized Vlahs, Serbs, or Orthodox Albanians. Nationalism was now ready to be slowly embraced by the masses through various mechanisms such as education, press and propaganda.

When the Greek state was eventually formed in the 1820s and recognized internationally in 1832, less than one-third of (assumed) Greek "nationals" were included within the boundaries of the established state. For this reason, its future was presented with a dilemma: the struggle between irredentism on the one hand, and internal reconstruction and modernization on the other.[22] The first American diplomat to Greece, Charles K. Tuckerman, recounted his observation about this dilemma in the 1860s:

> often a Greek may say to you in private that his countrymen are wasting their energies in chasing a phantom, which might better be employed in studies of political economy at home, he would not dare to advise any one of them to abandon the Great Idea nor does he himself believe that it should be abandoned.[23]

It seems that until its termination in 1922, following the failure of the Asia Minor campaign, irredentism with the name Great Idea (Megali Idea) was the primary policy of the Greek Kingdom. The logic of a Greek irredentist addressing the American public was such:

> Suppose that a foreign army, composed of people alien in civilization, feelings, religion and race to you, would overrun America; by fire and sword subjugate the American people, burn their churches and their schools, refuse to allow you to speak your own language, not allow you to educate yourselves in your traditions, compel you to accept their faith and in many instances to be their slaves night and day. Would you American people accept this condition of affairs as a course of Kismet, fate? Would you remain quiet and passive and never try to regain your place under the sun, your own home; to liberate yourselves from the yoke of the invader and thus regain your home country?[24]

These romantic and primordialist lines are certainly erroneous in the eyes of a contemporary student of nationalism studies, but they were mistaken at the time as well. There is no doubt that non-Muslims occasionally suffered at the hands of their Ottoman rulers, especially in provinces ruled by the local administrators, but there were never official policies of conversion, pressure to abandon native languages, prohibitions on schooling or church burning. Conversely, it is often claimed that the Greek Orthodox Church was able to preserve its institutions and tradition as well as a communal identity under Ottoman authority.[25] Tsolainos's lines are groundless but important because they portray how the Greek irredentists rationalized *Megali Idea* in their minds. *Megali Idea*, despite some nationalistic endeavors to trace its origins to the efforts of the thirteenth century Lascarid rulers of Nicaea to liberate Constantinople from "Frank" domination, was mainly a nineteenth-century phenomenon whose greatest achievement was the national integration of all Greeks.[26]

In the nineteenth century, the Orthodox Community of the Ottoman Empire was heterogeneous in multiple ways. It embraced not only ethnic Greeks but also various other groups; Romanians, Serbs, Arabs, Vlachs, Albanians, Macedonians, Bulgarians and so on, were included in its ethnic diversity, though there was some socio-economic differentiation among its members. For example, the polyglot primate of Phanar had little in common with the Turckophone tavern keeper of Niğde.[27] When it comes to the influence of Greek nationalism on these people, there were several standpoints. I classify the Ottoman Greeks in four categories in terms of their relation to Greek nationalism: 1) those who felt devoted to the Greek national cause; 2) those who developed proto-national community consciousness but were not yet Greek nationalists; 3) those who remained loyal to the Ottoman Empire and status quo; and 4) those (mostly humble peasants) who were simply indifferent to any political stance. As an example, the Phanariots distanced themselves from the ideals of Enlightenment after the Russo-Turkish rapprochement in 1791,[28] probably due to a fear of losing their privileged position in the Empire. The Ecumenical Patriarchate, on the other hand, initially resisted the inclusion of ethnicity in the definition of Greek national identity;[29] in the end, that meant the exclusion of non-Greek Orthodox Christians and, eventually, the loss of many members of its congregation as well as its power. Concerning the special case of the Ecumenical Patriarchate in relation to nationalism, only in the late nineteenth century, did a split appear between those who favored the nationalistic ideals and those who stressed its ecumenical character, and an external divide among the Orthodox clergy also corresponded to the internal confrontation.[30] Hence, there was no single Ottoman Greek response to Greek nationalism of the time.

After the foundation of the Greek Kingdom, a range of questions emerged concerning the prospective boundaries of the Greek state. In order to solve the boundary issue, the categorization of "Greek" had to be determined. What criteria should be embraced for "Greekness," the language, the religion or both? Should people of non-Greek ethnic origin (Vlahs and Slavs, for example), who nevertheless spoke the language fluently, be accepted as Greeks?[31] What would be the situation of the Turcophone Orthodox Christians of the Anatolian interior or the Greek-speaking Muslims of Crete or the Turcophone Protestants of Orthodox descent living in Cappadocia? Ethnicity was not considered the main determinant of "Greekness" in the early nineteenth century; instead, language and religion were the main criteria. However, many communities had "incongruent" religion-language combinations in the eyes of nationalists.

In the second half of the nineteenth century, the intellectual "irredentism" of the Greek Kingdom aimed at developing a sense of Greek national consciousness among the Orthodox Christians of Asia Minor. School teachers, trained at the University of Athens (and later in local Greeks schools like the seminaries in Heybeliada (Halki) and Zincidere (Flaviana), and who were frequently of Anatolian origin, propagated the gospel of Hellenism,[32] mostly in less provocative ways like teaching language and history. Despite the fact that the Patriarchate was irritated by the secularizing tendency of Greek nationalism and distanced itself earlier in the nineteenth century, it also stressed the importance of schooling in order not to lose its congregation to newly emerging national churches like the Bulgarian Exarchate and the Protestant and Jesuit missionaries. These two endeavors coincided and schools were opened in almost all Orthodox settlements in Anatolia. In the upcoming parts, education and enlightenment endeavors will be discussed, but before that another important phenomenon of the time for the Christians of the Anatolian interior will be examined: immigration to foreign lands (ξενιτιά, gurbet). As we will see later in this chapter, immigration, education and nationalism are all interrelated in our case.

Interrelated phenomena: *xenitia*, education and nationalism

– Why are you crying my kid? Asked the priest approaching [him].

Averkios answered with a stronger cry. He choked with sobs. The priest was lost. He did not know what to do. He caressed him; he asked again what the matter was but the child did not answer. And then, Ilias spoke. Nobody asked him though:

– His father is missing in foreign lands for six years.

"A!" said the priest smilingly.

– Haven't you seen Ioannis's father. He was away for eight years, not six and he came back. Come on, calm down [...] It is disrespect. God protects the walkers in foreign lands like patients.

Ilias spoke again demonstratively:

– And my father has been away for three years in Smyrna, and the year before last year he came to [visit] us.

– And mine! Added the dark haired child who is sitting in the back benches.

– And mine! Cried the third [child sitting] near him.

– My father comes regularly.

– Mine too!

[...]

– Listen, my class! *Xenitia* is one of the most important issues of our country and our tribe in general. Our dear compatriots are greedy money lovers. It is their great defect [...] they want to surpass the Turks economically. They

Figure 3.1 Tombstone of a tavern keeper's wife from Niğde in Karamanlidika in the yard of Zoodokhos Pigi Monastery in Istanbul. "In this tomb lies tavern keper Savva's wife H. Vithleem from the village Iloson of Niğde. May god mercy her soul. July 21, 1897."
Photograph: Gülen Göktürk

are attracted to mundane futility. And so today we observe that most of the men are struggling in Constantinople, Smyrna, Samsun, Adana, [and] Mersin [and] to deny the morals of modern Babylon. [...] Today our dear village has one hundred Christian families but in the past it had five hundred. This is the result of profiting.[33]

The priest, who was at the same time the teacher of a poor village called Kermira in Kayseri, faced the sorrow of his students during a class and tried to explain the reasons for immigration to foreign lands and blamed his compatriots for being greedy enough to empty the village in pursuit of wealth. The lines are

84 The path toward nationalism

from Christos Samouilidis's novel narrating the last days of Christians in a village of Cappadocia. The author of the novel worked for the Centre for Asia Minor Studies between the years 1955 and 1970, and interviewed a great number of Asia Minor refugees. Those interviews were the source of inspiration for the author and for this reason the book deserves attention. The excerpt in fact refers to three important phenomena occurring in Cappadocia at this time: education, immigration and population decline, all of which were interrelated and would lead to a transformation in the social identity of the Orthodox Christians.

For the priest, the reason for immigration was greed and competition with the Turks, though actually lack of resources drove people from Cappadocia to foreign lands. Immigration caused population decline among the Christians of Cappadocia and this meant becoming more vulnerable to Muslim Turkish culture. Many scholars have used this reason to explain their cultural resemblance to the Muslim Turks of the region and their speaking Turkish.

Toward the end of nineteenth century, the few Greek-speaking villages slowly became Turkish speaking as well; Andaval and Limna (today Gölcük) were two of these. In Andaval, for example, Greek was spoken up until 1884 but then it almost disappeared.[34] According to a CAMS informant, 150 men went to foreign lands from Andaval at the beginning of the twentieth century.[35] Women stayed in their hometowns and started to work in the fields of the Turkish village of Eskigümüş (Παλιά Ασήμια) to cope with their misery.[36] Similarly, the women of Limna who were left behind would work in the fields of nearby Turkish villages, and many of them married Turks to escape poverty.[37] Therefore, for these villages, *xenitia* and poverty were the reasons for Turkification both in lingual and religious terms. The situation of these villages clearly explains the reason for the anxiety of the above-quoted priest. Immigration, in the end, meant deserting one's ancestral homeland both physically and culturally, and it eventually indicated a sort of defeat for the Orthodox Christians in the ongoing contestation between themselves and the Muslim Turkish communities in the region. But the issue was not quite that simple, because on the other side of the coin the newly emerging schooling activities, supported by the money coming from brotherhood (αδελφότητα) organizations, established overseas created another opportunity to maintain and support the existing social identity and maybe even discover a new one, the national Hellenic identity. In the end, as I've mentioned, the combination of immigration, population decline and schooling all led to social identity transformation, unquestionably in varying degrees, from one locality to another.

Continuous mobility characterized the populations of villages in Cappadocia not only during the nineteenth century but also in earlier years. Up to the eighteenth century, there were various reasons for mobility, including the colonization policies of the Ottoman administration in newly conquered areas, concerns about security, poverty and clashes with nomads who were forced to settle by the government.[38] In the nineteenth century, however, the pull factors of economic development, especially in coastal areas, outweighed the push factors, such as the famine in Cappadocia of 1873–1875 that drove many families to fertile regions like Cilicia.[39]

Additionally, for the first time a physical and organic bond could be maintained between the immigrants and their homelands as a result of modern transportation networks like the railroad. The Istanbul–Bagdad and Izmir–Aydın railroads, while facilitating the transportation of people from one place to another, provided a link between the community at home and the community in foreign lands. This, in the end, not only eased the contact and transportation between the two, but also assisted the flow of both economic means and ideas from *xenitia* to *patrida*. The railroad was a discontinuity, a breaking point from the past. During this period, immigration was in three directions: to the financial centers of Asia Minor, to locations close to railroad stations and to the urban centers of coastal areas, and abroad. The areas that had a great increase in the Orthodox population were Ankara, Yozgat, the *kaza* of Sarımsaklı in the *vilayet* of Sivas in the North, the *sanjak* of Sis in the *vilayet* of Adana in the South and the whole area of Konya to the West.[40] Cappadocians eventually migrated to and settled in Istanbul, Izmir, Adana, Mersin, Samsun, Cairo, Alexandria, Athens and America in the late nineteenth century. Port cities like Izmir, Alexandria, Beirut and Thessaloniki attracted increased flows of capital, investors and immigrants after the opening of these ports to free trade as a result of the 1838 Anglo-Ottoman commercial treaty. Among these, Izmir and Alexandria (particularly after the British occupation in 1882) were preferred by the Cappadocians. As for Izmir, with the commercial treaties signed with European powers, the city enhanced its role as a center of export trade with agricultural products like figs and grapes. Other items such as silk, cotton, opium, rugs and carpets brought from interior towns were also assembled, packed and shipped to various European destinations from Izmir's port.[41] There was a flow of people toward places of economic opportunities from almost all cities, towns and villages of Cappadocia, so much so that by 1834 in seventeen Christian Orthodox settlements of Kayseri the rate of participation of immigration was thirty-eight percent.[42]

In addition to the growing transportation facilities, newly emerging trade possibilities with the entrance of European capital into the Ottoman Empire, the privileges given to European traders, and export opportunities were some of the other reasons for immigration to commercial centers, since it was the non-Muslims who were really benefiting from the new economic situation in the Empire.[43] There were two reasons for the flourishing of the non-Muslim bourgeoisie in the nineteenth century. First, international trade between the Ottoman Empire and the world markets depended mainly on agricultural products, and there were no landed estates in the hands of a land-owning class. Instead, there were a vast number of small peasant farmers producing diverse crops and it was almost impossible for foreign investors and merchants to control them. Mediators were needed to link these Ottoman peasants to the world economy. Second, the European merchants preferred to consult with the non-Muslim native merchant class as intermediaries to avoid the instability of inter-state relationships.[44] Certainly, not all Cappadocians were able to engage in commerce; most of them, in fact, continued to earn their livelihoods from unskilled jobs, since they were plain farmers in their place of origin and only those who originally dealt with trades and crafts were able to become rich. Consequently, the Cappadocians who originated from rich places were better able to get rich and be among the wealthiest of Greeks. Among them there were wholesalers from Niğde, Aksaray, Konya, Kayseri, Bor, Fertek and Tyana, who bought their merchandise and sent it to the major ports of Asia Minor.[45]

There were two patterns of immigration in the nineteenth century in Cappadocia. One was temporary immigration without family for terms of varying duration, and the other was permanent immigration without returning. During the initial years of immigration, men immigrated without their family and they made occasional visits to their place of origin to see their family for some months at a time. Later on, some men, after getting wealthy enough, started to take their families with them. Of course, it depended on the person, but the number of families did appear to decline in Cappadocia from the beginning of the twentieth century.

In the case of Pharasa, for instance, the inhabitants of the village had not previously immigrated because their mines held them in their homelands. In time, their mines ran out, and some of them started to go to Cilicia to work temporarily in cotton fields. When the harvest was complete, they returned to their families. Later on, they also discovered Izmir because it was connected to Cilicia by the sea. There, immigrants from Pharasa worked as porters, photographers and bodyguards of the rich. The males of Pharasa occasionally came to their village to get married and see their families.[46] For the males of Andaval, on the other hand, there were various destinations, including Istanbul, Romania, Bulgaria and America. In those places, they worked as porters, grocers or laborers.[47] Some of them were dry fruit merchants and moneylenders. In the last decades of the Ottoman Empire, they brought their families to foreign lands with them.[48] Every three years or so, they visited Andaval and stayed for a while; the young ones got married and had children.[49] For Endürlük, *xenitia* started very early around the last decades of the eighteenth century and when the exchange took place in 1924 there remained only 53 of the 600 or 700 households of previous times. Men started to take their families with them a few years before the Young Turk Revolution of 1908 (as noted by *Hürriyet* in its own words).[50] In the early phases of *xenitia*, men went abroad without their family and they visited them only every few years. In Vexe, all the men were abroad. Young boys, when they reached the age of 11, were sent to *gurbet*, and came back at the age of 19 or 20 to marry and then left again.[51] The destination for immigration was mainly Istanbul. A lot of males from Vexe were timber and dye merchants and a few of them were carpenters and they occasionally visited their villages.[52] Further to these examples, in Talas, men started to take their families with them after 1895, when before that only men went overseas.[53] From Talas, there were around 300 families in Izmir and Istanbul. The Onasis family was one who settled in Izmir. There were also immigrant families from Talas in Cilicia and in Karaman.[54]

For almost all CAMS interviewees, the reason for immigration was scarcity of resources and lack of trading activities in Cappadocia. An interviewee quoted Strabo to explain the reason of *xenitia*: "Cappadocia: an arid and stony country." According to the same interviewee, Cappadocians were only able to grow fruits, and such farming could only feed their families, leaving no surplus production to sell for money. Therefore, every Christian family started to send their sons abroad at early ages and sold their lands; in this way, the lands held by Christians changed hands and Cappadocia was eventually devastated, including the famous Gesi gardens, where the interviewee had grown up.[55] Another refugee made almost the same argument for his village Ai Kosten (Ai Konstantinos). There, men went to foreign lands since there was a lack of transportation and the surplus farm products remained in their hands. For this reason, their crops were very cheap. They could not survive under such conditions, and they went overseas to work as grocers, shoemakers and carpenters. Almost all families in the village were only able to live with the money coming from abroad.[56]

For the males of Prokopi (Ürgüp), *xenitia* started as early as 1800. Their first destination was Istanbul. There they worked as rowers and they brought loads from big merchant ships at the port. The rowers' brotherhood (Kayıkçı Kasası; originally named The Chest of Rowers, Ταμείο των Βαρκάρηδων) was in fact the first brotherhood organization founded in Istanbul. Later in the nineteenth century they started to go to Izmir, Samsun and Ankara to work as moneylenders, grocers and merchants.[57]

One of the few exceptions to the phenomenon of emigration from Cappadocia was Bor. From Bor, very few families emigrated, since Bor was a rich place that could maintain itself with sufficient trading activities for people to make a living. One of the few families who went to foreign lands was the famous Bodosakis family, who were poor and went to Adana. Generally, the males of Bor would only make seasonal migrations to bring goods and animals from places like Mersin, Tarsus, Aleppo and Arabia. Permanent immigration started from 1912 onwards, and the most common destinations were Istanbul, Adana, Izmir, Mersin, Tarsus, Ankara and America. There was a tendency among the immigrants from Bor to return home after making money and to invest in their homeland, so they rarely took their families with them.[58] Another exception was Tsouhour. There, immigration started quite late, around 1885. In 1922, there were around 100 men in Izmir from Tsouhour and only a few of them went to Adana for seasonal work.[59]

There were Orthodox Christians from almost every province and Orthodox village of Anatolia in Istanbul. Most of them were merchants, artisans, industrialists and plain laborers. For example, immigrants from Molu and Erkilet were mostly *araytzides* (αραϊτζήδες, arayıcı); their job was to find undamaged, useful items right after any big fires in Istanbul and to clean and sell them. They also looked for useful metals on the beach. Since they were constantly entering newly burned houses, many of them got sick at an early age.[60]

The general pattern of *xenitia* was men's immigration. Young males, mostly right after they finished elementary school (δημοτικό σχολείο), which was four to seven grades depending on the wealth of the locality, went to foreign lands to work with their fathers, relatives or compatriots as apprentices. When they reached the age of marriage, they wrote a letter to their parents to get their consent for a wedding. Then they came back and got married, stayed for a short while before leaving for foreign lands again. Depending on the distance between their homeland and place of immigration, they came back occasionally to visit their families. After learning the business as apprentices, they generally opened their own businesses and worked for themselves.[61] The pattern of *xenitia* was portrayed in lullabies and songs of the area. A lullaby from Zincidere depicts this situation very well: "my son will sleep, will grow up, will leave for foreign lands and will earn money."[62] Therefore, in the late nineteenth and early twentieth century, the Christian settlements of Cappadocia were deserted by men and mostly inhabited by women, children and elderly people.[63] Many anonymous women's songs demonstrate the hardship experienced by females at the time. The lyrics of one of them illustrate the longing of a woman left behind by her husband:

> *My agha,*[64] *it has been three years since you left,*
> *The saplings you had planted bear fruits*
> *All the aghas who left together with you came back*
> *Come, my agha, come quickly, aren't you allowed?*
> *Does not the cruel foreign land let you by?*[65]

The phenomenon of immigration was a major concern of intellectuals in the late nineteenth century. In his article in *Terakki* magazine, Iordanis I. Limnidis wrote about the immigration of boys at early ages. For Limnidis, many parents were sending their young sons to foreign lands to make money for their family as a consequence of widespread poverty in the region. For this very reason, boys were forced to leave school right after learning how to read and write, and rather than being enlightened by education they were broken away from their spiritual mothers, namely their teachers, and sent to faraway places like Istanbul and Izmir to work. Thus, poverty was the main reason for the lack of education and enlightenment in Anatolia.[66] For him, parents could have taken care of their children for a few more years until they finished their education, feed them at least until their adolescent years. But unfortunately, parents were ignoring the fact that their children, who could have brought them only 200 to 300 qurush a year, but could bring them thousands if they received an education for just a few more years. Accordingly, Limnidis warned parents to be more conscious about the importance of education and the negative outcomes of beginning work at an early age.[67] This excerpt shows just how interrelated immigration and education were. It also indicates the intellectual concern over the enlightenment of their fellow Cappadocians in the late nineteenth century.

There were two fundamental and quite contradictory outcomes of immigration: a decline in population in the region, and a flourishing of education and the enlightenment of the Cappadocian Orthodox. Through the money they made in foreign lands, Orthodox communities were able to build schools and other institutions as well as repair the old infrastructure in their homelands, so they initiated a sort of development campaign there. For Anagnostopoulou, this bloom was superficial, and caused their increasing economic and cultural dependence on coastal areas.[68] One way or another, Orthodox settlements in Cappadocia benefited in terms of wealth and education from male immigration. However, this did not prevent people from deserting their homelands. The Christian population in Cappadocia was constantly in decline as its emigration rate increased. Eventually, the region began to receive refugees from the lost lands of the Balkans and Muslim Caucasians escaping from Russia. Throughout the nineteenth century, the demography in the region continued to slowly change, and this transformation was finalized with the Exchange of Populations in 1923–1924.

As claimed by Livanios in respect of the Balkan Christians, the Cappadocian Christians had an understanding of boundaries that consisted of four layers: family, village, agriculture and Christianity.[69] Immigration transformed or even destroyed all of these layers. First, families were separated and family as an institution no longer offered a safety net for women, children and the elderly. Second, deserted villages became more vulnerable to outside influences and threats. Some depopulated Grecophone villages, for example, abandoned their vernacular and adopted Turkish. Due to poverty and fear of bandits, some women got married to Turks and became Muslims; the long preserved belongingness of Christian communities to their religious and communal identity was severely damaged. As for their previous occupation of agriculture, it was also damaged by loss of male presence in the fields. Not only the people left behind but also the immigrants faced this process of transformation in their lives. The immigrants came across co-religionists of different cultures, enlightenment efforts and nationalist ideals. In major cities of the Empire and in the Greek Kingdom, intellectuals were the producers and purveyors of these linguistic cultures through their publishing and schooling activities. Immigrants, though certainly in varying degrees, were affected by these novelties, and some of them wanted to transfer these novelties to the lives of their compatriots in their homelands. They therefore founded brotherhood associations to help educate and nationalize those left behind.

Community, schools and brotherhood organizations

Due to the fact that only a small group of privileged people were literate in agricultural societies there was a huge gap between upper and lower cultures. In Anderson's words, literate people were like small islands in big oceans of

90 The path toward nationalism

illiteracy. The Orthodox populations of the Ottoman Empire were no exception. Only a few people had the opportunity to receive an education from private tutors. A few were lucky enough to learn from the local priest how to read, write and memorize religious texts in old Greek. They spoke either a local Greek dialect or foreign languages in their scattered hometowns and none of these languages were found to be noble or historical enough to be imposed on masses of diverse backgrounds. In other words, as Hobsbawm declared, the "imagined" Greek nation was not supposed to speak *dimotika* or any other foreign language, like Turkish, since the actual or literal "mother tongue" (i.e., the idiom children learned from their illiterate mothers and spoke for everyday use) was certainly not in any sense a "national language." So the intellectuals realized the importance of education to teach the members of a prospective Greek nation an engineered language combining ancient Greek with vernacular Greek, called *katharevoussa*. This was a language that was designed by Korais to be "a hundred percent" Greek by replacing foreign words with ancient Greek words and the Greek Kingdom pursued a policy of teaching it even to the scattered communities of the Anatolian interior. This objective of enlightening the "prospective Greek nationals" living in exterior lands deviates from modernist conceptualizing, in which the state provides the means of education for its own citizens to unify them under a nationalistic ideal. Education was the intellectual branch of Greek irredentism. It worked hand in hand with the effort of the Patriarchate to protect its congregation from the secessionist churches and missionaries.

In 1839 and 1856, the Patriarchate was threatened by Imperial Edicts, according to which a mixed council consisting of lay participants (eight laymen, four cleric members of Holy Synod) was declared necessary in *millet* administration. The early resistance of the Church against early Greek (secular) nationalism and the secularizing attempts of the Edicts were simply the resistance of tradition against the new, in order not to lose its power and privileges. Afterward, however, the foundation of the Bulgarian Exarchate (1872) blew the wind in the opposite direction. Now, the Patriarchate deemed it necessary to employ every means to avoid losing members of its congregation, and even to regain the secessionists through instilling Greek consciousness on non-Greek-speaking Orthodox Christians through schooling activities. As a result, (intellectual) "irredentism" of Greek nationalism to educate "unredeemed" Ottoman Greeks coincided with the defensive schooling activities of the Patriarchate.[70]

The introduction of Greek nationalism to Cappadocian communities started in the 1870s and continued until the 1920s. Intellectuals, the *syllogoi* (societies) and the brotherhood organizations of the Orthodox settlements all assumed roles in the endeavor of nationalizing the Cappadocian Orthodox, most of whom were Turcophone. The involvement of the Patriarchate in educational activities was also a response to the increasing influence of Protestant and Jesuit Missionaries in the East. As a result, the first aim of education was to raise Orthodox piety, but in time a policy of linguistic "rehellenization" was added to previous efforts.[71] Before an examination of schools in Cappadocia, I will briefly discuss the general features of the Orthodox communities, with a particular emphasis on Cappadocia, in order to understand the administrative aspects of schools.

In most cases, the Greek Orthodox Community was organized under religious administrative units like parishes and dioceses. Apart from this, the council of the elderly (dimogerontia), established by local community leaders (τσορμπατ-ζήδες, çorbacı-kocabaş), was the secular authority. Consisting of eight to twelve members,[72] it was the body that dealt with the administrative and financial issues of the local community (koinotis or koinotita). The local community was so important that even when the members of a *koinotis* immigrated, they would establish a miniature community in their new settlement.[73]

Contrary to a common misunderstanding, the so-called *millet* system was a late Ottoman Empire phenomenon, rather than a classical institution. Non-Muslim institutions were in fact without legal status.[74] Further to this, despite the fact that in the nineteenth century there was no Orthodox settlement without community organization, the structures of the *koinotis* differed from one locality to another, and there was no single structure for communities of different localities. For example, the community of Smyrna had similarities with that of Thessaloniki but none with a community of Cappadocia. The priest held absolute power for organizing the community in Cappadocian settlements; however, this was not the case in coastal areas, especially in advanced communities like Smyrna. This situation can be explained by the socio-economic and geographical environments surrounding these communities. First of all, the people of Cappadocia, both Christians and Muslims, developed strong religious feelings, in part due to the fact that they were encircled by high mountains, virtually abandoned by the state and suffered in poverty. Second, they were deprived of the economic and cultural opportunities of the coast, and with the high rate of emigration throughout the nineteenth and early twentieth centuries, these communities recorded an increasing demographic decline. However, depending on the level of socio-economic development as a result of emigration, some of them gradually developed sophisticated structures similar to those of coastal communities. These were mainly places that maintained a significant population despite emigration, and where the emigrants maintained a close connection with their place of origin. Nevertheless, wealth did not automatically bring about a sophisticated community organization. For example, Konya had an economically powerful Orthodox population, but it only succeeded in organizing a well-structured community when the Bagdad railroad was built. The communities of Sinasos, Gelveri, Nevşehir, Ürgüp, Niğde and Kayseri, on the other hand, had sophisticated communal structures.[75] From the end of the nineteenth century almost all villages and settlements in Cappadocia had schools. The quality of schools and education changed from place to place in accordance with the population and wealth of the locality. For example, the first school in Sinasos opened as early as the 1780s and its education system changed in 1880 to produce better results. Similarly, Kayseri already had a school by 1792 and İncesu by 1814.[76] On the one hand, in Orthodox settlements like Gesi and Zile children continued to receive education from the priest in the traditional way (due

92 *The path toward nationalism*

to drastic population decline as in the case of Gesi or due to lack of wealth as in the case of Zile) but on the other, in some localities like Sinasos, Tenei and Nevşehir, there were special schools serving children of different age and gender groups. There were also many in-between situations. For example, Tsarikli (a village in Niğde) had a *dimotiko* school, but the children could go to school only for four months during the winter, since the assistance of children was needed for agricultural work. For this reason, very few of them successfully learned how to read Greek. The others only learned the basics of religion and chanting psalms.[77]

Overall, except for a few examples, every Orthodox Christian settlement in Cappadocia in the late nineteenth and early twentieth century had at least an elementary school (δημοτικό σχολείο), whereas up to the mid-nineteenth century education was usually acquired through private tutors, who were usually the local priests. Previously, children were taught how to read and write and arithmetic, and to memorize prayers, but the possibility of learning Greek was very rare.[78] This was the traditional way of education. During the nineteenth century, however, Cappadocian communities developed a formal education system, thanks in large part to their brotherhood organizations, school boards and benevolent compatriots; some of the education efforts did though remain relatively less developed or even traditional. The following part reveals the conditions of education in some developed Orthodox settlements in the region according to the Oral Tradition Archives of CAMS.

In Gelveri (Güzelyurt), there was one kindergarten (νηπιαγωγείο), one girls' school (παρθεναγωγείο) and one boys' school (αρρεναγωγείο). Beginning in 1890, Modern Greek was taught in the schools of the Turcophone village. The teachers forced children to speak Greek; those who spoke Turkish were beaten. Anyone who finished elementary school was able to speak *Katharevousa* and read Greek books and newspapers. According to testimonies, the children were also taught Turkish and French.[79]

Similarly, Tenei (today, Yeşilburç) had a big school founded in 1866 with a kindergarten and an urban school (αστική σχολή). These schools were originally separated but in later years they were combined. Children were taught Greek, Turkish and French, as well as Greek history, geography and the history of saints. The school had a library, too.[80]

Nevşehir had a very developed schooling system, with three kindergartens (νηπιαγωγείο), one girls' school (παρθεναγωγείο) and one boys' school (αρρεναγωγείο). There was also a middle school (γυμνάσιο) for Orthodox Christians. According to a CAMS interviewee, in school they received a good education; those who finished middle school in Greece were said to only know as much as those who finished elementary school in Nevşehir. In Nevşehir, the council of elderly (δημογεροντία) appointed the teachers. The two school boards (σχολική εφορεία) supervised and maintained the schools. The boards and the Council of Elders also collaborated on matters concerning the schools. The books, writing materials and salaries of the teachers were sent from Istanbul. The community

Figure 3.2 Greek language teacher Phillippos Papagrigoriou Aristovoulos in Nevşehir.
Source: Photography Archive of Centre for Asia Minor Studies

had an entire bazaar (çarşı) of its own in Istanbul; they rented the shops in it and sent the money to their homeland. On the boards, there were people who wanted to work for the progress of the community; they provided scholarships and sent successful children to Zincidere to continue their education in the Theological Seminary (Ιερατική Σχολή).[81]

Another community with a developed education system was Talas. There was one urban school, one girls' school and three kindergartens in town. In kindergarten, the children were taught the Greek language, arithmetic, measurement and songs. In the urban school, the children learned the history of the saints, history, catechism, ancient Greek, geography, French, Turkish, physics and chemistry. The school was free only for poor children and the community paid for all expenses, including the salaries of the teachers and supervisory bodies, and writing materials and heating. The salaries of the teachers were sent from Istanbul.[82]

94 The path toward nationalism

Prokopi (Ürgüp) also had a structured educational system. There was one girls' school, one urban school and one kindergarten. The girls' school had a theater stage where performances were presented. The annual spending of the schools was gathered from the incomes of community property in Prokopi and Istanbul, the annual tuition of the subscribers, the aids of beneficiaries, the proceeding records, offerings and tributes of the church, and from the taxes taken at name day celebrations, trials, funerals, baptisms, weddings and graveyards, as well as from the fees of theatrical performances and the money gathered through exhibitions of handcrafts. Immigrants in Istanbul founded a brotherhood organization in 1912, naming it Areti (Αρετή). The school board (σχολική εφορεία) took care of everything, including the provision of school materials, management of the school properties, repair of school buildings, appointment of teachers, tuition fees and so on.[83]

For the Orthodox Christian settlements of Anatolia, Zincidere was undoubtedly of particular importance, since the Theological Seminary (Ιερατική Σχολή, Kayseriye Mekteb-i Kebiri), the Cappadocian Central Girls' School, the Kindergartners Training College and two gender-separated orphanages were all located there.[84] It would, in fact, not be wrong to say that Zincidere was also a religious center for Cappadocia in addition to its role as an educational center, since the Metropolitan Bishop of Kayseri lived there along with the Monastery of John the Forerunner (Μοναστήρι του Ιωάννου του Προδρόμου). The Theological Seminary was at the top of the educational pyramid in the region and was at the level of gymnasium. It was established primarily to educate a competent group of clergy and a body of local teachers to serve in the community schools and churches of the region. The school was established in 1882 with the donations of Theodoros Rodokanakeis, a businessman from Chios, and carried his name for some year. The main mission of the school was to raise educated clergy in the struggle against the missionaries, since up until that time the Orthodox lower clergy was mostly illiterate, which was cause for ridicule and criticism by the missionaries.[85] Thus the Seminary was a means to compete with the missionaries at the ecclesiastical level. It would also work as a defense mechanism for the Community to consolidate itself. The program of the students at the school was full primarily with religious classes and with classes like pedagogy, foreign languages, experimental physics, chemistry, cosmology, algebra, trigonometry logistics, epistolography, gymnastics and Turkish language. The medium of education was Greek. Turkish was considered a foreign language and this created difficulties for the Turkish speaking students.[86] The Seminary operated for thirty-six years until the end of the First World War in 1918 with approximately 400 graduates.[87] It was among the best gymnasiums of the time.

The prospective teachers of the Seminary had to take exams at the University of Athens in order to be employed. Beginning in 1895, the graduates of the Seminary were accepted by the university with the official recognition of the Greek Ministry of Education.[88] According to the CAMS Oral Tradition Archives, through the last years of Orthodox presence in Cappadocia the Seminary successfully received children from other Orthodox settlements of Cappadocia. Some brotherhood organizations provided scholarships for those who wanted to further their education in the Seminary and become teachers or priests. Some teachers of the village Tenei were graduates of the Seminary.[89] Further, the first teacher of Zile, appointed in 1903, was a graduate of the Seminary.[90] In the case of the deserted village Gesi, the priest, who was simultaneously the teacher during the last few years leading up to the First World War, also studied in the Seminary.[91] I should note that employing teachers from Istanbul or Greece was costly for the communities of Cappadocia, and the teachers struggled with adapting to the conditions of the region. Additionally, the communities of Cappadocia were mostly Turcophone and knowledge of Turkish was an important criterion in order to be employed as a teacher by the communities. In an article in the periodical *Terakki*, for example, it was argued that a teacher had to speak the language of his/her students' mother tongue in order to be helpful.[92] In view of all these, the Seminary served the needs of Cappadocia very well, especially for the poor villages which were unable to appoint teachers from elsewhere.[93]

According to refugee testimonies, in the Turcophone villages of Cappadocia children were able to learn Greek through schooling. In some villages (for example, Gelveri), Turkish was prohibited from being spoken in schools.[94]

Figure 3.3 Teachers and graduates of the Theological Seminary (1908–1909).
Source: Photography Archive of Centre for Asia Minor Studies

However, some refugees disclosed that despite the best endeavors of teachers, children continued speaking Turkish at home.[95] Teaching the Greek language and Greek history was intended to generate national Greek consciousness in the minds of children, but its success was questionable. I believe that *Hellenization* attempts in Cappadocia were not successful until times of discontinuity, namely the nationalist Committee of Union and Progress (CUP) policies and the long war (1912–1922), and in my view the nationalization of these communities was only successfully completed after their expulsion to Greece. For earlier times we can talk about intermittent proto-nationalism and a broader Community consciousness which fluctuated between preservation of the status quo, conduct of daily business and sympathy toward the national Greek cause. An example is that of a prominent Cappadocian emphasizing the importance of learning how to write and read Turkish (in Arabic letters) for the Neapolitans (Nevşehirlis) in the *Anatoli* newspaper in 1891:

> We are in transaction with the subjects of Sultan and ninety-nine percent of our exchange is conducted in Turkish. Why don't we read and write it? [...] Why does not exist anybody who can read and write Turkish in each shop? [...] It is more useful to teach Turkish language to pupils than astronomy or theology.[96]

The importance attributed to the Turkish language was also visible in other issues of *Anatoli*. For example, in one of its issues from 1895, an announcement was made for those who wanted to learn to read and write Ottoman Turkish.[97] It seems that at both the public and the intellectual level, particular value was given to Turkish. For most Cappadocian Orthodox of the time, Turkish was the mother tongue and therefore it meant a comfort zone where people could easily express themselves; whereas for intellectuals it was a means to assuming a role in Ottoman society and, for this reason, the Orthodox had to learn to read and write in the Arabic alphabet.

In general, administration, control and supervision of Orthodox schools were undertaken by a mix of bodies including ecclesiastical and lay members at different levels of the organizational structure of the Community. At the top of the hierarchy were the ecclesiastical and national (ethnic) authorities in Istanbul, consisting of the Patriarch, the Holy Synod and the Permanent Mixed (clergy-laity) National (ethnic) Council. At a local level, there were three levels of educational administration: district, community and parish. At a district level, the head was the metropolitan; there were also Mixed Ecclesiastical Councils and Education committees, who were responsible for the "intellectual progress" in the district. At a community level, school boards, elected by the representatives from communal parishes, carried out direct administration and supervision of educational establishments. At a parish level, the elected school boards managed financial affairs, implementation of curriculums, appointment and dismissal of teachers, and so on. In practice, affairs were never actually this tidy since there were also brotherhood organizations and *syllogoi* (societies) which were very influential.[98]

It was the period of Ottoman reforms (1839–1876) that curbed the traditional privileges of the Patriarchate with the introduction of a mixed council consisting of both clerical and lay members to run communal affairs.[99] Before that the Church was the sole authority on the education of its congregation. Beginning with reforms in the second half of the nineteenth century, the secularized intelligentsia began to lead the educational efforts, rediscovering their ethnic past and attempting to revitalize Greek ethnic ties and sentiments. The middle class in particular became involved in educational matters and initiated privately funded cultural and educational societies (syllogoi) to promote the Helleno-Christian tradition; Athens became the ideological center of Hellenism during this period. Many of the individuals connected with the developing *syllogos* movement were well aware of the fact that the Ecumenical Patriarchate had neither financial nor administrative resources to reform and standardize the educational system of the Greek Orthodox Community of the Empire. During this process, the role of the Modern Greek state cannot be disregarded, as it aimed to enlighten the East, and the National University of Athens had a pivotal role in this mission as it became the intellectual center for both the Greeks of the Kingdom and the Ottoman Greeks.

The associations founded in Athens like the "Association for the Propagation of Greek Letters" (Ο Σύλλογος προς Διάδοσιν των Ελληνικών Γραμμάτων – established in 1869), the "Society of Anatolians, the East" (Ο Σύλλογος των Μικρασιατών, η Ανατολή – founded in 1891) and the Greek consuls in various localities of the Ottoman Empire, also started to get involved in the educational and communal affairs of the Anatolian Orthodox people. Istanbul, with its 300,000 Greek Orthodox, was the rival of Athens as another intellectual center for Greeks. Coupled with their numerical strength, the Greeks of the city were well represented in economic fields, including banking, shipping, manufacturing and commerce. A network of *syllogoi* bore witness to the highly-corporate life of the Greek community. One of them was the Hellenic Literary Society of Constantinople (Ελληνικός Φιλολογικός Σύλλογος Κωνσταντινουπόλεως) (EFSK), which was founded in 1861. The EFSK organized public lectures on topics like physics, chemistry, hygiene, physiology, history, ancient and modern philology, among others, to encourage the advancement and intellectual development of society. It also published a scholarly periodical. In addition to such efforts, it encouraged the intellectual advance of Ottoman Greeks by establishing a library and a public reading room in Constantinople. It inaugurated a series of competitions devoted to the topographical and ethnographical study of the various provinces of the Ottoman Empire. The presence and activities of the EFSK was an inspiration for many other *syllogoi* in Istanbul. There is no doubt that the Ottoman reforms provided an appropriate climate for the initiation of different societies that had both cultural and educational orientations. Finally, *syllogoi* helped the spread of middle-class values among the poor segments of the Community.[100]

98 The path toward nationalism

The *syllogoi* were known to be the most appropriate intermediaries between the wealthy Ottoman Greeks and the educational institutions or activities they wished to support. These societies tried to raise the national consciousness of Ottoman Orthodox Christians by supporting schools as well as non-school cultural activities, such as public lectures and competitions in the Greek language, history and culture, cultural contacts with the Greek Kingdom, publication of the works of ancient Greek authors, the creation of libraries and so on. However, their national-political goal was not always apparent; they aimed to create a sense of Greek ethnic national consciousness in a natural way by exposing people to Greek culture and its achievements and by teaching the Greek language. They did not talk about their *Hellenization* attempts out loud, although the educational activity of the *syllogoi* was influenced by the political precepts of the *Megali Idea* (Great Idea), and targeted supporting, encouraging and reinforcing the Hellenic consciousness of the Greek population of the Empire. In short, regardless of the private views and aspirations of their members and sponsors, the *syllogoi* never publicly espoused the irredentist precepts of the *Megali Idea*. Another reason for their stance was certainly the fact that their activities and publications were under strict Ottoman scrutiny. For example, the EFSK made statements of an openly political nature only after the Young Turk Revolution. All in all, the *syllogos* movement in its heyday aimed not only to found new schools and raise money for the maintenance of the existing educational institutions in the Ottoman Empire but also to utilize their members as carriers of intellectual irredentism. In other words, the most enduring legacy of the *syllogos* movement was its contribution to the maintenance of the Hellenic identity of the Greek inhabitants of remote parts of the Ottoman Empire.[101]

Coming back to Cappadocian immigrants, those who found themselves among the Greek intelligentsia in Istanbul began to become influenced by the atmosphere created by Greek nationalism, and many of them began to imitate the EFSK, and to get involved in educational activities that often resulted in the foundation of their own (relatively minor scale) societies. Not all immigrants were able to create such bodies; Gesi, for example, did not have a brotherhood organization in foreign lands. Although there were exceptions like Gesi, we cannot disregard the importance of brotherhood organizations in the development of the infrastructure and enlightenment of people in Cappadocian localities. For example, according to the first article of the regulation of the Brotherhood of *Agios Georgios*, founded in Istanbul in 1905 for the benefit of the village Aravan, the founding principles of the society were:

i   Supporting the school of Aravan by covering its annual budget deficit;
ii Repair and continuous maintenance of the water pipes of the village since the village has a water scarcity and it is an absolute necessity;
iii At a determined time of the year, it provides aid to the needy families of the village in accordance with the respective resources of the Brotherhood.[102]

Similarly, the regulation of the Brotherhood of *Nazianzos* of Gelveri, founded in 1884 in Istanbul, specified the purposes of the organization as such:

i   Protection of the Orthodox Christian schools of Gelveri;
ii Continuous progress of kindergarten (νηπιαγωγείο), girls' school (παρθεναγωγείο) and urban school (Αστική Σχολή);
iii Provision of books and writing materials for free for the successful and disadvantaged boys and girls.[103]

As another example, Stefo Benlisoy cites the objectives of the society of Papa Georgios, that of Nevşehir, as such:

i   Supporting the progress of education in Nevşehir;
ii Negation of propagation with necessary means and strengthening religious and national feelings;
iii Developing a contact mechanism between compatriots;
iv Improving the wills and wishes of compatriots about Nevşehir;
v   Spreading the national language.[104]

In a similar vein, the founding principles of Areti, the philanthropic society of Prokopi (Ürgüp) founded in 1909, were to improve the schools and financially support the students studying in the local schools.[105] As seen in the above regulations, the main reason for the establishment of brotherhood organizations was to support education efforts in their places of origin. Receiving education meant developing national consciousness and learning the "national language," Greek, an inevitable component of Hellenic identity not yet comprehended by the Orthodox of Cappadocia. As a secondary role, they financially supported the poor, providing scholarships for disadvantaged students or by supporting their learning of crafts. For example, the brotherhood organization of Tenei sent looms from Istanbul for the poor girls learning weaving. Later those girls worked for the Armenian carpet company (the original name of the company was "Halı Fabrikası") and were able to earn a living.[106]

As an interesting point, one of the means of collecting money for the schools was organizing theatrical performances (θεατρικές παραστάσεις) in the major theater halls of the time. Issues of *Anatoli*, especially in years 1890 and 1891, were full of invitations to such performances, as well as news and analyses about the attendance and interest of the Anatolian Christians.[107] *Anatoli*'s role in education cannot be disregarded. It had continuously supported schooling activities since its first issues in the 1850s. The development and enlightenment of Anatolia seem to be the reason for its very existence. The owner of the newspaper, Evangelinos Misailidis, was in fact known as the teacher of the Anatolians. Many articles were published to raise consciousness about the importance of education, not only during his supervision of the paper, but also after his death. An interesting excerpt from the newspaper:

100 *The path toward nationalism*

We shall open our eyes. We are no longer on our own. Railroads are being built in our Anatolia. American people will come to our motherland for work. If we remain illiterate, we could only be their servants.[108]

Returning to schooling activities, girls' schools and kindergartens had a particular importance in the acquisition of the Greek language at an early age. In the eyes of intellectuals, the role of women was to raise the children; therefore, if they knew the national language, they could teach it to their children. So, the primary objective of a girls' school was to teach women Greek. Kindergartens were also important for the acquisition of Greek by Turkish speaking Orthodox communities. Children were sent to kindergartens at 4 or 5 years of age with the intention of distancing them from their Turkish speaking family members and being taught Greek.[109] In addition to their role of planting an ethnic national consciousness in the minds of people from a nationalist intellectual point of view, the schools worked to safeguard against plausible, alien, religious or national proselytization (Roman Catholic, Protestant, Islamic or Slavic) from the perspective of the Greek Orthodox Church.[110] Through education, the position of Orthodox Christianity was strengthened in its competition with other faiths; in other words, in its struggle not to lose members in favor of other sects. In the case of Cappadocia, the primary rivals of Orthodoxy were Islam and Protestantism. As a final remark, among its other consequences, it could be surmised that the most important outcome of schooling was the expansion of nationalism from an elite level to a popular level by providing an ideological basis for already existing cracks, contestations and antagonisms between religious communities. It would not be wrong to claim that education initiated proto-nationalism in the minds of students and, thus, indirectly in the minds of their parents. It raised the consciousness of a broader Community as people became aware of their kinship with people living in remote places.

Prominent Orthodox figures of Greater Cappadocia and their stance toward nationalism

Owing to schools and immigration, an urban educated Cappadocian class emerged in the late nineteenth century. There were also many prominent Turcophone figures of Anatolian origin in the fields of politics, education, press and medicine.[111] Among those who dealt with commerce, the Onasis and Bodosakis families became the wealthiest in Greece. Additionally, the number of students who continued their education at the University of Athens grew steadily. Some of these people met nationalist romanticism much before their compatriots, and tried to help and enlighten them through the *syllogos* movement. Some of them, on the other hand, worked for and believed in the integrity of the Ottoman Empire, and served as deputies in the Ottoman Parliament, as we will see in the cases of Emmanouilidis and Carolidis.[112] I even came across a medical doctor from Niğde, Alexandros Yagtzoglou, who received his diplomas from the Universities of Athens and France, respectively, and who worked for the Ottoman army in the First World War and for the army of Mustafa Kemal in Turco-Greek War (1919–1922).[113] In view of the dissimilar standpoints of these educated Cappadocians, and despite what nationalists wanted to believe, people had complicated feelings of belongingness and nationalism was often too strict for complex individual concerns. On the one hand there were strict communal boundaries based on religious affiliation, and nationalism strengthened these boundaries, particularly during years of discontinuity or crisis; on the other hand, individuals were torn between their various identities. In the early twentieth century, for example, one could be a devoted Christian and an enthusiast of Ancient Greek Civilization, a loyal citizen of the Ottoman Empire, a critic of Young Turk policies, a sympathizer of royalists in the Greek Kingdom, an opponent of Venizelists and an admirer of Asia Minor and the Turkish language all at the same time. Before the age of nationalism, all these viewpoints could be accommodated in a single Christian identity. In the end, being a Christian only indicated not being a Muslim or a Jew, and competition between religious communities did not necessarily mean that there was conflict, as borders were impervious. Unlike pre-modern religious identity, national identity was stricter and less permeable; the Other was regarded as the foe, and homogeneity was more acceptable than diversity. Under the strictness of nationalism, individuals juggling with various states of belonging were forced to pick sides.

Emmanuil Emmanuilidis was one of those individuals who was forced to change sides as a result of the nationalist aggression of the Young Turks. Having lived most of his life as a devoted Ottoman citizen, but passing as a Greek patriot, Emmanuilidis was an interesting figure and one of the few prominent and educated Cappadocians. He was born in Tavlusun, Kayseri, in 1860 and studied law in both Istanbul and Athens. He worked as a lawyer in Izmir for many years. In the aftermath of the Greek Ottoman War of 1897, he published the journal *Aktis* (ray), in *dimotika* [the popular Greek vernacular] as a reaction against the purists using *katharevoussa*, and despite fierce opposition. Emmanuilidis served as a deputy in the Ottoman Parliament due to his close relations with the local branch of the Committee of Union and Progress and represented Izmir and Aydin provinces between the years 1912 and 1919. With a certain distance from the two established perceptions of nationalism adopted by the Greek intellectuals, who had been known either as *Yunancılar* (the Hellenists who supported the unification of "unredeemed Greeks" under the Hellenic state) or as *Bizansçılar* (the Byzantinists who supported the replacement of Ottoman rulers with Orthodox Christians), Emmanouilidis was an Ottomanist who believed in collaboration with Muslim Turks for the integrity of the Empire.[114]

Like Emmanouilidis, Pavlos Carolidis was an Ottomanist who spent most of his life in Athens as a university teacher. During his years in Athens, he devoted himself to the Enlightenment of his compatriots from Asia Minor. Similar to the biography of Emanuilidis, Carolidis was born in the town of Endürlük (Andronikio), near Kayseri, in 1849. His parents were wealthy Turkish speaking landowners. He studied first in Smyrna at the Evangelical School (Evageliki

102 The path toward nationalism

Sholi), and then in Istanbul at the Patriarchal Academy, also known as the Supreme School of the Nation (Mekteb-i Kebir, Megali tou Genous Sholi). He later moved to Athens, where he studied history at the university. He continued his studies in Munich, Strasburg and Tubingen, Germany. Following his lengthy studies, he worked as a professor in Istanbul, Izmir and finally at the University of Athens upon the encouragement of the Greek Prime Minister Charilaos Trikoupis (1832–1896). In Athens, he became a member of the Society of Anatolians, the East (see above), and played a prominent role within the Asia Minor–Athens network.[115] Among the twenty-four deputies of Greek origin, Carolidis represented Izmir in the Ottoman Parliament after the 1908 elections.[116] Though an independent member of parliament in 1908, he was elected within the CUP in 1912. As an Ottoman patriot, he valued the integrity of the Empire.

Unlike these two Ottomanists, Ioakeim Valavanis was a Greek nationalist of Cappadocia origin. Born in Aravan, Niğde, Valavanis completed his education first at the Supreme School of the Nation in Istanbul, and later receiving philology and philosophy degrees from the University of Athens. He was also known for his three-volume book, *Νεοελληνική Κιβωτός* (*Yunani–i Cedid'in Sandukası*, Modern Greek Ark), an anthology of Modern Greek poets and prose writers.[117] His other educational works were *Απανθίσματα Ελληνικών Γραμμάτων* (Anthologies of Greek Literature) and *Αναγνωσματάριον εκ του Ηροδότου* (Reading book from Herodotus). Valavanis devoted himself to the enlightenment of his compatriots about their ethnic identity. In his *Mikrasiatika* (1891), he complained about the indifference of Anatolians to their ethnic origins. He wrote once that

> if you ask a Christian, even one speaking as a corrupted Greek: "What are you?" "A Christian (Christianos)," he will unhesitatingly reply. "All right, but other people are Christians, the Armenians, the Franks, the Russians ..." "I don't know," he will answer, "yes, these people believe in Christ but I am a Christian." "Perhaps you are a Greek?" "No, I'm not anything. I've told you that I am a Christian, and once again I say to you that I am a Christian!" he will reply to you impatiently.[118]

With these lines, Valavanis was pinpointing the indifference of humble people to Greek nationalism. He was right. Even in the late nineteenth century, many people had not yet embraced the Greek national cause and remained unresponsive to it. Conversely, Valavanis was a Cappadocia origin Greek nationalist and always a critic of his compatriots since he found them ignorant.

Another prominent figure from the Greater Cappadocia area was Evangelinos Misailidis, who was born in Kula in 1820 and died in Istanbul in 1890. Like the intellectuals mentioned above, he went to the *Evangeliki Sholi* (Evangelical School) in Izmir and continued his education at the University of Athens as a student of philology. Afterward, he worked as a teacher in Alaşehir for a while. Misailidis was one of the most important people in the Turcophone Christian community of the time. He spent his entire life trying to enlighten his compatriots through the press. His publications contributed greatly to the progress of the *Karamanlidika* language. He published several journals like *Mektep-i Fünun-i Meşriki* (School of Eastern Sciences, 1849) and newspapers (*Pelsaret-il Maşrik* – Eastern Herald, 1845; *Şark* – East; *Fünun-u Şarkiyye, Risale-yi Havadis* – News Bulletin, Scientific East, 1850–1851; *Kukurikos,* 1876–1881) the most famous of which was the long-lived *Anatoli* (1851–1912 or 1922).[119] In addition to his contributions to the press, Misailidis is known because of his novel *Temaşa-i Dünya* (1872), which was one of the first novels written in the Turkish language. Throughout his life, Misailidis published ninety-two books in *Karamanlidika*, which constitutes thirty percent of total *Karamanlidika* publications.[120] Having read many issues of his *Anatoli*, I can confirm that Misailidis was a devoted Orthodox and an admirer of Greek culture and history. A careful reading of his articles in *Anatoli* and his novel indicates his ethnic Greek consciousness and he invited his fellow compatriots to discover their origins. He was also a modernist, aware of the importance of knowledge, science, literature, hygiene and history. He aimed to enlighten his reading public on all of these issues. However, it is not easy to decipher if he was an admirer of Greek irredentism or an Ottoman patriot. In the end, he published under Ottoman scrutiny and during the reign of Abdülhamid II under strict censorship. Under such conditions, *Anatoli* did not hesitate to praise the Sultan at every possible occasion. Especially in times of crises between the Ottoman Empire and the Greek Kingdom, the paper took an ostensibly neutral stance.

Originally from the Black Sea region, raised in Cappadocia, Ioannis Kalfoglou was another important personality of the Turcophone Orthodox Community. He learned Greek only later in his life and adopted it as the language of culture and the Greek national ideology.[121] After finishing his studies at the Seminary in Zincidere (Ροδοκανάκειος Ιερατική Σχολή, later known as Καππαδοκική Ιερατική Σχολή),[122] he followed in the steps of Misailidis and proceeded to publish almanacs in *Karamanlidika* to enlighten his compatriots. Between the years 1892 and 1898, he worked as the editor of Misailidis's newspaper *Anatoli*.[123] His major work was the "Historical Geography of Asia Minor" [originally Mikra Asia Kıtasının Tarihi Coğrafyası], in *Karamanlidika*.

Except for Ioannis Kalfaoglou, all the above-mentioned personalities were graduates of the University of Athens. Certainly there were other Cappadocian graduates of the university whose names are not stated here. It seems that there was an intellectual-educational link between Cappadocia and Athens in contrast with the common belief that Cappadocia was an isolated place. Before the nineteenth century it might have been, but in the nineteenth century things changed: technology and transportation developed, Western capital entered the Ottoman Empire, new opportunities opened up and all these induced a new flow of immigration from Cappadocia. This time, however, immigration did not break the connection between the migrants and those left behind. Rather, various links were maintained, including economic, educational, intellectual and sociopolitical ties between the Greeks living in big cities and in the Kingdom, and the Cappadocians. Though it was on a relatively minor scale in comparison with those, for example, between Ionia and Athens, an intellectual-educational connection was also built between Cappadocia and Athens. The schools founded in Cappadocia with the help and aid of the immigrants and societies in foreign lands tied the educated Cappadocians to the rest of the Hellenic world. It is true that immigration left the Orthodox settlements in Cappadocia deserted but it helped to strengthen the religious identity (and later helped to develop a national identity) of the Orthodox of the region.

A channel for greater community consciousness: the *Karamanlidika* press

More often than not, nationalism is pioneered by intellectuals and professionals. Intellectuals develop the basic definitions and characterizations of the nation, and the intelligentsia are the most enthusiastic consumers and purveyors of nationalist myths. The question is how nationalism moved from the elite to the general populace. In the nationalization process of the Orthodox Christians of Cappadocia, schools, associations and the press were the channels for nationalist ideas. The success of these channels was controversial, but it would not be wrong to claim that such efforts planted the first seeds of nationalism and inspired local intellectuals to spread the gospel of nationalism and certainly created a Community consciousness that linked Cappadocians to the broader Orthodox Community. The general schema of the process was: A) a group of people from an Orthodox settlement emigrated to a large commercial city where they met co-religionists who had already developed a nationalist consciousness; B) in their new environment they were influenced by the endeavors of their co-religionists to enlighten and educate the Community in line with Hellenic identity, mostly propagated by the Kingdom; C) the relatively wealthy ones came together and initiated an association/brotherhood to assist and enlighten the village by means of schools and the church; and D) several intellectuals were raised in local schools and helped appraise their local community on many issues from national consciousness to hygiene.

The intellectual propagation of nationalism was not always evident, but penetrated through the teaching of the "ancestral language and history." In this struggle of enlightening the Community, the publications, especially those in mother tongue Turkish, were of special importance. Many newspapers and periodicals were published in *Karamanlidika* like *Aktis* (1910–1914), *Zebur* (1866), *Mikra Asia* (1873–1876) and *Nea Anatoli* (1912–1921) in the last decades of the Empire.[124] In this book, I refer to *Anatoli*, *Terakki* and the missionary paper *Angeliaforos*.

Enlightenment of fellow compatriots was the main concern of *Anatoli*. In its initial years, the mission of *Anatoli* was to bring progress to Anatolia. When we look at the first issues of the paper published between the years 1851–1854, many articles concerned the geography and history of Orthodox settlements in interior Anatolia and the different Greek dialects spoken in Cappadocia. It seems that *Anatoli*'s primary target was to create awareness and appreciation for the motherland. Additionally, extreme emphasis was devoted to education and schools. Many news and articles were about schooling activities in various Cappadocian towns, gratitude for those working for the foundation and development of schools, condemnation of those who did not work enough for the schools and the importance of education in general. From an article written by Misailidis early in 1851:

> each human being comes to life as an animal but in school he leaves the state of animality and develops into a human being; he learns way and method and becomes distinguishable from animals in school. He recognizes his God and begins to contribute to world in every means and serves to his people and his God and works for the benefit of everyone [...][125]

People generally tend to disapprove of the new. When the education movement began in the second half of the nineteenth century, many were suspicious about its benefits. At the time, *Anatoli* played a prominent role in raising awareness about schooling. For example, a letter from Kermira was received by the newspaper in 1852, which gave information about fundamentalists, including local prelates, who were trying to prevent children from going to schools and families from contributing to school expenditure.[126] Similarly, in 1852 a group of people in Niğde tried to prevent the establishment of a school using religious arguments, despite patriarchal support.[127] It seems that in the early phases of the education movement in Cappadocia there were reactionaries who tried to preserve the traditional against the potential attack of the progressive. *Anatoli*'s stance was tough against the fundamentalists. It always pursued a progressive path and even in its early years it aimed to inform its readers about any advancement in science, medicine and technology, and also about the history of the Ottoman Empire and Anatolia, as well as about the origins and importance of the Greek and Turkish languages.

In the 1850s, *Anatoli* encouraged the Anatolian Orthodox to open schools and work for progress. Those were the initial years of schooling activities and there were many fundamentalists who condemned the schools, portraying them as working for evil. In the 1890s, however, in almost all Orthodox settlements of Anatolia there were schools. At this time, *Anatoli* was concerned about the advancement of these schools and supported them in every respect. First, it assumed the role of publishing invitations for theatric performances for the benefit of specific schools of Orthodox settlements, and encouraged Anatolians to attend those activities and contribute to the financing of schools. It also criticized those who attended performances but behaved disrespectfully during the show.[128] Second, news about schools and orphanages and their progress were frequently published; schools of a special kind like the Seminary in Zincidere were introduced to the readers,[129] and the employees of these institutions and their benefactors were praised for their devotion to the cause of enlightenment. In the end, *Anatoli* was always committed to the education and enlightenment of its fellow Christians. As part of its mission, it continuously published news from home and abroad, articles about scientific advancements, translated pieces about child-rearing and other issues of human development, and French, Greek and Turkish serial novels. For Şimşek, *Anatoli* promoted a secular medium in the community and tried to strengthen the consciousness of citizenship rather than solely promoting religious identity.[130] Although a valid interpretation of the newspaper, one should not disregard *Anatoli*'s sensitivity about Orthodoxy; the newspaper informed its readers about the "true faith." Throughout its years of publication, *Anatoli* assumed the role of protector of religion, especially against the missionaries.

During its years under the editorship of Ioannis I. Kalfoglou (1892–1898), *Anatoli* was under considerable financial burden due to reader indifference. Many readers did not pay their subscription fees. At first, they were warned politely; Kalfaoglou himself wrote an open letter, addressing readers as "wisdom lover Anatolians" (Ilimperver Anadolulular), that explained the sacrifices of *Anatoli* over the preceding fifty-five years, and graciously requested that Anatolians appreciate their work.[131] In later issues he was much more explicit in his warnings. Almost every issue included a criticism of those who did not pay their fees. The last warning article was exceptionally harsh, with the title "Why doesn't Anatolia progress?" (Anatoli neden terakki etmiyor?); the "education lover Anatolians" were now labeled as "freeloaders" (otlakçı) due to their continued unwillingness to pay their debts. Not only was that, but the newspaper staff was aware that often a single issue of the newspaper circulated among several people. For the editor, this behavior of Anatolians was ruthless, and their disregard of *Anatoli* was the reason for the backwardness of Anatolia.[132] These lines indicate that the cadre of *Anatoli* assumed the role of teacher of their fellow compatriots and the paper itself was a means for enlightenment. The founder of the paper, Evangelinos Misailidis, was referred to as the "teacher of Anatolia" (Anadolu Hocası)[133] in the paper in the years after he passed away. It is apparent that the administrators of *Anatoli* always took their position seriously, and for this reason they were offended by the indifference of Anatolian Christians.

Subscription to *Anatoli* went from around 500 in 1890 to closer to 300 in 1895. This was less than half of the expected numbers, according to editors of the paper, and for this reason a discussion started in December 1895 as to whether or not there was really a need for the continuation of *Anatoli*. This discussion was initiated by the previous editor of the paper, Nikolaos Soullidis.[134] As a response to Soullidis, one of the writers of the paper came up with an idea and appealed directly to the rich personalities of Anatolia to help the paper financially. Several other letters and articles about the problem were also published until the first months of the next year and all of them agreed on the fact that *Anatoli* was important for Anatolians both as a means for progress but also to save Orthodox Anatolians from the clutches of the Protestants and Jesuit missionaries.[135] Adding to that, *Anatoli* was defended on the basis that it informed its readers about their religion in their mother tongue, in contrast with the Patriarchate which totally disregarded the Turcophone Anatolian Christians and published the "Ecclesiastical Truth" (Εκκλησιαστική Αλήθεια) only in Greek, a language that was not spoken by thousands of Anatolian Christians.[136]

As opposed to *Anatoli* and *Angeliaforos*, *Terakki* was a short-lived periodical published in the heart of Anatolia, in Nevşehir. For this reason, teachers and prominent figures of the region would write articles for the periodical. As with *Anatoli*, *Terakki* targeted progress for the Anatolian Orthodox. In the preamble of the first issue of the periodical, the low number of publications in *Karamanlidika* was discussed in a critical way, and the endeavors of Evangelinos Misailidis to enlighten Anatolia were commended.

One interesting part was the promise for the language of the periodical. The administrators stated that the language of *Terakki* would be plain Turkish, but also argued that some meanings could not be expressed with simple words, and asked for pardon if they occasionally used high-level language.[137] Although the administrators of the periodical were careful about language, by its second issue *Terakki* had already started to receive letters of complaint. A grocer, for example, asked for simple Turkish, a language that could be understood even by grocers, with an emphasis on his occupation.[138] There was a particularly interesting point about the letter of the grocer. Cappadocian Orthodox were known to be grocers in big cities. There was even a character called "*Karamanlı Bakkal*" (Karamanli grocer) in a traditional Ottoman shadow theater. Referring to a common occupation of Cappadocians, *Terakki* had published an article in its first issue in which it had claimed that Anatolians had to follow technology and science rather than traditional ways unless they wanted to continue to be grocers.[139] Therefore, most probably the writer of the letter was being sarcastic in his letter and referring to this article.[140]

I have come across complaints about the use, or lack thereof, of plain Turkish in three *Karamanlidika* publications that I referenced for this book. The Anatolian Orthodox, if they did not receive higher education in community schools, or if they attended Ottoman schools, did not have any knowledge of Ottoman Turkish. They did not know the Ottoman alphabet, nor did they use Arabic and Persian words. Most barely learned how to read *Karamanlidika* in local elementary schools. For this reason, they constantly demanded plain Turkish from the editors. The editors, on the other hand, were individuals educated in higher institutions and capable of using both Ottoman Turkish and Greek (and Katharevousa), and their purpose was educating ordinary folk and raising their intellectual level, rather than publishing in line with popular standards. To this end, the publications promoted not only learning Greek but also writing and reading in Ottoman Turkish. As a remarkable example, *Terakki* magazine answered the complaints it received from its readers about the language with these lines:

> If the reason of publication of *Terakki* is to serve for the public, it has to explain itself with a medium level language; [by this way] the Anatolian could get opinion as well as he could be able to learn the Ottoman language that he already knows or does not know.[141]

108 The path toward nationalism

Anatoli, Terakki and other publications in *Karamanlıca*, despite the low number of subscribers, commonly reached thousands of Turcophone Christians around Anatolia, since one single paper was circulated among many people. The most important benefit of this printed material was that their reading public in Anatolia now had the necessary means to "imagine" the presence of other members of their greater Community. They could now picture how their co-religionists in Pontus, Athens, Thrace and Macedonia were living. Anderson's argument for Europe applies in our case: "print capitalism made it possible for people in growing numbers to think about themselves, and to relate themselves to others, in profoundly new ways."[142] It would be an exaggeration to name the print press as the first example of print capitalism in the Ottoman Empire, but it certainly had an effect on people developing a consciousness about such matters as their communal (in terms of their broader Community of co-religionists, millet), religious and/or national identity.

In furtherance of the creation of a "Community" consciousness, publications helped to create a single literary language called *Karamanlidika* for the Anatolian Christian. Although there were already *Karamanlidika* publications before the nineteenth century, they were mostly religious works and were only accessible to a few people. The development of *Karamanlidika* as a literary language was made possible especially through the endeavors of Evangelinos Misailidis and his enduring newspaper *Anatoli*. Unlike previous times, when the use of Turkish in written form was rare and incoherent, the proliferation of *Karamanlidika* started to create a unified culture with a special devotion to education and enlightenment, and bonded Orthodox communities of different settlements together. For a still agrarian society, these developments should be evaluated within the elite endeavor. As previously mentioned in this chapter, the elite, not only through publications but also through societies, assumed a great role for the realization of the enlightenment of the Anatolian Orthodox.

In concluding this part, I want to stress a few points. It is true that schools, other educational activities and the press aimed to revive a sense of ethnic consciousness in the Orthodox populations of Cappadocia. One part of this story concludes that these attempts were successful, and several people were advantageous enough to receive education and follow newspapers. Some of them were even lucky enough to continue their academic path abroad. Yet the other part of this story means that a lot of men found themselves living and working in foreign lands indefinitely from a very early age, due to economic hardship and lack of education. This was also true for men and women of relatively poor settlements. Schooling, the press and the endeavors of the *syllogoi* and brotherhood organizations were indeed successful, but only to a limited extent. They could successfully inculcate a comprehension of Greek language and create proto-national bonds, but it was not until the times of violence and discrimination after the Young Turk Revolution (1908) and the Balkan Wars (1912–1913) that the national identity of ordinary people started to truly forge; their nationalization could only be finalized after their transfer to Greece and reception by the ideological apparatus of the Greek Kingdom.

Notes

1 İ. Ortaylı, *İmparatorluğun En Uzun Yüzyılı*, p. 48.
2 V. Roudometof, From Rum Millet to Greek Nation: Enlightenment, Secularization, and National Identity in Ottoman Balkan Society, 1453–1821, p. 32.
3 A. D. Smith, *Nationalism and Modernism: A Critical Survey of Recent Theories of Nations*, p. 17.
4 See E. Gellner, *Nations and Nationalism;* E. Hobsbawm, *Nations and Nationalism since 1780: Programme, Myth, Reality*; B. Anderson, *Imagined Communities: Reflections on the Origin and Spread of Nationalism*; D. Stamatopoulos, From Millets to Minorities in the 19th Century Ottoman Empire: an Ambiguous Modernization, p. 253.
5 P. Van der Veer, *Religious Nationalism*, p. 15.
6 A. Smith, *Nationalism and Modernism: A Critical Survey of Recent Theories of Nations*, pp. 45–46.
7 E. Gazi, Revisiting Religion and Nationalism in Nineteenth-Century Greece, p. 95.
8 P. Van der Veer, *Religious Nationalism*, p. 2.
9 H. Erdem, "Do not Think of the Greeks as Agricultural Laborers": Ottoman Responses to the Greek War of Independence, p. 81.
10 See B. Anderson, *Imagined Communities: Reflections on the Origin and Spread of Nationalism*, p. 88; P. Mackridge, *Language and National Identity in Greece 1766–1976*, p. 44; U. Özkırımlı, & S. A. Sofos, *Tormented by History: Nationalism in Greece and Turkey*, p. 22.
11 D. Stamatopoulos, From Millets to Minorities in the 19th Century Ottoman Empire: An Ambiguous Modernization, p. 255.
12 P. Mackridge, *Language and National Identity in Greece 1766–1976*, p. 33.
13 For the issue of "Russian Expectation," see P. Kitromilides, *Enlightenment and Revolution: The Making of Modern Greece*; P. Kitromilides, *Enlightenment, Nationalism and Orthodoxy: Studies in the Culture and Political Thought of Southeastern Europe*.
14 E. Gazi, Revisiting Religion and Nationalism in Nineteenth-Century Greece, p. 96.
15 T. G. Tatsios, *The Megali Idea and the Greek-Turkish War of 1897: The Impact of the Cretan Problem on Greek Irredentism, 1866–1897*, p. 13.
16 A. Koraes, Report on the Present State of Civilization in Greece, pp. 158–159.
17 T. G. Tatsios, *The Megali Idea and the Greek-Turkish War of 1897: The Impact of the Cretan Problem on Greek Irredentism, 1866–1897*, p. 10.
18 V. Roudometof, From Rum Millet to Greek Nation: Enlightenment, Secularization, and National Identity in Ottoman Balkan Society, 1453–1821, pp. 28–29, 30, 33.
19 U. Özkırımlı, & S. A. Sofos, *Tormented by History: Nationalism in Greece and Turkey*, p. 78, 83. Byzantium was not rehabilitated into school manuals until the end of the nineteenth century, the Byzantine Museum was not founded until 1914, and the first professors of Byzantine Art and Byzantine History were only appointed at the University of Athens in 1912 and 1924, respectively; appropriation of the Middle Ages with Greek national historiography took some time. Koulouri & Kiousopoulou quoted in A. Liakos, Hellenism and the Making of Modern Greece: Time, Language, Space, pp. 209–210.
20 I. N. Grigoriadis, *Instilling Religion in Greek and Turkish Nationalism: A "Sacred Synthesis,"* pp. 3, 32–35.
21 U. Özkırımlı, & S. A. Sofos, *Tormented by History: Nationalism in Greece and Turkey*, p. 23.
22 T. G. Tatsios, *The Megali Idea and the Greek-Turkish War of 1897: The Impact of the Cretan Problem on Greek Irredentism, 1866–1897*, p. 3.
23 C. K. Tuckerman, *The Greeks of To-day*, p. 124.
24 K. P. Tsolainos, Greek Irredentism, p. 160.

25 P. Mackridge, *Language and National Identity in Greece 1766–1976*, p. 34.
26 T. G. Tatsios, *The Megali Idea and the Greek-Turkish War of 1897: The Impact of the Cretan Problem on Greek Irredentism, 1866–1897*, p. 10.
27 R. Clogg, The Greek Millet in the Ottoman Empire, p. 186.
28 V. Roudometof, From Rum Millet to Greek Nation: Enlightenment, Secularization, and National Identity in Ottoman Balkan Society, 1453–1821, p. 21.
29 I. N. Grigoriadis, *Instilling Religion in Greek and Turkish Nationalism: a "Sacred Synthesis,"* p. 36.
30 D. Stamatopoulos, From Millets to Minorities in the 19th Century Ottoman Empire: An Ambiguous Modernization, p. 266.
31 D. Livanios, Making Borders, Unmaking Identities: Frontiers and Nationalism in the Balkans, 1774–1913, p. 16.
32 R. Clogg, Anadolu Hıristiyan Karındaşlarımız: The Turkish Speaking Greeks of Asia Minor, p. 79.
33 C. Samouilidis, *Καραμανίτες: Οι Τελευταίοι Έλληνες της Καππαδοκίας*, pp. 22–24.
34 Karolidis quoted in R. Dawkins, *Modern Greek in Asia Minor: a Study of the Dialects of Silli, Cappadocia and Pharasa with Grammar, Texts, Translations and Glossary*, p. 11.
35 CAMS, Cappadocia, Andaval, Paraskevas Ignatiadis.
36 CAMS, Cappadocia, Andaval, Makrina Karadagli.
37 CAMS, Cappadocia, Limna, Anastasia Prodromou.
38 S. Anagnostopoulou, *Μικρά Ασία: 19ος Αιώνας -1919: Οι Ελληνορθόδοξες Κοινότητες από το Μιλλέτ των Ρωμιών στο Ελληνικό Έθνος*, pp. 230–231.
39 H. Hatziiosif, *Συνασός: Ιστορία Ενός Τόπου Χωρίς Ιστορία*, p. 247.
40 S. Anagnostopoulou, *Μικρά Ασία: 19ος Αιώνας -1919: Οι Ελληνορθόδοξες Κοινότητες από το Μιλλέτ των Ρωμιών στο Ελληνικό Έθνος*, pp. 234–235.
41 S. Zandi-Sayek, *Ottoman Izmir: The Rise of a Cosmopolitan Port, 1840/1880*, p. 5, 24.
42 Renieri quoted in P. P. Kapoli, *Πόλη και Μετανάστευση στην Οθωμανική Αυτοκρατορία: Κωνσταντινούπολη και Καππαδόκες Μετανάστες (1856–1908)*, p. 58.
43 G. Augustinos, *The Greeks of Asia Minor: Confession, Community, and Ethnicity in the Nineteenth Century*, p. 80.
44 Y. D. Çetinkaya, *The Young Turks and the Boycott Movement: Nationalism, Protest and the Working Classes in the Formation of Modern Turkey*, p. 15.
45 S. Anagnostopoulou, *Μικρά Ασία: 19ος Αιώνας -1919: Οι Ελληνορθόδοξες Κοινότητες από το Μιλλέτ των Ρωμιών στο Ελληνικό Έθνος*, p. 237.
46 D. Loukopoulos, Η Ξενιτειά. *Deltio*, p. 508.
47 CAMS, Cappadocia, Andaval, Paraskevas İgnatiadis.
48 CAMS, Cappadocia, Aravan, Haralambos Koumr.?
49 CAMS, Cappadocia, Andaval, Haralambos Pasalis.
50 CAMS, Cappadocia, Endürlük, Isaak Karamanoglou.
51 CAMS, Cappadocia, Vexe, Evgenia Tokatloglou.
52 CAMS, Cappadocia, Vexe, Lazaros Farsakoglou.
53 CAMS, Cappadocia, Moutalaski, P. Kiostoglou, Lioudakis Oktovrios.
54 CAMS, Cappadocia, Moutalaski, P. Kioseoglou.
55 CAMS, Cappadocia, Kesi, V. Leontiadis.
56 CAMS, Cappadocia, Ai Konstantinos, Iordanis Aleksandridis, Pantelis Lazaridis.
57 CAMS, Cappadocia, Prokopi, Eustathios Hatzieuthimiadis.
58 CAMS, Cappadocia, Poros, Ioannis Kamalakidis, Amfil. Amfilokiadis.
59 CAMS, Cappadocia, Tsouhour, Kostas Misailidis, Iak. Hairoglou.
60 CAMS, Cappadocia, Erkilet, Anastasios Isakidis.
61 CAMS, Cappadocia, Tenei, Kurillos Terkendoglou.

62 «το αγόρι μου θα κοιμηθή, θα μεγαλώση, θα ξενιτεύση, και θα κερδίση λεφτά ... » Renieri quoted in P. P. Kapoli, *Πόλη και Μετανάστευση στην Οθωμανική Αυτοκρατορία: Κωνσταντινούπολη και Καππαδόκες Μετανάστες (1856–1908)*, p. 27.
63 As a consequence of male immigration and high rates of maternal mortality during child birth and pregnancy, there were too many orphans in Cappadocia. In the latest years of Christian presence in Cappadocia, in some settlements many women were saved by the doctors who studied abroad and came back to serve their communities. K. Nikolaidou-Danasi, *Καισάρεια Τόμος Α': Η Μονή Τιμίου Προδρόμου στο Ζιντζίδερε (Φλαβιανά). Το Πνευματικό και Εκπαιδευτικό Κέντρο της Καππαδοκίας Κερμίρα, Μερσίνα, Ποτάμια*, pp. 144–146.
64 A title of respect used for men.
65 "Ağam sen gideli üç yıl oldu. Diktiğin fidanlar hep meyve verdi. Seninle giden ağalar geldi. Tez gel ağam, tez gel elvermiyor mu? Zalim gurbet sana yol vermiyor mu?" CAMS, Cappadocia, Gelveri, D. Loukidou, M. Haztzopoulou. For the female songs about foreign lands, see. G. Göktürk, *Zalim Gurbet Sana Yol Vermiyor mu? Geride Kalan Ortodoks Kadınların Gözünden Gurbetliğe Bakış*.
66 I. Limnidis. (July 16, 1888). Anatol'da İlm Niçin İleri Gitmiyor? *Terakki*, 5.
67 I. Limnidis. (August 15, 1888). Anatol'da İlm Niçin İleri Gitmiyor? *Terakki*, 7.
68 S. Anagnostopoulou, *Μικρά Ασία: 19ος Αιώνας -1919: Οι Ελληνορθόδοξες Κοινότητες από το Μιλλέτ των Ρωμιών στο Ελληνικό Έθνος*, p. 238.
69 D. Livanios, *Making Borders, Unmaking Identities: Frontiers and Nationalism in the Balkans, 1774–1913*, p. 10.
70 D. Kamouzis, *Elites and the Formation of National Identity*, p. 16, 19.
71 P. Kitromilides, *Greek Irredentism in Asia Minor and Cyprus*, p. 7.
72 S. Anagnostopoulou, *Μικρά Ασία: 19ος Αιώνας -1919: Οι Ελληνορθόδοξες Κοινότητες από το Μιλλέτ των Ρωμιών στο Ελληνικό Έθνος*, p. 371.
73 See G. Augustinos, *The Greeks of Asia Minor: Confession, Community, and Ethnicity in the Nineteenth Century*.
74 A. Ozil, *Orthodox Christians in the Late Ottoman Empire: A Study of Communal Relations in Anatolia*, p. 122.
75 S. Anagnostopoulou, *Μικρά Ασία: 19ος Αιώνας -1919: Οι Ελληνορθόδοξες Κοινότητες από το Μιλλέτ των Ρωμιών στο Ελληνικό Έθνος*, pp. 325–326, 361–364.
76 H. Hatziiosif, *Συνασός: Ιστορία Ενός Τόπου Χωρίς Ιστορία*, pp. 310–324.
77 K. I. Karalidis, *Τσαρκλί Νίγδης Καππαδοκίας*, pp. 61–62.
78 S. Benlisoy, F. Benlisoy, *19. Yüzyılda Karamanlılar ve Eğitim: Nevşehir Mektepleri*, p. 25.
79 CAMS, Cappadocia, Gelveri, K. Sotyropoulos, G. Dopridis.
80 CAMS, Cappadocia, Tenei, Efterpi Koursoglou, Stefanos Giapitzoglou, A. Kuriomidis.
81 CAMS, Cappadocia, Neapoli, Vithleem Kalavoutsoglou, Foteini Georgiadou, Evronia Georgiadou, Marika Trellopoulou.
82 CAMS, Cappadocia, Moutalaski, Mihail Giavroglou, P. Kiostoglou.
83 CAMS, Cappadocia, Prokopi, Efstathios Hatziefthimiadis, Georgios Isaakidis.
84 There was a school for the Muslims at the Turkish neighborhood as well as a separate school for the Protestants. The fact that the schools coalesced with the church affiliation confirms the competition at inter-communal level. See K. Nikolaidou-Danasi, *Καισάρεια Τόμος Α': Η Μονή Τιμίου Προδρόμου στο Ζιντζίδερε (Φλαβιανά). Το Πνευματικό και Εκπαιδευτικό Κέντρο της Καππαδοκίας Κερμίρα, Μερσίνα, Ποτάμια*, p. 41.
85 S. Benlisoy, *Education in the Turcophone Orthodox Communities of Anatolia during the Nineteenth Century*, pp. 102, 254–255.

86 K. Nikolaidou-Danasi, *Καισάρεια Τόμος Β': Η Κατά Καισάρειαν Ροδοκανάκειος Ιερατική Σχολή. Ανδρονίκιο, Μουταλάσκη, Στέφανα*, pp. 57–91. Also for the teachers of the Theological Seminary, see the same book, pp. 35–52, 463–516.
87 K. Nikolaidou-Danasi, *Καισάρεια Τόμος Α': Η Μονή Τιμίου Προδρόμου στο Ζιντζίδερε (Φλαβιανά). Το Πνευματικό και Εκπαιδευτικό Κέντρο της Καππαδοκίας Κερμίρα, Μερσίνα, Ποτάμια*, pp. 91–92.
88 Kayseriye'deki Kappadokiki Ieratiki Sholi. (March 12, 1895). *Anatoli*, 5012.
89 CAMS, Cappadocia, Tenei, A. Kuriomidis.
90 CAMS, Cappadocia, Zile-Kayseri, Eleftherios Hatzipetros.
91 CAMS, Cappadocia, Gesi, D. Manolaka.
92 Anatol'da Hemcinslerimiz Rumca Tahsilinde Niçin Suupet Çekiyorlar? (September 30, 1888). *Terakki*, 10.
93 For statistics about schools I used refugee testimonies because they gave the latest information about the schools. Another source for education statistics was *Xenophanes*; however it only informs us about the years 1905–1906. These two sources do not fully match. See Στατιστική της Επαρχίας Ικονίου, *Xenophanes (3)*, pp. 44–47; Στατιστική της Επαρχίας Καισαρείας (Στατιστικός Πίνακας), *Xenophaness (3)*, pp. 230–233.
94 CAMS, Cappadocia, Gelveri, K. Sotiropoulos, G. Dopridis.
95 CAMS, Cappadocia, Gölcük-Limna, Neofitos Apostolidis, Kosmas Serafimidis.
96

> Biz teba-i şahaneden ve ez cümle alış-veriş içinde bulunuyoruz. Ahz-u itamızın yüzde doksan dokuzu Türkçe'dir. Niçin yazıp okumayalım? [...] Niçin her dükkanda bir Türkçe yazıp okuyan bulunmasın? [...] Mekteplerde Astronomia veyahud teologia okutmaktan ise lisan-ı Türki'yi layıkı ile belletmek daha evliyadır.
> Y. Gavriilidis, (January 24, 1891)

Nevşehirlilere Hem Tavsiye Hem Rica. *Anatoli*, 4288.
97 "Lisan-ı Osmani'yi tahsil etmek arzusunda bulunanlara az vakit zarfında yeni usul üzere tarif olunur. Arzu edenler gazetemize müracaat etsinler." *Anatoli*, February 21, 1895, 4948.
98 Papastathis quoted in A. Kazamias, The Education of the Greeks in the Ottoman Empire, 1876–1923: A Case Study of "Controlled Toleration," pp. 354, 355.
99 R. Clogg, The Greek Millet in the Ottoman Empire, pp. 195–199.
100 See D. Kamouzis, Elites and the Formation of National Identity, pp. 20–22, 29, 37. Also see G. Vassiadis, *The Syllogos Movement of Constantinople and Ottoman Greek Education 1861–1923*, pp. 51, 60–65.
101 See G. Vassiadis, *The Syllogos Movement of Constantinople and Ottoman Greek Education 1861–1923*, pp. 209–210, 230–236. Also see A. Kazamias, The Education of the Greeks in the Ottoman Empire, 1876–1923: A Case Study of "Controlled Toletation," p. 355.
102 *Κανονισμός της εν Κωνσταντινουπόλει Αδελφότητος της Κώμης Αραβάν: Ο Άγιος Γεώργιος*.
103 *Κανονισμός της εν Κωνσταντινουπόλει Φιλεκπαιδευτικής Αδελφότητος Καρβάλης: Ναζιανζός, Ιδρυθείσης τω 1884*.
104 S. Benlisoy, İstanbul'da Yaşayan Nevşehirli Ortodokslar Tarafından Kurulan Papa Yeorgios Nam Cemiyet-i Islahiyyesi, p. 37.
105 S. Benlisoy, İstanbul'a Göçmüş Ürgüplü Ortodoksların Kurduğu Bir Cemiyet: "Areti" Maarifperveran Cemiyeti, p. 7.
106 CAMS, Cappadocia, Tenei, Efterpi Koursoglou, Stefanos Giapitzoglou.
107 Dahiliye. (January 22, 1891). *Anatoli*, 4287.

108 "[...] Gözümüzü açalım. Bundan böyle biz bize kalmıyoruz. Anadolumuzda demir yolları yapılıyor. Geçim için ta Amerika'dan memleketimize ademler gelecektir. Cahil kalır isek hizmetçilikten başka işe yaramayacağız [...]" Anadolumuzun Mektepleri. *Anatoli*, February 24, 1891, 4295.
109 S. Benlisoy, *Education in the Turcophone Orthodox Communities of Anatolia during the Nineteenth Century*, p. 116.
110 A. Kazamias, The Education of the Greeks in the Ottoman Empire, 1876-1923: a Case Study of "Controlled Toletation," p. 362.
111 For a list of prominent people of Asia Minor, see Ch. A. Theodoridou, *Διακριθέντες του Ξεριζωμένου Ελληνισμού: Μικράς Ασίας - Πόντου - Αν. Θράκης - Κωνσταντινουπόλεως, Τόμος Β'*.
112 Other deputies of Cappadocian origin were Pant. Kosmidis (Istanbul, 1908-1912); Mihalakis Stelios (Limni, 1908-1913); Anas. Mihailidis (Izmit, 1908-1918); Georg. Kourtoglou (Niğde, 1908-1912); Aris. Georgantzoglou; (İzmir, 1908-1911); Ananias Kalinoglou (Niğde, 1912-1918); Theod. Arzoglou (Samsun, 1914-1918); I. Gkevenidis (Karahisar, 1914-1918); Vang. Meymeroglou (İzmir, 1914-1918); Vikt. Tsormpatzoglou (1914-1918). M. Harakopoulos, *Ρωμιοί της Καππαδοκίας: από τα Βάθη της Ανατολής στο Θεσσαλικό Κάμπο. Η Τραυματική Ενσωμάτωση στη Μητέρα Πατρίδα*, p. 50.
113 CAMS, Cappadocia, Niğde, Alexandros Yagtzoglou. For his short biography, see Ch. A. Theodoridou, *Διακριθέντες του Ξεριζωμένου Ελληνισμού: Μικράς Ασίας - Πόντου - Αν. Θράκης - Κωνσταντινουπόλεως, Τόμος Β'*.
114 V. Kechriotis, Osmanlı İmparatorluğu'nun Son Döneminde Karamanlı Rum Ortodoks Diasporası: Izmir Mebusu Emmanuil Emmanuilidis, p. 39. For the English version of this article, see. V. Kechriotis, Ottomanism with a Greek Face: Karamanli Greek Orthodox Diaspora at the End of the Ottoman Empire.
115 See V. Kechriotis, Ottomanism with a Greek Face: Karamanli Greek Orthodox Diaspora at the End of the Ottoman Empire; V. Kechriotis, Atina'da Kapadokyalı, İzmir'de Atinalı, İstanbul'a Mebus: Pavlos Karolidis'in Farklı Kişilik ve Aidiyetleri; Ch. A. Theodoridou, *Διακριθέντες του Ξεριζωμένου Ελληνισμού: Μικράς Ασίας - Πόντου - Αν. Θράκης - Κωνσταντινουπόλεως, Τόμος Β'*, pp. 42-43.
116 C. Boura, The Greek Millet in Turkish Politics: Greeks in the Ottoman Parliament (1908-1918), p. 195.
117 I. H. Kalfoglou (1894). Ιωακείμ Βαλαβάνης: Νεοελληνική Κιβωτός. *Ημερολόγιον: η Ανατολή*. Karamanlidika Book Collection, Centre for Asia Minor Studies.
118 Valavanis quoted in R. Clogg, Anadolu Hıristiyan Karındaşlarımız, p. 67.
119 E. Balta, Karamanli Press Smyrna 1845- Athens 1926, pp. 109-110.
120 See M. Erol, Evangelinos Misailidis; E. Balta, Gerçi Rum Isek de Rumca Bilmez Türkçe Söyleriz: The Adventure of an Identity in the Triptych: Vatan, Religion and Language.
121 I. Petropoulou, Foreword. In I. Kalfoglou, *Ιστορική Γεωγραφία της Μικρασιατικής Χερσονήσου*.
122 Many distinguished people taught at the Theological Seminary in Zincidere. One of them was Ilias Emmanouilidis. Being originally from Zincidere, Emmanouilidis was also a medical doctor. Anastasios Nikolaidis, as another distinguished figure, was born in Kermira in a Turcophone family. After completing the Theological Seminary and the gymnasium of Chios, he worked as a teacher in his home town Kermira and afterwards in Moutalaski and Mersina. For the teachers of the Seminary and its prominent graduates, see K. Nikolaidou-Danasi, *Καισάρεια Τόμος Α': Η Μονή Τιμίου Προδρόμου στο Ζιντζίδερε (Φλαβιανά). Το Πνευματικό και Εκπαιδευτικό Κέντρο της Καππαδοκίας Κερμίρα, Μερσίνα, Ποτάμια*.
123 S. T. Anestidis, Introduction. In I. Kalfoglou, *Ιστορική Γεωγραφία της Μικρασιατικής Χερσονήσου*.

114 *The path toward nationalism*

124 See S. Tarinas, *Ο Ελληνικός Τύπος της Πόλης*. For publications in Karamanlidika; E. Balta, *Karamanlidika: Nouvelles Additions et Complements I*; E. Balta, *Karamanlidika: XXE siècle: Bibliographie Analytique;* E. Balta, *Karamanlidika: Additions (1584–1900)*; E. Balta, Karamanli Press Smyrna 1845- Athens 1926; E. Balta & Matthias Kappler,(Eds.),*Cries and Whispers in Karamanlidika Books*.
125 E. Misailidis. (December 11, 1851). Akıl Potası Nedir? Sholeion'dur! *Anatoli*, 47.
126 An anonymous letter from Kermira. (October 28, 1852). *Anatoli*, 90.
127 Dahiliye. (April 8, 1852). *Anatoli*, 62.
128 Dahiliye. (January 22, 1891). *Anatoli*, 4247.
129 Kayseriye'deki Kappadokiki Ieratiki Sholi. (March 12, 1895). *Anatoli*, 5012.
130 Ş. Ş. Şimşek, The Anatoli Newspaper and the Heyday of the Karamanlı Press, p. 117.
131 I. I. Kalfoglous. (August 31, 1895). Ilimperver Anadolululara. *Anatoli*, 5097.
132 Anatoli Neden Terakki etmiyor? (December 4, 1895). *Anatoli*, 5172.
133 Hemşehrilerimize. (February 7, 1891). *Anatoli*, 4293.
134 N. Soullidis. (December 5, 1895). Anatoli Gazetesi Ser Muharriri Rıfatlı Ioannis Kalfaoglou Efendi'ye. *Anatoli*, 5173.
135 A. Grigoriadis. (December 8, 1895). Anatoli'nin Devamına Lüzum Var mı Yok mu? *Anatoli*, 5175.
136 I. Sadeoglou. (February 26, 1896). İzhar Hissiyat. *Anatoli*, 5235.
137 Erbab-ı Mütalaaya. (May 15, 1888). *Terakki*, 1.
138 Bir Mektup: Terakki İdaresine. (June 30, 1888).*Terakki*, 4.
139 M. I, Portakaloglou. (May 15, 1888). Terakki. *Terakki*, 1.
140 For an article about *Terakki*, see M. Orakçı (2014). Karamanlıca Bir Gazete: Terakki.
141 "Eğer Terakki'nin neşrinden maksat ulum-u maarife hizmet ise, bunu orta derecede bir lisan tasvir etmek lazımdır, ta ki Anadolulu yazılan şeyden fikir ala, hem de aynı zamanda, az bildiği veya hiç bilmediği Osmanlıca lisanını da öğrenmiş ola." Bafralı Yanko. (September 30, 1888). Muharrerat: 8. Nüshadan Mabat. *Terakki*, 10.
142 B. Anderson, *Imagined Communities: Reflections on the Origin and Spread of Nationalism*, p. 36.

4 *Halasane ta pragmata* (Things spoiled)

The refugee narrative in testimonies has always been filled with dichotomies. There were good Turks and bad Turks, local Turks and refugee Turks, the years before the Young Turk Revolution and after it, local Greeks and refugee Greeks, life in Turkey and life in Greece, Christianity and Islam and so on. Concerning these dichotomies, one constituent was always relatively good and the other was always relatively bad. "Goodness" and "badness" were determined in accordance with the other component of dichotomy. Relativity prevails and there is no other measure to test the components. For instance, the testimonies of the refugees in the CAMS Oral Tradition Archives portray a relatively peaceful world in the years before the Young Turk Revolution (1908). The Hamidian years were the "good old times" in their narratives. Doumanis interpreted these accounts in an overly positive way and referred to the Hamidian years as a *belle époque* for the Orthodox Christians. It is questionable whether the period of Abdülhamit's reign was really quiet and peaceful. In the nearby Armenian settlements in Cilicia and Cappadocia in 1894–1896 Armenians were persecuted, and the refugees themselves expressed their fear of being killed even at the time of their testimonies. Furthermore, the press was under strict scrutiny and censorship.

I concede that refugees talked about those years in a relatively positive manner and their perceptions drastically changed for the period after the Young Turk Revolution; however, we should evaluate their narratives in accordance with their displacement and loss of homeland after the Turco-Greek Population Exchange and the hardships that they met in their new country, not to mention the persecutions, exile, confiscations, economic boycotts, hunger and ethnic violence they experienced during the "long war" (1912–1922). In the end, oral history is not solely about the past; it is also about the present and future expectations. Therefore, when they were narrating the Hamidian years their perception of the time in question was tainted by the experiences they went through later. It should also be noted that the refugee testimonies did not tell us anything about the years before the Hamidian era, since almost all of the refugees were born during and after the reign of Abdülhamit. So yes, the Hamidian years were perhaps better than the years after the Young Turk Revolution, but it was definitely not a *belle époque*.

116 Halasane ta pragmata *(Things spoiled)*

In the context of Cappadocia, fortunately, we do not need to talk about any great violence and persecutions suffered by the Greeks of Western and Northern Anatolia, since their population was small and their settlements were scattered. Orthodox settlements in Cappadocia were half empty and consisted mainly of women, children and the elderly because of male immigration throughout the nineteenth century. In a traditionally male-dominated world, where clashes occurred due to male aggression, this situation prevented Muslim–Orthodox clashes. Poverty-stricken Orthodox women started to work in the fields of Muslims and even got married to Muslim men due to economic hardships. Remarkably, in some villages, rather than fighting with each other, Orthodox and Muslim individuals were brought closer together.

According to many interviewees of the CAMS, the Balkan Wars created great distrust and suspicion between Muslim and non-Muslim communities in Cappadocia and the situation got worsened after the declaration of the First World War. For some of the interviewees, inter-personal intimacy between Christians and Muslims continued until late into 1922, and then everything got worse. Many settlements of Cappadocia suffered additionally from famine during the war years and under such conditions they were forced to help the Turkish army. Zincidere, for example, became the center for recruitment where the conscripted Turkish soldiers coming from the periphery were transferred to battlefields. The army took whatever they had from their hands. They also took the orphanage. The orphans, mostly Armenians, were distributed among the locals. Other than the orphanage, buildings of the schools and all the facilities of the monastery were used for military needs. For example, in 1916 the building of the Theological School became a hospital for the wounded soldiers.[1]

There is a common understanding that Cappadocians were mostly indifferent and did not take sides during the "long war." Some scholars explain this on the basis of the isolated location of the region, both from the main centers of Hellenism and from the battlefields. I disagree with this point of view for three reasons: first, Cappadocian Christians were not indifferent to the war; they had diverse views and perspectives about the war. Second, they were living among the Muslim masses and most of the male population was away from the homeland so they remained relatively silent out of necessity. Third, Cappadocia was not an isolated region in the early twentieth century; it had strong familial, socio-political, religious, intellectual and educational ties with coastal areas. There were Cappadocian immigrants in big coastal cities and they had strong bonds with their homelands and there was a flow of students from Cappadocia to Istanbul and Athens; the Greek Kingdom had been interested in Cappadocia for a long time and Greek consulates had already been opened in some Central Anatolian *vilayets* like Konya (established in 1906). In this way, Athens, in collaboration with the Ecumenical Patriarchate, mobilized its diplomatic powers to create the feeling of the "mother country" for Greece.[2] Newspapers and publications were also in circulation in the region, and Cappadocian dioceses had been under the hierarchy of the Greek Orthodox Patriarchate for some time. In consideration of all these factors, again I suggest that although the Cappadocian

Orthodox were ostensibly indifferent to war, they actually had some perspective and stance. Due to their small number, however, they hesitated to publicly declare their political stance. The lack of male power was a fundamental factor in their silence.

How and why, then, did the Orthodox in Cappadocia gradually become nationalized? This is an important question, but the answer is not complicated and the case of the Cappadocians is not that different from the cases of the Orthodox in other Ottoman territories. As related above, educational activities were aimed at instilling a national consciousness into the Cappadocian communities, most of whose maternal language was Turkish. It initiated the "nationalization" process and created the "imagination" of the broader Community, thus generating proto-national bonds. However, its success concerning the adoption of the Greek language was controversial; refugee testimonies show that people resisted, be it consciously or unconsciously, the adoption of the Greek language. Added to that, the memories of intellectuals and European travelers also showed that many of them resisted accepting the national Greek identity since they regarded it as an attack on their Christian identity. It seems that national identity was very rigid for individuals who had diverse or even contradictory identities.

Nationalism stipulates that to be an ethnic Greek one had to be a Greek-speaking Orthodox Christian with a sense of attachment to the Greek cause. For ordinary people, the Greek national identity was not as important and influential as it was for Greek intellectuals. Their identity was shaped by their religion, and by village and familial bonds. Their maternal language, Turkish, was not alien to them, as Greek nationalists regarded it. Speaking Turkish meant speaking without effort. I believe that Cappadocian Christians of the time occupied a third space, outside of Turkishness or Greekness, as a quasi-literate rural community. It was not until their settlement in Greece did most people adopt a national identity; Turks were no exception. National identity was alien to traditional communities. For Orthodox Christians, the economic boycott of 1914, the continuous wars, the Greek campaign in Asia Minor and the exile they suffered all forged the communal belongingness that originated from religion and was strengthened by the walls between the Self and the Other. Their previous relations with the Turks, the competitive nature of co-existence or religious millenarianism had nothing to do with nationalism. They were first exposed to nationalistic ideals at school, but they couldn't fully grasp its meaning until the onset of war, and afterward they began to treat nationalism like a security blanket. Nationalistic policies, wars and violence were a discontinuity from the past; there was now a legitimate atmosphere to make the masses believe the nationalistic cause of the elite and politicians. Nationalism was a new phenomenon but it settled and fed on the existing features of relations and belongingness. Schools and publications planted the first seeds, but to a great extent it was the war years that made most people believe in a national cause, and their nationalization was finalized after their settlement in the Greek state and their reception by its institutions.

Economic boycott

The increasingly nationalistic policies of the Young Turks generated a discontinuity from the past. Such policies affected Orthodox Christians all over Anatolia. Cappadocians may have been the luckiest of all Orthodox Christians, but their testimonies show that things radically changed in their lives as well. According to general refugee chronicle, "things spoiled: χαλάσανε τα πράγματα."

The Young Turk Revolution was initially a movement promising equality for all citizens of the Ottoman Empire regardless of their religious beliefs. During its first phases, it indeed created an atmosphere of freedom and generated a genuine feeling of hope for non-Muslims. In fact, they thought that the revolution would open posts for them in higher positions in the state administration, and help them to strengthen their position in the economy. With a few exceptions, such as the Patriarchate, whose authorities feared losing their traditional power, Orthodox Christians supported the revolution.[3] In time, however, several issues, such as general military conscription, the boycott movement first against foreigners and later against local non-Muslims, and finally persecutions, including exile and confiscation, alienated Orthodox Christians from the Ottomanist ideal of the revolution. Cappadocians were no exception. The question here is why the Young Turks chose to diverge from their original ideas about creating a multinational federative state with a liberal constitution. For Mourelos, the successive defeats between 1911 and 1913, the almost total loss of the Ottoman territories in North Africa and the Balkans and the change in the ethnic composition of the population, with a predominantly Turkish element, resulted in the creation of strong nationalist tendencies.[4]

Particularly from 1913 onwards, the Young Turk program evolved into a triptych: Westernization, Turkification and Islamization. The latter two went hand in hand because Turkification could only be effective on the Muslim population. The Muslim religion played a facilitating role in the Turkification of the Muslim population, and the Turkish state bourgeoisie was the instrument of modernization of society. These two policies would eventually de-Ottomanize the state, society and Anatolia.[5] By early 1908, the Committee of Union and Progress (CUP) had already initiated a movement of Turkification in the economy by means of eliminating foreign elements from the Turkish economy through the boycott movement. Different foreign merchants and the business activities of foreign countries such as Austria-Hungary, Bulgaria, Italy, the United States and Greece within the Ottoman Empire were the targets of this policy. The reasons for the boycott movements were mainly political. For example, Austria-Hungary's annexation of Bosnia-Herzegovina was the reason for boycotting Austrian products. Intensification of the boycott of European products affected non-Muslims severely. Non-Muslim merchants had been benefiting from the absorption of the Ottoman economy into the world capitalist economy throughout the nineteenth century and they had been operating under the protection of the Great Powers. Accordingly, when a Muslim protest spoke out against foreign states, including Greece, the native merchants acting in close collaboration with the Great Powers and those who could benefit from the opportunities provided by the capitulations suffered just as much as the foreign merchants. As the boycott movement strengthened its network and organization, the resentment of non-Muslim communities increased.

The call for a National Economy (Milli İktisat) gradually led to a demand for a Muslim Turkish dominance in the Ottoman economy. In 1909 and, particularly, 1910 the economic dominance of non-Muslims in the Ottoman Empire slowly became one of the main targets of this political and economic protest movement. The movement slowly moved against native non-Muslims, who subsequently suffered greatly. The protests against Crete's call for *enosis* (union) with Greece provoked a wave of political meetings. Ottomans started to call for a boycott against particularly Greek merchandise in the years 1910–1911. The boycott organizations, which mainly comprised port workers, persons of note and low-ranking bureaucrats, were reactivated during the mass meetings against Greece. Within a short time, problems emerged regarding the definition of what was Greek. The boycott officially targeted the Hellenes, the citizens of the Greek state and exempted the Greek citizens of the Ottoman Empire. Yet the Greek community and the Patriarchate argued that the Ottoman Greeks were also influenced by the boycott, since both groups had deep and close bonds.[6]

Emmanuil Emmanuilidis, a deputy of the CUP between the years 1912 and 1919, wrote about the boycott movement in 1914 in his memoir, saying, economic boycott was declared in mosques, societies and in newspaper articles for the sake of God and the prophet. Muslims were prevented shopping from the non-Muslims and the transactions were annulled. If one rejected it, he was beaten severely and the object was destroyed. The law was named "national revival" (milli uyanış).[7] The boycott movement affected the Cappadocian Orthodox merchants as well. The resentment against the movement was quite clear in a refugee testimony:

> In 1908, the Young Turks appointed Tahir Bey to our city. He visited firstly the Orthodox and Armenian Churches and then gathered the Turks in Paşa Mosque. He made them promise before our eyes and said: "Donkeys! You have surrendered the city to Christians; I don't see any single trading activity in your hands; Christians made you their slaves." Afterwards, the wealthy Turks of Bor initiated a company to dispose of us but they could not succeed. We started to lose. Turks confidentially entered Christian trade; they were buying for cheaper and were able to bring better goods. The Young Turks encouraged them to enter trading. In time, especially during the time of Kemal [Mustafa Kemal Paşa], things got worse. Young Turks started to force Turks to abandon shopping from Christian stores.[8]

In another testimony, an interviewee recalled how Christian possessions changed hands during the long war:

120 Halasane ta pragmata *(Things spoiled)*

They bring you an illiterate Turk to be employed. After a while they want you to take him as your partner. In a few months he wants to change his work and by this way you lose your own shop. In the end, shopkeepers were forced to be dependent on Turkish aghas and merchants.[9]

The Turkification of the economy, particularly through the boycott movement, and the subsequent ethnic cleansing policies led to the final and irrevocable decline of the Greek Ottoman bourgeoisie.[10] In 1914, right after the outbreak of the First World War, thousands of Greeks were forced to either convert to Islam or leave Western Anatolia and Thrace for Greece. This policy was justified by security concerns in coastal and border areas; the Turkish army claimed to be caught between two fires: foreign enemies and internal enemies.[11] Around the time of the 1914 cleansing operation, the Ottoman diplomatic minister in Athens, Galip Kemali (Söylemezoğlu), proposed to the Greek authorities that the Muslims of the Greek administrative provinces of Macedonia and Epirus should be exchanged with the rural Greek population of the Smyrna province and Ottoman Thrace. Greek Prime Minister Venizelos seemed to approve of this idea of exchange on condition that it would be voluntary and that the persecution and forced migration of Greeks would cease. The outbreak of the First World War, however, prevented the project of exchange.[12]

Administrative harassment was followed by the persecutions of bandits (başıbozuk) in Western Anatolia. Among them were the Cretans who suffered at the hands of the Greeks and who wanted to take revenge.[13] To a lesser extent, bandits persecuted people in Cappadocia, especially after the termination of the Turco-Greek war. Among these settlements there were Bereketlimaden and Gürümce (Κουρούμτζα).[14] According to Ottoman sources, 163,975 people were forced out just from Northwestern Anatolia to Greece.[15] Exile policies continued throughout the Great War. The Black Sea region and, to a lesser degree, Cappadocia were no exceptions, and the reasons for exile were always security concerns and the rebellious activities of the Orthodox. Refugee testimonies show how the Orthodox suffered after the Young Turk Revolution. As previously mentioned, interviewees usually made a distinction between the years before and those after the Young Turk Revolution: "before *Hürriyet*, our Turks never harmed us; only the foreigners would bully us."[16] "We got along well with the Turks and lived like brothers; after the constitution, however, they got wild and wanted to kill all the Christians but the governor (mutasarrıf) of Niğde did not let them do it."[17] Testimonies also reveal the times of exile:

> Two-three years before the Exchange, Turks forced many Orthodox to exile from Western shores to interior lands. All of them were fifteen to sixty years old males. We hosted in our village around sixty men from Isparta. They stayed for several days and left our village for nearby villages. Only ten of them stayed in our village. We helped them.[18]

Halasane ta pragmata *(Things spoiled)* 121

In 1919, expatriate Christians from Antalya, Isparta, Alanya and Silifke came to our village. They stayed with us and we all left with the Exchange.[19]

The boycott movement and, later, the exile policies of the Young Turks were part of the general policy of economic and political homogenization. Non-Muslims were no longer seen as members of a whole that used to comprise the Ottoman nation; now instead it was the Turkish nation. Muslim groups could be absorbed by the Turkish nation in the long run, but non-Muslims were seen as betrayers and their presence was regarded as harmful for the prospective Turkish nation. Tolerance was rapidly replaced by persecution. The constitutive Other of the Self had become a "constitutive foe" for a nation to be realized. In the end, all nations require a "foe" to come into being. The nationalist aggressiveness of the CUP leadership raised the communal borders at a societal level; however, individual responses were still torn between resentment of the state and the need to protect the existing, to remain in one's hometown, to survive and to continue economic transactions.

General military conscription and the long war (1912–1922)

Under the CUP administration, compulsory military service entered the lives of the Orthodox in 1909, one of the first causes of resentment. The idea was first tabled in 1855 when the *jizya* tax levied upon non-Muslims was abolished in order to achieve equal citizenship for everyone. At the time, military service was made compulsory for everyone, and the decision became official with the Reform Decree (Islahat Fermanı) in 1856. However, non-Muslims were reluctant to serve in the army and the decision was not applied. A tax in lieu of military service called *bedelat-ı askeriye* was open to anyone, including Muslims, who did not want to be conscripted.[20] In August 1909, the compulsory military service law was enacted and most of the non-Muslim deputies supported the idea to retain equal citizenship.[21] At the grassroots level, however, non-Muslim people and their religious authorities did not like the idea of compulsory military service. For instance, in Tarsus, the Christian community did abide by the inspection related to the call for recruitment. In Niğde, some soldiers of the reserve were claimed to be in America when the Balkan War broke out.[22] Many young Christian men, especially Greeks, who were wealthy enough and had overseas connections, opted to leave the country or obtain a foreign passport. To exemplify this, many males of Sulucaova (Kayseri) were exempted from military obligations when they either left for Western countries or paid a certain amount of money.[23] Some of the deserters were not able to go to America or Europe; for them either Egypt or a *vilayet* away from their military zone was a destination.[24] Several of them, rather than leaving the country, changed their nationality or paid a larger amount called *bedel-i nakti* (along with the prosperous Muslims) but they too were nonetheless conscripted during the First World War. Most non-Muslim soldiers worked in labor battalions

122   Halasane ta pragmata *(Things spoiled)*

(amele taburları) doing repair work on roads and railways, or carrying supplies to the front, and most were unarmed.[25] Sir Samuel Hoare noted that conscription of non-Muslims in labor battalions was the most effective way of exterminating the Christian populations employed by the Young Turks.[26] From another perspective, it was not so until the Balkan War when hundreds of Greek and Bulgarian soldiers and later some Armenians changed sides. For this reason the Ottomans took away their weapons and put them behind the front.[27] Below you will find refugee testimonies that highlight the consequences of general military conscription from the perspective of ordinary people.

> Greeks were also conscripted in the Balkan Wars. The ones who did not have forty-four golden liras were recruited. [In our town] sixty men paid the amount and one thousand two hundred men joined the army. It seems that they were not good soldiers because in the European War [they call the World War the European War] they were recruited not in the army but in the labor battalions.[28]

> Beginning from Hürriyet [they also call it Syntagma which means constitution in Greek], it began to be difficult for us because before we were paying an amount not to become soldiers. With Hürriyet, they recruited us as soldiers. The rich people could settle their children wherever they wanted since they had money. The ones who suffered were the children of poor people. They served as soldiers.[29]

> During the war [1914] they recruited me, my brother and my father in the army [...] We laid out the roads.[30]

> We hid inside *keleria* (cellars) not to become soldiers during seferberlik [campaign]. I was recruited only for ten or twelve days. Afterwards, I brought a false document showing that I am forty-five and I was not taken as a soldier again.[31]

According to refugee testimonies, the conditions in the army were much worse for non-Muslims since they would be working in labor battalions and the wars were continuous. For this reason, those who could afford *bedel-i nakti* did not serve in the army. Among the poor, many deserted from the Ottoman army and hid in cellars (underground settlements of Cappadocia), which they called *keleri*.

Deserters were not few in number but there were also people who continued to serve in the Ottoman army and, later, in the army of Mustafa Kemal during the Turkish–Greek War (1919–1922). People had various attachments and most of their behavior was shaped by fear during the long war. While some people tried to show their attachment to the Turkish cause, many others sought to run away or to be dismissed. Also, we cannot disregard the perplexed people whose national attachment was shaped by either self-interest or personal antipathy to

Greek or Turkish nationalists. An interesting figure with a confused mind was Kosmas Serafeimidis. Blocked by the trenches of the Turkish nationalists in Mersin, he went to Lesvos Island in 1920 in order to volunteer for the Greek army in Izmir. He was a Turkophone Orthodox, and was rejected for this reason. Later, we see him as a volunteer in the Turkish army; eventually he reached Izmir and became a postman in a local post office.[32] There were different soldier stories recounting a variety of attachments of individuals. It seems that although soldiers fought for either the Turkish or Greek national cause, their national identities were still fluid and were mostly shaped by fear, weariness and resentment, and changed according to the circumstances. For example, Sergeant (Çavuş) Ioannis from Karacaören fought in the Ottoman army from 1914. In 1920 he was recruited by the army of Mustafa Kemal; in 1923 he was dismissed and returned to his village.[33] Similarly, Eleftherios Iosifidis worked in the labor battalions of the Turkish army in Sivas between the years 1921 and 1922.[34] Dimitrios Misailidis, on the other hand, deserted from the Ottoman army in 1914 and lived in the mountains with a false Turkish identity until the armistice. In 1919 or 1920 he was recruited to the army of Mustafa Kemal, when he again deserted with his compatriots.[35] Alexandros Yagtzioglou, a gynecologist from Niğde, was recruited by the Ottoman army in 1914 and served in the Black Sea, Iraq and Iran until 1918. Between 1919 and 1924, he drew closer to the army of Mustafa Kemal.[36] Deserters, dismissed soldiers and voluntary fighters, among other things, the Orthodox of Cappadocia responded in many different ways during the ongoing wars. Some of them believed in the Greek cause and expected to be saved by Greece. However, there were also individuals who were continually altering sides in line with the shifting conditions. We cannot even be sure that people supported the Greek cause with nationalistic feelings. It might still have been millenarianism; they may have desired to be saved from the Muslims, as devoted Christians who believed that their punishment by God to be dominated by the "infidel" had to end. One way or another, continuous wars and the ultimate displacement of peoples strengthened the borders of communities, and the final separation of communities completed their nationalization through ideological state apparatus.

The war years brought endless hardships. The number of losses had never been so huge. Death was not a natural phenomenon at the time. Thousands of people killed each other and there was no sacred cause behind it, as not only soldiers but also civilians lost their lives. This abundance of loss created an emptiness in people's souls. What was the reason for all this suffering? At this time, the ideal and feeling of nationalism arrived to save the masses from emptiness and misery. People understood that all the hardships suffered up to that time were for the benefit of the nation. Losses and despair suddenly became meaningful. National identity was no longer something to be escaped; it was not an alien element that swallowed religious identity, but rather a security blanket at a time when religion remained inadequate to answer the question of why. Up until that time it was an empty concept for ordinary people, but now it became a sanctified cause for the sake of which millions could die.[37]

The Turkish–Greek war and the movement of Papa Efthim

During the war years, the Anatolian Orthodox met a problem that they had never faced before. For the first time, they realized that they could be forced to leave their motherlands. The Armenians had already experienced this, and the same could happen to them as well. In this sense, Papa Efthim was in a way a savior for many of the Orthodox. Efthim was a realist whose decisions were in line with the changing circumstances of the time. He was also a passionate personality who was always sought for leadership.

Efthim, originally from Akdağmağden, was appointed a priest in Keskin Maden by the Metropolitan of Trabzon in 1918. He established the "Turkish Orthodox Church" (1921) and aimed to separate the Turkish speaking congregation of the Anatolian interior from the Ecumenical Patriarchate, with the support and direct involvement of the Ankara government.[38] For him,

> The Orthodox community was "deservedly" (emphasis is mine) outraged as a consequence of Phanar's disastrous inimical activities towards the government. It was Phanar's irrational policies that were responsible for all the suffering they had been living through at the hands of the Turks, so it was natural that the Turks raged against the Orthodox Christians due to the activities of the Patriarchate in Istanbul. The Turkish government had protected the interest, life, property and honor of the Orthodox community for five hundred years; therefore, the Orthodox community should have been obedient and loyal.

The landing of Greek troops and the support by Phanar of the Greek cause threatened the lives of thousands of Anatolian Christians; Efthim claims that these were his reasons to cozy up to the Ankara government and initiate the project of the Turkish Orthodox Patriarchate in Anatolia.[39]

The Ankara government followed an open policy of separating the Anatolian Orthodox from the Phanar. The reason for this support, according to Benlisoy, was to weaken and counter the Greek and foreign propaganda on the "Turkish atrocities" toward the Anatolian non-Muslim by providing assistance to Papa Efthim and the "Turkish Orthodox Church" project. It was also a way to oppose the Greek territorial claims on Asia Minor since the Turkish national Church was demonstrating that there were no "unredeemed Greeks" in Anatolia but Christian Turks. As an indicative example of these concerns, the former Minister of Justice and deputy of Saruhan Refik Şevket Bey informed the government by a memorandum dated July 26 that the foundation of a Turkish Orthodox Patriarchate would curb the power of the Phanar and at the same time would show that there was no minority issue in Anatolia.[40]

The support given to the Turkish cause by Papa Efthim doesn't seem exceptional. Beginning in 1919, telegrams and petitions, allegedly from Orthodox Christians to the Ankara government claiming that they were Turkish and they were against the inimical activities of the Patriarchate against the Turkish cause, were published in newspapers like *İkdam*, *Hakimiyet-i Milliye*, *Sada-yı Hak* (İzmir), *İstikbal* (Trabzon) and *Yeni Şark*. By 1921, the number of telegrams had increased and they repeated their wish for the foundation of a Turkish Orthodox Patriarchate. The telegrams came from various parts of Anatolia, including Safranbolu, Isparta, Samsun, Kastamonu and Sivas. As an example, eleven notables and the local priest, in the name of the 2749 Orthodox residents of Safranbolu, sent a petition to Ankara asking for the foundation of a Turkish Orthodox Church in a proper locality of Anatolia. The Christian notables of Safranbolu affirmed that they were Turks in their language, tradition and origins but because they were under pressure from the Patriarchate that served Pan-Hellenic ideals, they could not express in public their real nationality (milliyet-i asliyemiz). The petition was published in *Hakimiyet-i Milliye* on May 1, 1921. Benlisoy suggests that we cannot be sure whether these letters represent the real wishes and loyalty of the Anatolian Christian communities to the Ankara government. They might even be fabricated, forcing the Orthodox communities to express such opinions, or perhaps simply some of them were real and some were false.[41] No matter how the Orthodox expressed their will during wartime, we can suppose that people were anxious about the possibility of losing their lives, their traditional routines and, of course, their homelands, leading them to pursue every possible way to save themselves. For this reason, they seem to be hung between Turkishness and Greekness during the Turco-Greek War.

The Turkish Orthodox Patriarchate was eventually founded on September 21, 1922, in Zincidere, Kayseri. It was not an exceptional event when we consider the previous endeavors of Slavic churches and even the Greek national Church to separate themselves from the Ecumenical Patriarchate.[42] However, it remained weak and unrecognized after the termination of the war and the uprooting of much of the Anatolian Orthodox population due to displacement as a result of the Population Exchange.

With regard to Papa Efthim himself, as claimed in the manuscript of a refugee from Keskin Maden, he veered between Greek and Turkish nationalisms. In fact, he changed his side in accordance with the changing circumstances during the war. According to an interviewee of CAMS, in the first years of the Greek occupation in Western Anatolia, Efthim brought to the village a Greek fiver that had Venizelos's picture on it, and this made the community very happy. For the interviewee, Efthim was like the biggest gift from God; whatever he said or wanted was a holy command or a national mandate for the community. During the war, he was continuously going to Ankara, and they knew that he had good relations with Mustafa Kemal. It is because of this that the Christians of Keskin Maden were saved from exile; four days after their uprooting they returned to their village, thanks to Efthim. Through the last phases of the war, Papa Efthim was mostly away wandering around Christian settlements. Once he gathered the community in Keskin and warned Orthodox Christians that they needed to change their attitude in order to stay in Turkey. He aspired to power and wanted to be the patriarch of the Turkish Church, and with this in mind he chose to become Turk.[43] In refugee testimonies, only in

126   Halasane ta pragmata *(Things spoiled)*

respect of Papa Efthim was becoming "Turk" not associated with becoming Muslim. Efthim was a unique case of a "secular" approach to ethnicity in refugee narration. As we heard in the previous chapter, refugees often labeled women who got married to Turks and converted to Islam as having been "Turkified."

Refugee testimonies about Papa Efthim provide us with contradictory views about him and his Turkish Orthodox Patriarchate movement:

> I don't know where Papa Efthim was from. We had learned how he had his own separate church in Poli (the City; short version of Constantinople in Greek). Christians would not go to his church because they knew how he became Turk. This could be a lie because an acquaintance of mine told me that a woman in Istanbul saw the Virgin Mary in her dream and [the Holy Mother] asked her "Why don't you go to the church of Efthim?" and ordered "go to his church." If he was bad, why would she see that dream? At the time we learned how he visited the villages and made goodness. We waited for him like we waited for the God. They wanted to take for exile fifty men of our village. When he came (Efthim), we found him. In two days he brought our people from exile. He was friends with many Turks. Whomever he wanted, he brought from exile because he was supported by Kemal.[44]

> We were not harmed by the Turks until the time brigands emerged in 1919 but they did not touch us thanks to Papa Efthim.[45]

> I met Papa Efthim in Prokopi. Kemal sent him to make a tour with deputy of Adrianoupoli [Edirne] Tanis Bey in Greek villages to persuade the Christians to proceed with Kemal [Mustafa Kemal Paşa] in order not to leave their villages [...] Later that day he invited the council of elderly and some rich people of Prokopi to school. He called me too. When we gathered, he started to talk about Kemal and tried to persuade each one of us to demand to stay in our village. "We knew the Turks very well. We have been living with them since the years of our great grandfathers. What would we do in Greece? Kemal wants our good" he said. He also told about his relation to Kemal (how he met him etc.). We listened to him but we did not want to stay with the Turks. We did not even want to hear about it. We wanted to come to Greece but now we don't find it as we expected.[46]

We can never know Papa Efthim's motivation to become "Turk." It is very likely that he wanted to protect the Anatolian Orthodox from being deported and his desire coincided with the Ankara government's policies of abolishing the Phanar. As a passionate person, he could also satisfy his ego of becoming a patriarch by completely breaking with the Phanar in the end. For Psomiades, Patriarch Meletios IV (Patriarch from 1921) was against any disciplinary action against Papa Efthim and the other prelates supporting him, like the Metropolitan

Halasane ta pragmata *(Things spoiled)* 127

of Konya Prokopios, and bishops Meletios and Yervas; he was even prepared to set up "a special ecclesiastical province" to meet their demands.[47] However, Efthim was zealous and his extremism also proved an embarrassment to the Ankara government.[48]

Papa Efthim's movement remained weak after the uprooting of the Anatolian Orthodox as a result of the signing of a convention concerning the exchange of populations between Greece and Turkey. At the beginning of the Lausanne negotiations, Turkish speaking Christians were thought to be exempt from the Exchange. İsmet Paşa argued that Anatolian Christians never demanded treatment different from that enjoyed by their Turkish compatriots. Venizelos and Lord Curzon also didn't oppose the idea that the Turkish speaking Orthodox could remain in their place. As negotiations continued, the Turkish delegation persisted with its anti-Greek sentiment and wanted to expel the Ecumenical Patriarchate and replace it with the Turkish Orthodox Patriarchate of Papa Efthim; the Greek delegation as well as American and British representatives were firmly opposed to the idea. In the end, Venizelos assured the Turkish delegation that the Patriarchate would stay only to meet the ceremonial needs of the Greek community in Istanbul. Venizelos's last move changed the minds of the Turkish diplomats about the Anatolian Orthodox, because thousands of people could be hard to deal with should they insist on being loyal to the Greek Orthodox Patriarchate. As for the Greek point of view, the presence of thousands of Orthodox Christians as the congregation of a Turkish Church would be able to curb the power of the Greek Orthodox Patriarchate and even terminate its presence in the long term.[49] Finally, the Anatolian Orthodox was the very last group of people to leave Turkey during the Exchange; Papa Efthim and his family were exempted by a special resolution; his movement remained weak. The number of followers of the Turkish Church has been debated, but it probably consists of very few people.

According to Clogg, if promoted more sensitively, the project of the Turkish Orthodox Patriarchate would have been beneficial for the Anatolian Orthodox. In the end, ordinary Anatolians, most of whom had only slight information about Greece, were uprooted and suffered incomprehensively during and after their journey to Greece and their reception at the hands of the indigenous Greek population was not always a happy one.[50] It would also be an opportunity for Turkish nationalism to embrace more civic values because the presence of Turkish Christians in the country could prove that Turks might have other religious beliefs as well. The Anatolian Orthodox were unfortunately abandoned easily both by Turkish and Greek politicians. During the Lausanne negotiations, their future was locked onto the future of the Greek Orthodox Patriarchate. Greece was not ready to receive another flow of refugees (or exchangees) and Turkey could accept the Anatolian Orthodox only if the Greek Orthodox Patriarchate were expelled from the country. As a result of the negotiations, Turkey was forced to accept the perpetuation of the Patriarchate and Greece was forced to accommodate a new mass of refugees. Turkish politicians always regarded the Phanar as a Trojan horse and wished to reduce its power to that of a local church. The presence of almost 100,000 Anatolian Orthodox, the potential congregation of the Greek Orthodox Patriarchate, caused problems for the country in the long run due to their nationalist stance.

In terms of nationalization, Cappadocians maintained a heterogeneous position until the long war, and their nationalization would not be fully completed until their accommodation by Greece following their expulsion. For the time between the 1870s and the 1920s, there were Greek nationalists who received an education in Athens and Istanbul, and there were proto-nationalists who received an education from nationalist teachers in their homelands. There were also illiterate traditional people who were still strongly attached to their religion, and there were Ottomanists among the elite who supported the well-being of the Empire and status quo among the Cappadocians. Refugee narratives make a distinction between times before and after *Hürriyet*. According to testimonies, "things spoiled" after the Young Turk Revolution. The nationalist policies of the CUP, which first aimed at a "national economy" and second at a "religiously homogeneous" country, created a lot of resentment among the Cappadocian Orthodox, as it did among the Orthodox of other regions. Before the *Hürriyet*, they had relatively few problems with the Ottoman state apparatus and its officials. Consequently, there is a "before and after *Hürriyet*" dichotomy in which "before *Hürriyet*" is restricted by the life duration of refugees who could have born in the 1860s at the earliest. The years before *Hürriyet* may have been relatively better compared to the hardships experienced afterward, but it was also a period of censorship of the press, persecution and strict Islamist policies.

For ordinary people, even as late as the Turco-Greek War (1919–1922), people's identities were entangled between saving their lives and resentment against nationalist Turkish policies. As a small community with little male power among the Muslim masses, the Anatolian Orthodox remained relatively silent and passive during the war years. For this reason, the "nationalization" process of the Cappadocian Orthodox could only be completed after their expulsion to Greece. All in all, the competitive ecosystem or the antagonistic tolerance model worked well with almost no inter-communal conflict in Cappadocia until the time of discontinuity, a time marked by continual war, which I call the "long war," the nationalist policies of CUP including boycotting movement, exile and intolerance. All these strengthened the communal borders and started to create a "national" awareness; however, complete nationalization occurred only after the final separation of peoples with the Exchange and absorption of refugees into the Greek nation through ideological state apparatus.

Notes

1 See Maria Porloglou Kosmidou, Kermira; Eleni Serafeimidou, Zincidere; Annika Haritonidou, Gesi, *Η Έξοδος, Τόμος Β΄*, pp. 67, 83, 92; K. Nikolaidou-Danasi, *Καισάρεια Τόμος Α΄: Η Μονή Τιμίου Προδρόμου στο Ζιντζίδερε (Φλαβιανά). Το Πνευματικό και Εκπαιδευτικό Κέντρο της Καππαδοκίας Κερμίρα, Μερσίνα, Ποτάμια*, p. 91.

Halasane ta pragmata *(Things spoiled)* 129

2 M.Harakopoulos, *Ρωμιοί της Καππαδοκίας: από τα Βάθη της Ανατολής στο Θεσσαλικό Κάμπο, η Τραυματική Ενσωμάτωση στη Μητέρα Πατρίδα.* p. 48.
3 See E. Ahladi, İzmir'de İttihatçılar ve Rumlar: Yunan-Rum Boykotu (1908-1911).
4 See Y. G. Mourelos, The 1914 Persecutions and the First Attempt at an Exchange of Minorities Between Greece and Turkey.
5 S. Anagnostopoulou, *Μικρά Ασία: 19ος Αιώνας -1919: Οι Ελληνορθόδοξες Κοινότητες από το Μιλλέτ των Ρωμιών στο Ελληνικό Έθνος,* pp. 524-526.
6 Y. D. Çetinkaya, *The Young Turks and the Boycott Movement: Nationalism, Protest and the Working Classes in the Formation of Modern Turkey,* pp. 90, 119-120.
7 See E. Emmanuilidis, *Osmanlı İmparatorluğunun Son Yılları.*
8 CAMS, Cappadocia, Bor, Sofoklis Fakidis, Dim. Haralambidis.
9 CAMS, Cappadocia, Bor, Papakostis Papadopoulos.
10 H. Exertzoglou, The Development of a Greek Ottoman Bourgeoisie: Investment Patterns in the Ottoman Empire, 1850-1914, p. 100.
11 E. Emmanuilidis, *Osmanlı İmparatorluğunun Son Yılları,* p. 153.
12 See Y. G. Mourelos, The 1914 Persecutions and the First Attempt at an Exchange of Minorities Between Greece and Turkey; M. Bjørnlund, The 1914 Cleansing of Aegean Greeks.
13 M. Bjørnlund, The 1914 Cleansing of Aegean Greeks, p. 47.
14 See *Η Έξοδος Τόμος Β': Μαρτυρίες από τις Επαρχίες της Κεντρικής και Νότιας Μικρασίας.*
15 R. Gingeras, *Sorrowful Shores: Violence, Ethnicity, and the End of the Ottoman Empire, 1912-1923,* p. 40.
16 CAMS, Cappadocia, Limna-Gölcük, Mihail Savvidis.
17 CAMS, Cappadocia, Nigdi-Niğde, Konstantinos Haleplidis Elisavet Hasirtzoglou.
18 CAMS, Cappadocia, Ağırnas, Avraam Avramidis.
19 CAMS, Cappadocia, Zincidere, Katina Piniatoglou.
20 The amount of the tax in lieu of military service paid by Muslims and non-Muslims was unequal (8000 *kurus* and 5000 *kurus,* respectively). One from every 180 non-Muslim men were to be conscripted. Therefore, 180 people paid the tax of one man. In the end, the amount paid by every non-Muslim was more or less equal to previously collected *jizya* (cizye) tax. See U. Gülsoy, *Cizyeden Vatandaşlığa: Osmanlı'nın Gayrimüslim Askerleri,* pp. 85-101.
21 U. Gülsoy, *Cizyeden Vatandaşlığa: Osmanlı'nın Gayrimüslim Askerleri,* pp. 141-144; M. Hacısalihoğlu, Osmanlı İmparatorluğunda Zorunlu Askerlik Sistemine Geçiş: Ordu-Millet Düşüncesi, p. 63.
22 U. Gülsoy, *Cizyeden Vatandaşlığa: Osmanlı'nın Gayrimüslim Askerleri,* pp. 156, 171.
23 M.Harakopoulos, *Ρωμιοί της Καππαδοκίας: από τα Βάθη της Ανατολής στο Θεσσαλικό Κάμπο. Η Τραυματική Ενσωμάτωση στη Μητέρα Πατρίδα.* p. 65.
24 U. Gülsoy, *Cizyeden Vatandaşlığa: Osmanlı'nın Gayrimüslim Askerleri,* p. 156.
25 See E. J. Zürcher, The Ottoman Conscription System In Theory And Practice, 1844-1918.
26 See G. Kritikos, Motives for Compulsory Exchange.
27 Cemal quoted in U. Gülsoy, *Cizyeden Vatandaşlığa: Osmanlı'nın Gayrimüslim Askerleri,* p. 156.
28 CAMS, Cappadocia, Prokopi, Eust. Eu8imiadis, Elisavet Isaakidou.
29 CAMS, Cappadocia, Tynana, Vas. Seferiadis.
30 CAMS, Cappadocia, Misti, Mak. Damianoglou.
31 CAMS, Cappadocia, MistiGeorg. Mpolasih.?
32 CAMS, Cappadocia, Limna, Kosmas Serafeimidis.
33 CAMS, Cappadocia, Karatzoren, Ioannis Misailoglou.
34 CAMS, Cappadocia, Zile, Eleftherios Iosifidis.

35 CAMS, Cappadocia, Akso, Dimitrios Misailidis.
36 CAMS, Cappadocia, Niğde, Aleksandros Giagtzoglou.
37 I am particularly inspired by Jay Winter's lecture entitled "Sites of Memory, Sites of Mourning" in Open Yale courses for the class "History 202: European Civilization, 1648–1945" in this paragraph.
38 See F. Benlisoy, S. Benlisoy, *Türk Milliyetçiliğinde Katedilmemiş bir Yol: 'Hıristiyan Türkler've Papa Eftim*, pp. 25–32.
39 See *Papa Efthim Efendi'nin Orthodoxos Ahaliye Müracaatı ve Patrikhaneye Karşı Müdafaanamesi*, pp. 1–19.
40 F. Benlisoy, S. Benlisoy, Türk *Milliyetçiliğinde Katedilmemiş bir Yol: "Hıristiyan Türkler" ve Papa Eftim*, pp. 67, 102, 137.
41 F. Benlisoy, S. Benlisoy, *Türk Milliyetçiliğinde Katedilmemiş bir Yol: "Hıristiyan Türkler" ve Papa Eftim*, pp. 42–48.
42 The Orthodox Churches in Greece, Romania, Bulgaria, and Albania declared their independence or autocephality unilaterally in 1833, 1865, 1870 and 1922–1937 respectively. F. Benlisoy, S. Benlisoy, *Türk Milliyetçiliğinde Katedilmemiş bir Yol: 'Hıristiyan Türkler' ve Papa Eftim*, p. 53.
43 CAMS manuscripts, Galatia, Keskin Maden, Nikos Fotiadis.
44 CAMS, Cappadocia, Neapoli-Nevşehir, Sofronia Georgiadou.
45 CAMS, Galatia, Keskin Maden, K. Giorgiadis.
46 CAMS, Cappadocia, Prokopi, Sythimios Sofoulis.
47 See H. J. Psomiades, *The Oecumenical Patriarchate under the Turkish Republic: The First Ten Years*, pp. 61–62; T. Ergene, *İstiklal Harbinde Türk Ortodoksları*, pp. 25–26.
48 R. Clogg, Anadolu Hıristiyan Karındaşlarımız: The Turkish-Speaking Greeks of Asia Minor, p. 82.
49 See O. Yıldırım, *Diplomacy and Displacement*, pp. 75–76; H. J. Psomiades, *The Oecumenical Patriarchate under the Turkish Republic: the First Ten Years*, p. 62.
50 R. Clogg, *Anadolu Hıristiyan Karındaşlarımız: the Turkish-Speaking Greeks of Asia Minor*, p. 83.

5 Tolerating the heretics
The distinctive case of the Greek Protestants

The years before and after the Young Turk Revolution were different from each other concerning the practice of co-existence. In both cases, however, non-Muslims were left in the position of being either tolerated or not tolerated. The only thing they could do in their relation with the ruling polity was to consent. In this chapter, I will investigate the position of Orthodox Christians as "tolerators" in their relations with the Protestants, some of whom had familial bonds with them. The situation is complex and the scope of reaction toward the Protestants varied from persecution to negative tolerance, though there were some anomalies, like the case of *Zincidere*, which was a non-conflictual center of seemingly irreconcilable denominations, namely Orthodoxy and Protestantism.

Conversion to Protestantism in the nineteenth century was regarded as an attack not only on dogma but also on tradition for the Orthodox. It would also mean *denationalization* since Orthodox Christianity became the main component of "Greekness" after the foundation of the Kingdom of Greece (1832). Interestingly, during the years of the long war, the boundaries between the Orthodox and the Protestant communities ostensibly faded away in some regions of the Black Sea. Nonetheless, this situation did not eventually end up in total acceptance of Protestants by the Orthodox in contemporary Greece.

It is difficult to find a term for a person who was originally Orthodox Christian, later became Protestant and Turkish speaking, and had not yet encountered or was to encounter nationalistic ideals. He or she cannot simply be called Protestant because of the need to distinguish between previously Orthodox newly Protestant communities and the missionaries and Armenian Protestants in Anatolia at that time. To make it easier for me and for the reader I have decided to call them Greek Protestants. Here, the term Greek does not refer to their ethnicity, but to their previous membership of the Greek Orthodox congregation.

The studies on Protestantism in the Ottoman Empire have always focused mostly on the activities of missionaries, not on the Protestants themselves. On one side, the missionaries praised themselves on their work and their success in converting people to the "genuine" path of God. On the other side, those who faced the "evil" objectives of the missionaries decried proselytism. In Turkey, most of the studies about Protestantism focus on the educational activities of the missionaries, their inimical positions during the grand war and the

132 Tolerating the heretics

"damage" done to Turkish culture and society.[1] In such nationalist scholarship, there is an obvious enmity. For Greeks, the studies focus on the rivalry between the missionaries and the Church authorities. In fact, the enmity in ecclesiastical sources of the time was especially counter-missionary.[2] As expected, the Church authorities did not want to lose their members either to denominations like Catholicism and Protestantism or to Islam. The religious authorities wanted to protect the community borders and keep their congregation intact. Further, in the nineteenth century, loss of members also meant loss of the prospective members of recently created nations. Deringil calls this situation *denationalization*. Indeed, the converts were seen as potential traitors of the nation. Additionally, religion was the main component of Greek national identity and proselytism was an attack not only on the religious dogma but also on the hundreds of years of tradition and could not be accepted. All these concerns indicate that there was competition between denominations and this competition was the determinant of inter-communal encounters.

However, scholars and ecclesiastical sources give us no information about the Protestants themselves. What was the motive behind their conversion? How did they convert? How did it change their lives? What were relations between Protestants and other communities like? What was the scope of tolerance toward the Protestants exercised by the Orthodox? The focal point of this chapter is particularly the Greek Protestants and I aim to paint a picture of the lives of converts by pursuing answers to these questions as much as I can on the basis of reader correspondence in the missionary newspaper *Angeliaforos*, the testimonies of Protestant refugees of *Zincidere* and *Merzifon* in the CAMS Oral Tradition Archives, the memoirs of missionaries, articles in The Missionary Herald and relevant materials I found in the Greek Historical Evangelical Archive (Ελληνικό Ιστορικό Ευαγγελικό Αρχείο) in Athens.

The missionary activities and the genesis of the Protestant Greek communities

In the year 1819 the first American missionaries arrived in Western Asia to spread the Gospel of Christ to Muslims, Jews, crypto-believers like the Dönmes and to the adherents of syncretic religions like the Alawites. The missionary work was a part of American millennialism to unite the world, the great pillars of the Papal, Judaic and Islamic faiths, under the umbrella of Protestantism around the year 2000 or earlier;[3] but in the Ottoman territories their success was very limited.[4] Even forty-five years after their arrival on Ottoman shores the missionaries were still struggling at the hands of Turkish authorities in consideration in their efforts to convert Muslims. According to correspondence presented to both houses of Parliament in the UK dating to 1864, "Turkish Protestants" (ten to thirteen people) were imprisoned and ill-treated at the Police Department for endangering public peace and the situation caused significant trouble in the country.[5] Just a few years before the Reform Edict of 1856 had introduced freedom of religion to all subjects of the Empire, and the missionaries regarded it as authorization to convert Muslims.[6] Nevertheless, in practice not only conversion but also any sort of move against Islam or propagation was not tolerated. For example, Abdülhamit II, when he came to the throne in 1873, cautioned the missionaries not to attempt to convert Muslims, just as his predecessors had.[7] All in all, the Turkish officials kept scanning the reports of the American Board of Commissioners for Foreign Missions (the ABCFM) with suspicion and for this reason the Board remained very wary of information about "Turkish converts." Correspondingly, the number of "Turkish Protestants" remains unknown, and it may be that the missionaries did not insist on this effort in order to avoid jeopardizing their presence in the country.[8]

Under such conditions, the missionaries changed their targets. They limited their mission to trying to correct the faults of Islam and to proselytizing among the native Christians and Jews. They regarded the oriental Christian sects as ignorant, illiterate, superstitious and idolatrous in their faith.[9] Initially, they aimed to reform the Armenian Church and revive the knowledge of the Gospel among the Armenians. However, this early position failed and their converts were excommunicated by the Armenian Church.[10] As a result, in 1846, Protestant Armenians were asked to sign a charter of faithfulness in order to be accepted again by the main Church. Those who did not sign the charter were excommunicated, their properties confiscated by the Patriarchate, their debts discharged by force and those who were indebted to Protestants were prohibited from paying their debts.[11]

The missionaries were also not welcomed by the Greek Orthodox Church. The Greek Ecclesiastical Committee at Izmir published charges against the English and American Missionaries in 1836, claiming that they could not be ignorant, given that three of the Gospels, the Acts and the Epistles were written in their own language, Greek; thus, missionary translations would darken rather than clarify their meaning. The Greek Ecclesiastical Committee also emphasized the unifying function of their religion in keeping their nation distinguished.[12] The same year, a thesis was written by the publisher Kyriakos H. N. Lamprylos[13] in Smyrna in an attempt to record the efforts made by missionaries and to show how they strived to proselytize to attract people to them. According to this publication, the missionaries distorted the meaning of Scriptures to support their heresy and frequently targeted uneducated people. For Lamprylos, the poor and the wretched were confused by the ideas presented by missionaries, which in the end caused more harm than good.[14]

Jewish authorities were also highly uncomfortable with missionary activities, and regarded the activities of missionaries as "ecclesiastical imperialism" and a threat to their traditions and sacred language. Rabbis went to extreme measures to prevent people from attending missionary services, including standing on the corner of missionary houses to prevent Jews from entering. Due mainly to this resistance, the ABCFM decided to annul their mission to convert Jews in 1855.[15] So, it is well established that the missionaries were not welcomed by any of the religious communities in the Ottoman Empire. They were seen as a threat and their presence in the country generated anxious competition, particularly for non-Muslim denominations, until the collapse of the Empire.

There is a widespread impression that the Protestants in Anatolia at this time were only of Armenian descent. While it is true that Armenians substantially outnumbered the Greeks, the latter was still a very significant population. By 1884, remarkable success was achieved by the missionaries in Istanbul, Bursa, Izmir, Merzifon, Talas, Sivas, Bahçecik (Bardezag) and Gürümce.[16] In Kayseri and the surrounding area, there were eleven Protestant churches with members of both Orthodox and Gregorian descent.[17] Indeed, in places such as Ordu, Greek Protestants actually outnumbered Armenians. In fact, by 1899 Ordu's Protestant population was so heavily Greek that Armenians decided to withdraw from the shared church, where both communities had worshiped in their common language of Turkish, so as to be able to use their native tongue.[18] According to a Greek source, the total number of Greek families subscribing to an Evangelical faith throughout the Black Sea region was around 500,[19] while in Asia Minor the first Greek Evangelical community was established in the village *Demirtaş* (ten kilometers north of Bursa) in 1867 and the total number of the Greek Evangelicals leading up to the Turco-Greek Population Exchange (1923) throughout Asia Minor was roughly around 200 to 250 families.[20]

Özsoy suggests that the missionaries targeted the Armenians more often than the Greeks because of the difficulties associated with the strong sense of nationhood that the Greek Kingdom was providing, the tough central authority of the Patriarchate and the challenges of infiltrating large groups with strong ties in their settlements.[21] Özsoy's argument seems accurate given the conversion of the Greek Orthodox Arabs of the Church of Antioch. Conversion of Arab Orthodox in Syria, Lebanon and Palestine occurred mainly due to the fact that the Church lacked cohesion, as the upper clergy were Greek not Arab, and the priests who took care of daily affairs were poorly trained, incompetent and hardly educated. Additionally, they lacked the organization and discipline necessary to hold the congregation together.[22] Conversely, however, the Lebanese Maronite Community as a coherent body was much more reactionary and cruel toward the missionaries and converts, especially until 1847 when Protestant *millet* was recognized by an imperial decree, legitimating the place of Protestant converts.[23]

For Asia Minor and Greece, particularly in the second half of the nineteenth century, the Orthodox Church was constantly working to prevent missionary activities and to strengthen community ties, mainly through publications and increasing involvement in schooling activities. The Orthodox Church used two starkly different channels of opposition against the missionaries. One was theological; since Protestant churches lack Episcopal succession and an unbroken communion with the ancient church in order and doctrine,[24] they were in opposition to the standards of Christian truth accepted by privileged leaders, meaning they could be called heretics.[25] The other opposition was more culturally focused, as the missionaries posed a challenge to Orthodox traditions and customs, so threatening the cultural unity of the previous few centuries. The reaction of the Church, however, was not only to try and preserve the integrity and purity of faith, but also to defend ecclesial authority.[26] As it happens, behind closed doors Orthodox authorities knew that the missionaries were right in their claims that the local priests and monks of Orthodoxy were illiterate. In this sense, the missionaries' first impact on the Greek Orthodox Church was a positive one, as the church authorities now felt the need to educate both the priests and the congregation. For instance, the Metropolitan Bishop of Kayseri Paisios Kepoglou (1832–1871) translated the religious books to *Karamanlidika* and taught the word of God in Turkish in order to protect the local Christians from the outflow of Protestantism.[27] With similar concerns, many articles were published in Greek newspapers and in the magazine of the Patriarchate on this subject (Εκκλησιαστική Αλήθεια; Ecclesiastical Truth). As an example, in the Greco-Turkish newspaper *Anatoli*, various articles were published to call for the conservation of Orthodoxy. The following passage is from one of those articles:

> The Orthodox Christians are not informed about their religion and the metropolitan bishops do not take it seriously. They do not even employ priests in some villages and in such villages the number of Orthodox is in decline. Additionally, in the last years, Turcophone Christians are distracted since the Evangel, the Epistles and the prayers are being read in Greek; hence, they prefer the churches where the services are conducted in Turkish.[28]

After setting the problem, the writer of the article lists some strategies to avoid losing members to other religions and denominations:

> 1) Sunday classes (Κυριακόν Μάθημα) must be serviced; 2) metropolitan bishops must employ two or three preachers (ιεροκήρυξ); 3) illiterate people should no longer be accepted as priests; 4) scripture classes should be taken seriously in schools; 5) capable teachers must undertake religious classes.[29]

Evidently both religious authorities and intellectuals were aware of the "threat" created by missionary activity. The presence of Evangelical missionaries, along with Catholics, challenged the comfort zone of the Orthodox Community, whose borders were already occasionally threatened by the ruling Muslim polity, which created another field of competition between the Orthodox Church and the missionaries. Interestingly, the motive to cope with them generated a strong sense of religious identity and initiated a process of enlightenment through education among the Orthodox. Thus, the competition with Evangelicals created an atmosphere of *Protestantization*. In Gazi's theorization, the objective of the missionary was not solely the conversion of people. The missionaries also aimed to reinforce a more "secular" version of religious beliefs, strongly related to the image of a reformed and "enlightened" individual.[30] They themselves described their mission as *direct evangelization, literary effort* and *education*[31] and an introduction of practical gospel which makes for better living, both material and moral.[32]

For example in *Merzifounta* (Merzifon, Marsovan), there were Greek Orthodox pupils studying in American College Anatolia[33] and later there were Greek Orthodox orphans in the American orphanage.[34] In 1903, the Greek Orthodox students of the American school founded the Greek Athletic Club of Pontus (Ο Ελληνικός Σύλλογος Πόντος). As it was argued by the authorities that the name Pontus carried political implications, the Club was later renamed as Greek Literary and Athletic Society. Americans were always cautious about keeping a neutral position in political matters.[35] The Club functioned in three fields: philology, music and sports. By 1913 the number of members of the school reached 180. This does not mean that those students converted or were victims of proselytism from an Orthodox point of view. They emphasized that they were living with persistent beliefs in tradition and were faithful to Orthodox progeny.[36] However, in terms of adopting Western culture, their situation was obviously *Protestantization*.

Protestantization, not only in the Ottoman Empire but also in the Greek Kingdom, was experienced by sections of Greek Orthodoxy, who eventually adopted certain Protestant particularities, including piety, moral individualism and the use of the vernacular for the improvement of faith.[37] As a result, the missionary effort and the responses to it created an atmosphere of competition; and the Evangelicals, while criticizing the low level of education of the Orthodox priests, continued to attract people through native pastors and preachers with sound theological views.[38]

In addition to high ranking prelates, local priests waged war against the missionaries. *The Missionary Herald* reported many complaints about persecution of the Protestants by local clerics. As previously mentioned, another channel of criticism against the missionaries were the newspapers of the time, which frequently reported clashes between local authorities and Protestants from surrounding provinces. For instance, in an issue of the Greco-Turkish newspaper *Anatoli*, it was reported that in Izmir the Metropolitan Bishop and some others burned the books that missionaries had distributed to draw people from Orthodoxy.[39] In another issue, it was claimed that even if the Protestants and Jesuits tried hard to deceive the members of the Greek Orthodox Community, they would be unsuccessful and this was the reason that they targeted the Armenians.[40] It was also contended in the paper that a Greek would always remain Greek and an Armenian would always remain Armenian and any attempt to invite a Christian to another Christian sect would not be licit in Christianity.[41] In *Terakki*, a warning article was published in 1888 for those who had doubts about their denomination. The article claimed that doubts meant accepting going to Hell.[42] For the converts themselves, excommunication was the worst possible punishment. In nineteenth-century Sinasos, it was even forbidden to greet the excommunicated who had broken the rules of the community. However, the actual frequency of this punishment remains unconfirmed. Stefo Benlisoy affirmed that most of the time the achievements of the missionaries were transitory, and many people returned later to their original form of worship.[43] Despite these obstacles, beginning in the nineteenth century,

Figure 5.1 Greek students of the American College in Talas with their Greek teacher, H. Bogdanos (third from right, seated) and next to him, the American director.
Source: Photography Archive of the Centre for Asia Minor Studies

a Protestant community with both Armenian and Greek converts did in fact start to emerge, and its number increased year by year until the *millet* status of the Protestants was officially recognized by the *firman* of Sultan Abdülmecit in November 1847.[44]

Regardless of this official legitimacy, the authorities of the Greek Orthodox Church used every means possible to keep their congregation united, and the Orthodox prelates continued to respond to Protestant criticisms of their faith. For example, the Metropolitan Bishop of Kayseri Efstathios Kleovoulos (1871–1876) wrote letters to three missionaries (W. A. Fransworth, S. Bartlett, O. Barrows) who temporarily settled in Talas, Kayseri, in 1872 to convert the local Christians. In the first letter, Kleovulos expressed his resentment to the missionaries trying to attract people among the Orthodox congregation, some of which were illiterate, ignorant and easily swayed by novelties. He stressed that their mission could only be appreciated if they tried to spread the word of Christ among the pagans and idolaters.[45] In the second letter, he claimed that the missionaries exploited curiosity about science to attract people, and that if they aimed at providing goodness to the world through science and politics, they should have kept themselves away from the faith

138 *Tolerating the heretics*

Figure 5.2 The Oratory House of Evangelicals (Δζοαράν) in Zincidere with its congregation on the left (Source: Agapidis, 1950) and its current state on the right.
Photograph: Gülen Göktürk

of Anatolians. He also added that the Orthodox had learned the Evangel in their own language and had become martyrs for the sake of it ages before the discovery of America and they did not really care whether the missionaries translated the holy scripts into 170 different languages.[46] Lastly, in his third letter, Kleovoulos likened the missionaries to lazy birds that nestle in nests of other birds.[47] Kleovoulos was clearly very uncomfortable with the activities of the missionaries; nevertheless, their presence even in the region of the residence of the Metropolitan Bishop could not be terminated. Interestingly enough, the place of his residence, Zincidere near to Talas, became one of the centers of Protestantism in Cappadocia. Between the years 1876 and 1877, the Protestant community in Talas comprised 300 people, Greeks and Armenians in equal numbers. In Zincidere, however, most of the Evangelicals were from the Greek Orthodox Community.[48] There were around twenty to twenty-five Protestant households in town and they had a newly-built building that was used both as a school and a church. They named it "Dzoaran" (Δζοαράν).[49] This is curious because Zincidere was already a center for Orthodoxy with its schools, orphanages and the Seminary, as well as with the monastery of Ioannis Prodromos (John the Forerunner) as well as the residence of the Metropolitan Bishop of Kayseri. During my investigation about Orthodox–Protestant cohabitation in the village, I did not come across any conflict between the two communities until their uprooting in 1924. In the following years, Zincidere continued to be a center for the two different Christian sects in Cappadocia.

During this time, missionaries were not just relocating and settling in Ottoman territories, but also in the Greek Kingdom and during the early years of missionary work, the missionaries also met opposition there. The national Greek Church was increasingly antagonistic toward the so-called *Loutherikalvinoi* (Lutheran-Calvinists), imposing such strict restrictions on them that they could not even work as private tutors in a family without official permission. Even when they conducted their Sunday services in their own private houses, the ecclesiastical authorities often watched the houses to ensure that no Greek attended. Anti-heresy and anti-proselytism departments were established to neutralize Protestant influence, while the Holy Synod circulated encyclicals condemning the missionary publications; moreover, a number of civil laws were passed outlawing proselytism, the violation of which was punishable by fines, imprisonment, or both. Consequently, missionary schools were closed down in 1842 and the American missionary Jonas King was put on trial for proselytism (1845–1852).[50] In the Kingdom, the Church and the State cooperated against the missionaries. In the Ottoman Empire, however, the state seemed indifferent to them unless they tried to convert Muslims. For Makdisi, the Ottomans were operating under the "constraints of the day and age";[51] that is to say, their position against the proselytization of non-Muslims was one of pragmatism.

Compared to their contemporaries in the Kingdom, the patriarch and the prelates remained relatively passive in their struggle against the Evangelists in the first decades of the 1800s. By adopting the "my enemy's enemy is my friend" doctrine, Patriarchal circles were flexible toward missionaries due to their shared hostility toward the Catholics.[52] Because of this, Archimandrite Hilarion of Mount Sinai, the supervisor of the Patriarchal Press, allowed Protestant tracts to be printed there between the years 1818–1820. For Clogg this shows that the first missionaries to the Ottoman Empire and Greece primarily wanted to promote a kind of Protestant reformation within Orthodoxy.[53]

The missionaries frequently used the press and schools for proselytizing and *Protestanization* purposes. From the missionaries' point of view, newspapers had an important missionary influence, and a considerable portion of their readers were non-Protestants.[54] The objective of missionary papers like the Armeno-Turkish *Avedaper* and the Greco-Turkish *Angeliaforos* was to deepen the spiritual life of the Protestant population, and to serve as a conduit for sharing information about their annual meetings, their work in education, and their situation at a local level, thus helping to establish a sense of fellowship among them.[55] I reviewed the issues of *Angeliaforos* published between 1889–1890 and 1903–1904. For *The Missionary Herald*, the majority of the subscribers of *Angeliaforos* had no other paper and no other means of contact with the outside world. Additionally, the paper was a means to respond to the insults and criticisms of the Greek Orthodox Church authorities. This can be seen in a published reply to a sermon of an Orthodox deacon, who accused Protestantism of being a fake faith, a claim that was rebutted by the statement that Protestantism would not accept any church under the power of a patriarch, only those under the power of Jesus Christ.[56]

A BUILDING OF THE AMERICAN HOSPITAL, TALAS

Figure 5.3 The American Hospital in Talas.
Source: *The Missionary Herald*, 1914

Like the press, schooling occupied a very important place in missionary activities. People had to be educated because uneducated people could not follow them, read the Bible, understand the sermons or develop a world view that binds him/her to the West. Schools were an inevitable target for missionary activities. Accordingly, as Protestants increased in number, their demand for teachers, preachers and priests increased. While on the one hand they raised an educated generation for religious purposes, on the other, they created an economic and socio-cultural sphere of life in the East designed to connect it to Western capitalism,[57] and cultivated an inner drive that would transform "nominal" into "enlightened" Christians,[58] another central aspect of *Protestantization*. For Augustinos, even though the missionaries were unable to achieve any great religious transformation either in Islam or Eastern Christianity, they provided an example and an opportunity for aspiring Eastern Christians in their industriousness, initiative and enterprise. They left a permanent legacy of philanthropic and educational work, and of girls' education. Additionally, they made a significant contribution to the development of bourgeois culture, primarily among Anatolian Greeks.[59] As a matter of fact, by 1899, the total number of schools, including primary schools, girls' schools, boys' schools, colleges and theological schools, in Western Turkey was 136.[60]

Tolerating the "heretics": a glimpse of Protestant life in Anatolia

In this section, I will paint a picture of the lives of individual Protestants and their relations with the other religious groups. My sources are very limited, and because of this scarcity I will not be able to clearly portray the Greek Protestant residents of Cappadocia. I believe that the information about Greek Protestants of other regions such as Pontus and North Western Anatolia can provide a general picture of the lives of Evangelicals in Anatolia. I should also note that the people I talk about were either Turcophones or in good command of Turkish in order to follow the Greco-Turkish missionary newspaper *Angeliaforos*. As for the testimonies of CAMS Oral Tradition interviewees, they were Turcophone Greek Protestants from Zincidere, Cappadocia and Merzifon, Pontus.

For all publications, each missionary was responsible for printing in one particular language. They were, in general, in command of three or four languages besides English, but several educated Armenians of literary ability also undertook proof-reading and translation purposes.[61] In other words, the literary productions of the missionaries were supported by educated Armenians.

The Turcophone Evangelical communities of Anatolia – if they did not attend any college or higher school – were mostly capable of understanding only plain Turkish, like their Orthodox compatriots. Thus, the incomprehensibility of the language used in the publications was a problem for many readers. In a letter, they complained about the language of *Angeliaforos* as such:

> We are sorry to declare that the language of the newspaper is complicated and because of this we are losing most of the information. With this letter, we demand from the editor and the people of pen who are writing externally to the paper to be careful about this for the benefit of the reading public. The benevolent people, who are writing articles with devotion to the newspaper, aim to enlighten the minds of the community. This is the mission of *Angeliaforos*. If it is published with its real purpose and in accordance with the agreement of 85 (1885) promising more plain language, more people will buy it and it will serve to benefit the larger communities. […] Since we, as the subscribers of the newspaper, are not students, we do not know Arabic and Persian words and we do not have time to learn them.[62]

Angeliaforos was a way to create bonds between the scattered Protestant communities. Through this correspondence they obtained news from other parts of Anatolia and spread the news in their own locality. For example, in a letter from Zincidere, Stefanos I. Serinidis informed the reader of details from his town; everything from mentioning the cold relations among community members, to the fact that many youths of their locality had begun obtaining education in local and overseas American schools.[63]

The life of the Protestants was not easy. Both missionaries and new converts were disliked by the Greek Orthodox and Armenian Church authorities, and faced dislike from their kin, as they were taught by local prelates (who regarded the Protestants as harmful to their religion) to target their dogma and tradition and treat them as an enemy who diminished their members and attacked their comfort zone. Unlike that between Orthodox and Muslim communities, the contestation between the members of Orthodox and Protestant communities was tough and often violent. As previously mentioned, in their relations with the Muslims the Orthodox were the tolerated people who could only wield consent. In their relations with the Evangelicals, however, they assumed the role of "tolerators" due to their demographic superiority and their historical status in the Ottoman society. Bağçeci, in line with his research in Ottoman archives, lists many conflicts between Gregorian and Protestant Armenians all over Ottoman territories, including physical abuse, proselytism and the boycotting of Protestants by Gregorian Armenians as a reaction to their conversion.[64] Such conflicts were also recounted in *Angeliaforos*. In an anonymous letter from Everek (Develi) to the newspaper, it was stated that a local notable preached in a Church warning the local Christians not to read the Bible distributed by the Protestants, and not to be gentle in a quarrel with them even if they themselves were wrong. The sermon also invited the local Christians to call the Protestants *porod*, which means mangy, wounded and bruised in Armenian. Additionally, he preached that they should not let Protestants enter their houses. His sermon influenced other Christians who also started to call the Protestants *porod* and irritated them with nasty behavior. A Protestant called Zakar, for example, was attacked by Armenians when he was in his shop, but was saved by Muslims. A Protestant woman was harassed by a group of Armenian women as a result of the agitation of a priest when she was bringing water from a fountain.[65]

From these accounts, it seems that Muslims did not regard Protestants as a threat to their religion. For Cyrus Hamlin, the founder and first president of Robert College, the Muslims were more sympathetic to the Protestants than the local Christians since they were not worshiping the same icons.[66] Hamlin was wrong in this. The reason for Muslim sympathy or indifference was that they weren't required to defend their religion, and as such they did not regard the missionaries as a threat to integrity of their community; apostasy from Islam was prohibited and the Sultan had already warned the missionaries not to approach Muslims. The local Christians, however, were struggling to keep their congregation intact in the face of missionary influence. This was especially important because their religion was what kept them together as a community; they did not want to become divided like the Armenians. In their perspective, "to leave one's church was to become alien from one's people."[67] Therefore, local Christians were in competition with Protestants just as much as they were with Muslims, but the latter were the dominant ruling party, forcing Christians into a passive position. Against the missionaries and local converts, however, they had more power and were occasionally intolerant. Their harassments seemed to be a cause of great dread for Protestant life. Correspondence in *Angeliaforos* written by Hacı Savvas, describes an attack on a Protestant colporteur by a Metropolitan Bishop:

> In order the collect the tax called *kapnika*, the Metropolitan Bishop every year walks around the coastal villages and uplands. In his tour, he also serves Liturgy for the souls of the dead people [...] When he was in an upland called Çambaşı, in a village called Armut Eli, accidentally a colporteur called Yannis Deliyannidis who is under our administration came to the village with a bag full of Bibles. When the bishop was informed that a Protestant colporteur was in the village on his way to church for Liturgy service, he ordered that he be sent away from the village until he was back from the church. In compliance with his order, a henchman found him in a house when he was taking a bath and kicked him [...] When the colporteur felt better; he got the guts and went to the Bishop to ask for justice. When the colporteur approached him, the Bishop went crazy and asked for his revolver. The bishop and his henchman beat and injured the colporteur severely [...][68]

The Missionary Herald also reported many types of harassment against Protestants by the Orthodox. For example, in Ordu, the Protestant congregation suffered from repeated stoning and endless abuse and insults.[69] In another case, Yani Savva, a Greek Protestant from Magnesia, was the subject of a painful persecution. He was of a wealthy and very respectable family, and was rich himself in lands and flocks of sheep. From the time that Savva became a Protestant, being a man of much personal influence, he had been a particular object of hatred on the part of the Greek Bishop and primates in Magnesia. Since there were complaints coming from the local Greeks and men of religion, the Turkish administrator of the region decided to punish him. First, heaviest irons were put upon him, then he was sent to Smyrna as a prisoner and later to Gallipoli as an exile.[70]

Joining the Protestant congregation sometimes had other sorts of negative outcomes for individuals other than direct persecution. One example of this was the alienation of converts from family and relatives. *The Missionary Herald* reported many stories relating to the isolation of individual Protestants from their kin. For instance, a letter from Izmir in the magazine dated 1886 told of a Greek convert's family cutting off contact following his conversion by no longer writing to him. Likewise, another Evangelist gave up his business and his fiancée. Further, two girls who had already become Protestants only had the courage to come out openly a full year and a half after their conversion due to the opposition of their family.[71] However, inter-communal and inter-personal relations between the members of Orthodox and Protestant denominations were not always bitter. Although rare, there were also places where Orthodox and Gregorian Churches had positive attitudes toward Protestants. One of those places was *Marsovan* (today, Merzifon) where the presence and good work of

144 *Tolerating the heretics*

ON THE CAMPUS OF ANATOLIA COLLEGE IN 1920

Figure 5.4 Anatolia College, Merzifon.
Source: *The Missionary Herald*, 1921

the Anatolia College and the hospital created a relatively peaceful atmosphere.[72] In another case, in *Sardovan* (today Serdivan), a Greek village in Adapazarı,[73] the Protestants were almost never persecuted by the Orthodox, who even attended Protestant services.

As far as the Anatolian Protestants are concerned, it is quite curious how nonetheless they increased in number and formed communities. One correspondent to *Angeliaforos* explained the Protestant community in Bartın in this way:

> It is not an exaggeration to claim that twelve years ago, there was no community of the Bible and the people did not even know what Protestant was. When this town was sleeping, the name of Protestant was heard due to the arrival of a precious clock-seller Hagop Apelyan from Merzifon. One year later, I came to this town as a result of my father's demand who is dealing with his own work and I started to help him. By this way our number became two. Every week we gathered in our room to pray. One and a half years after our union, another youth joined us. [...] Thus, we became three people. [...] Even though in those years we heard swear words from the

Tolerating the heretics 145

children of the neighborhood and were faced with difficulties, these hardships were overcome due to our friendship and conciliatory words.[74]

A missionary letter set out the way a group of pilgrim women of both Armenians and Greeks were attracted by the missionaries in Ordu:

> The deck of the Russian steamer was crowded with Greek and Armenian pilgrims to Jerusalem, and we soon found opportunities of seed-sowing on the way. "You will not find Christ at Jerusalem," I said, after pleasant conversation with some of the women. "What!" exclaimed an aged mother, "is he not there? Then there is no use in our going." […] "No," I replied, "he is not there in *person*; but in spirit he is here and everywhere and you need not take the long journey to the Holy City to find him." […] We left among them a number of tracts and portions of Scripture in their own tongue, with prayer for the divine blessing.[75]

For the newly converted it was important to legitimize their position and their beliefs in the eyes of their ex-coreligionists. Either by criticizing their religious beliefs or by criticizing those who accused them of having false beliefs, they tried to obtain a position in their locality. This was also a matter of competition to gain new members from other denominations and not to lose members to these other sects. In correspondence from Ünye, Ilias El. Meymaridis criticized a youth for spreading false beliefs and the Armenian and Greek Orthodox people of his region for being ignorant. In this letter, he warned his fellow Protestant co-religionists not to encourage false beliefs:

> The Armenians and Greeks of our community are non-religious, if not faithless. On Sundays, they are going to coffee-houses to play backgammon rather than going to church. When our community is under such conditions, a heathen youth who thinks he is wise coming from Ordu deceived some of our ignorant youth with such words: "God exists; it is important to be a good person; there is no need to the Holy Book." […] The heathens, who think that there is no need for the Holy Book and it is more important to be a good person, are very much mistaken. Because in our century, there still exists savages not accepting the Holy Book, lacking of moral values and eating human flesh. Conversely, the ones who accepted the Holy Book – like the people of the Fiji Islands who used to eat human flesh – became good people […] For this reason; some wise heathens abjured and started to obey the Holy Book. Voltaire, the head of the heathens, once said that he was compelled to believe since he was scared of death.[76]

The Protestant communities were rarely established as a result of a spontaneous coming together of individual Protestants. The local Protestant preachers, the colporteurs and the missionaries themselves were moving around Anatolia to spread the Evangelical message. For example, in a letter from Nikolaos

Kuzudzakoglou, an Armenian preacher called Zenot Filcyan, who was sent to Trabzon as a representative of the Christians (Protestants), was praised for his devotion to spreading the Evangel in their locality.[77] Likewise, the correspondence of Kosmas Korpoglou wrote about the genesis of the Evangelical community in Keskin after the appointment of a graduate of Merzifon College, Agop Der Gazarian, to their town as a preacher.[78] The missionaries or the preachers, when they were new in a locality, organized gatherings and said prayers in private houses. There were two different types of gatherings, one for Bible instruction and one for prayers. Likewise, in correspondence from Samsun, Hacı Antonoglou stated gatherings for the youths to clarify some issues from the Bible and to generate will for religious matters.[79]

The importance of education was always stated in *Angeliaforos*. However, in correspondence, I rarely encountered information about the schools. Instead, I came across short lines about scholarships for the ordinary people of Anatolia, including Protestants not yet affluent enough to send their children to school. Hence, scholarships were important for youth access to education. In relation to this, in his correspondence, Gavrieloglou, the treasurer and the clerk of a youth company in Samsun, declared his contribution to youth education at Anatolia College and asked wealthy readers to contribute to this duty and provide scholarships.[80] Another correspondence cited with pleasure the admittance of a poor pupil from Denek Maden to Saint Paul School in Tarsus with a scholarship of half his tuition.[81]

The rationality behind conversion certainly changed from individual to individual. From a lay point of view, poor people became Protestants for upward movement in the socio-economic strata. From an Orthodox point of view, "they (the missionaries) mainly targeted the uneducated people who did not know how to distinguish the words and fooled those."[82] There is no information to hand that economically disadvantaged people chose to become Protestants; the correspondence in *Angeliaforos*, and the few testimonies in the Oral Tradition Archives, in fact, show that some Protestants were already well situated before their conversion. However, it would not be wrong to claim that Protestantism provided advancement in people's lives. In the end, they at least had the opportunity to learn how to read and write, and to read the Bible in their own language. This advancement was especially significant for women.

Protestants who received an education in the missionary schools learned science and foreign languages and thus developed a broader world perspective. Additionally, Protestantism introduced these people to the capitalist culture of West and imbued them with a sense of enlightenment. This can be seen in refugee testimonies of the CAMS Oral Tradition Archives, in which I came across narratives of the Protestants from Zincidere. For example, Viktoria Seirinidou, born in Zincidere in 1889, received her education first in the American College in Talas; afterward, she went to Arsakeia Schools in Corfu (Αρσάκειο Κερκύρας) and Athens (Αρσάκειο Αθηνών).[83] She worked as a teacher in American schools in Izmir and Gedik Paşa (Istanbul), and as a director at Talas American College. Right before the Asia Minor catastrophe, she went to Athens. Many of her friends received assistance from the missionaries to go to Athens. Another missionary provided scholarship for seventeen women, who worked as teachers in American schools, to go to the United States. In this way she went to the U.S. and studied dental medicine in Boston. She ultimately continued her life as a dentist in Piraeus and Athens.[84] The story of Viktoria Seirinidou represents a great achievement for that time as she was able to enjoy a working life dominated by or, arguably, solely for men. Her narrative proves to a degree that, through the assistance of the missionaries, Protestantism provided people with the necessary means to realize and obtain self-actualization. The CAMS interviewer described Viktoria as a smart, determined, courageous person who was not fanatical like many other Protestants. This statement is important in understanding the stereotypical image that Protestants had in the eyes of the ordinary Orthodox.

There is no information to support the other view that uneducated people were attracted to Protestantism, but we can suppose that most Anatolians at that time were uneducated or insufficiently educated to be able to fully comprehend religious texts. Another idea which bears consideration was that perhaps the native Christians regarded conversion as salvation, or as an opportunity to leave the country for Britain or America, especially during times of crisis and persecution. I only once came across such a statement in *The Missionary Herald*, where a man from a mixed Armenian and Turkish village asked if he could go to America with his family following his conversion. The missionary response was that he could not, arguing that Protestantism was not a changing of nationality but a changing of heart.[85] I do not have the necessary sources to answer this question clearly. This might have been a factor in individual choices. Comparing the rate of conversion before and after persecutions such as massacres, exiles and boycotts may shed some light on the issue.

I came across two other Protestant oral tradition accounts, neither of whom were economically disadvantaged. Eleni Serafeimidou's family were Turcophone Protestants from Zincidere. Her father Hatzisavvas was a tobacco merchant in Amasya who came to Zincidere once every five years. Hatzisavvas was not a Protestant and he rejected one of his sons after he converted to Protestantism. The punished son went to Merzifon to study at the American College. He returned to Amasya to see his father after finishing school but was once again shunned. Eventually, missionaries hired him to work in the American Consulate in Izmir and he later went to the U.S. As for Eleni, she lived with her mother in Zincidere with the help of her brothers, as her husband lived and worked in various places including Batumi, Athens and Patras. He sold the Bible on Filellinon Street in Athens before the First World War. They had six children and her daughters were living in the U.S. when the interview was conducted in 1954.[86] The Haritonidis family, like the Serafeimidou family, was wealthy enough for a good life. Nikolaos Haritonidis was a Turcophone grocer from Zincidere. Their surname was Sarmousakoglou in Turkish documents; his father (Ayan Ioannis) was a sculptor in the Ottoman palace. After finishing community school he went to Istanbul, where he worked as a grocer for fifteen years. He

148 Tolerating the heretics

later came back to Zincidere and opened a grocery store. In 1914, he worked as a housekeeper in an American orphanage in Zincidere, after the Americans left the village because of the war. Upon their return in 1918, he continued to work as a housekeeper in American schools and in the orphanage. Nikolaos came to Athens after the Americans left the village. All the personnel and children of the American schools were called to leave Turkey, but the Evangelists were not included in the Exchange. None of them, according to Nikolaos, went back to Turkey to sell their properties. He worked as a moneylender in Athens, and although he learned Greek at school, he would continue to read his Bible in Turkish until he died in 1958.[87]

Inter-communal relations during the long war (1912–1922)

As we have seen, the Greek and Armenian Church authorities clearly waged war against the activities of missionaries and even against the Evangelicals themselves. They also provoked the members of their congregations to reject the Protestants vehemently. Through these methods they attempted to close their community borders to Greek Protestants, but shutting the door on Protestants was not so simple, largely due to the familial bonds they had with Orthodox Christians. In the case of the Arab Protestants of Syria, Lebanon and Palestine, Sabra believes that the converts tended to remain in close contact with their families and their larger Orthodox environment, though he claims these interactions were often followed by envy and resentment as converts began to fare better economically, socially and educationally and they often adopted a condescending attitude toward their relatives and friends.[88] Although familial bonds could not be easily removed, Greek Protestants lived through hardships originating from the preaching of the Orthodox and Gregorian clergy. The issue was complicated and the behavior of other Christians toward them varied from persecution to negative tolerance, since they may have had close kin. Additionally, even if they converted to Protestantism, most continued their old customs of cultivation, nutrition, trading, child-rearing and so on, and they still shared the same geographical territories. Therefore, the two communities had many intersecting zones. However, despite their common roots, shared spaces and similar customs (with the exception of religious ones), the Greek Protestants exhibited a different trajectory of community development and, because of the prejudices they faced, over the course of time they became a closed community in contemporary Greece. Only during the long war (1913–1922) did wartime hardships minimize the differences between the two communities and allowed room for some of the Greek Protestants to become part of the Greek nationalist movement, especially in the Black Sea region.

Events in the first two decades of the twentieth century forced people to pick sides according to the hardships they lived through. During the years of war the peoples of the combat zones inevitably got politicized and some even got nationalized. Traditional religion-based forms of self-definition were replaced by nationalistic ones. The Greek Protestants also found themselves at a time of discontinuity and had to choose their side. We know that some of them adopted Greek nationalism, as happened in Pontus where Greek Protestants joined bandits to fight against the Turks. We also know of Greek Protestants that left Turkey during the war or in the following Exchange of Populations – with the exception of a few families like the Kantartzi family from Ordu who stayed in their homeland, sold their property in a proper way and left in 1925,[89] although Greek Protestants, like Greek Catholics, were excluded from the procedure.[90] According to Greek Protestant scholars Papageorgiou and Kalfas, even though the Treaty of Lausanne excluded the Protestants, they sacrificed everything and came to Greece. They preferred the hardships and great risks, including death, of refugee life over the idea of remaining in Turkey away from their compatriots. For these scholars, even if they believed in different sects and had disputes in doctrinal matters, the Protestant and Orthodox Greeks were still one community. For example, in the Black Sea region, Protestant Greeks were just as impressed by the spread of Greek nationalism as their Orthodox compatriots had been in the first decades of the twentieth century, and since they fought for the autonomy of Pontus, Protestant Greeks were not excluded from the persecutions of the Young Turks.[91] Unfortunately, we know very little about the position of the Greek Protestants in Cappadocia. Like their Orthodox compatriots, they were mostly isolated from the areas of conflict. We do not know if they were indifferent to Greek or Turkish nationalism, or whether they sided with one or the other. How would they respond, for example, to the Papa Efthim movement, which claimed that the Anatolian Orthodox were of Turkish origin? What would have been the position of the Anatolian Protestants if his movement had been successful? We can only speculate what would have happened to Turcophone Greek Protestants of Anatolia if the Anatolian Orthodox had stayed in Turkey. We only know that all the Greek Protestants left Turkey, either for Greece or the U.S.,[92] during and after the long war.

There are several possible reasons for the emigration of Protestant Greeks from Turkey. Many were probably unaware of the fact that they were not included in the Exchange Protocol so they simply joined the crowd. Some probably left Turkey because of their family bonds with the Orthodox Greeks and their desire to accompany their loved ones. And we can assume that some left because of their fear that the persecutions of the Turks would continue. An example of this occurred in Gürümce (Κουρούμτζα) in February 1922 when the local bandits (κομητατζήδες) put all the Christians, including Protestants and Orthodox Christians, in the Orthodox Church of St George (Η ορθόδοξη εκκλησία του Αγ. Γεωργίου) and burned them to death.[93] There were about fifty Protestant families in the village and 110 to 120 inhabitants were killed in the fire while the rest of the community went to Greece and resettled in the village of Neos Mylotopos in Giannitsa (Νέος Μυλότοπος).[94] For the Pontus region things were different. When the Exchange of Populations protocol was signed in 1923, most Greek Evangelicals had already been driven out of their homes and exiled to Syria. Çambaşı (Ordu) was one of those villages deserted long before the Exchange.[95]

According to a CAMS interviewee, the Greek Protestants left Zincidere with the personnel of the American schools and orphanage.[96] Like the Protestants, most Greek Catholics (Uniates), who were not included in the Exchange Protocol, left Turkey for Greece in 1923, fearing for their future in Turkey, despite the severe opposition of the national Greek Orthodox Church to the Uniates and the support they received from the Greek state.[97] So, the Greek Protestant exodus from Turkey could be or could not be related to their sympathy toward the Greek cause. As with other communities of the time, their self-definition and belongingness were determined by factors including fear of death or expulsion, kinship relations, nationalist propaganda, their relations with the Armenian Protestants and the opportunities presented by the Americans to local converts. Thus, we cannot determine a rigid form of identity for the Greek Protestants at this time; it was probably fluctuating between their religious identity and relations with the Americans on the one hand, and their blood ties with the Orthodox on the other.

As I discussed in the previous chapter, Greek nationalism consequently evolved into a religious nationalism and excluded those who were not Orthodox Christians, like the Cretan Muslims, Catholics, Uniates and Protestants. In the first Greek constitution of 1822, the first article declared, "The established religion of the Greek State is the Eastern Orthodox Church of Christ; the government of Greece, however, tolerates every other religion, and its services and ceremonies may be practiced without interference."[98] This means that the Greek national identity was built upon confessional identity. As we have seen above, the Protestant Church from the beginning found itself in profound otherness with regard to the Orthodox Church, not only in the Kingdom but also in the Ottoman Empire. As for the official Greek nationalism's perspective on Greek Protestants, there was suspicion about the fact that they did not share that fundamental marker of Greek identity, Orthodox Christianity, just like the Greek Catholics of the Aegean and Ionian Islands[99] and the Greek Uniates.[100]

Up until the years of turmoil there was competition between Orthodox and Protestant communities focused on not losing members to the other and trying to keep the groups intact. A religious dispute between the two denominations was prevalent and Protestant arguments about Orthodoxy created severe resentment both in ecclesiastical circles and among its pious believers. Despite the official legitimacy they received from the Ottoman administrators and the support of missionaries and American diplomats, Greek Protestants were still in a passive defensive position in their relations with Orthodox people. It was the Orthodox who tolerated or persecuted the Protestants, since they were dominant both in number and power due to their economic, demographic and administrative advantage in the Empire.

At an inter-personal level, things were much more complicated due to the kinship relations that discouraged hostilities. Conversely, we could talk about competitive living together at an inter-communal level. The Protestants were either tolerated negatively – so long as they did not proselytize – or harassed as a result of their activities, whereas during the years of turmoil things became much more complicated and people's belongingness fluctuated. In those years, some Greek Protestants cooperated with the Greek forces and devoted themselves to the Greek cause. We do not have enough information about the others and with the sources at hand we can only speculate. Some were likely indifferent to either Turkish or Greek nationalism, and perhaps even felt themselves closer to the Americans, as many of them eventually decided to emigrate to the U.S.

Notes

1 For such scholarship, see H. Ertuğrul, *Azınlık ve Yabancı Okullarının Türk Toplumuna Etkisi*; İ. P. Haydaroğlu, *Osmanlı İmparatorluğunda Yabancı Okullar*; H. Özsoy, *Kayseri'de Amerikan Misyoner Faaliyetleri ve Talas Amerikan Koleji*.
2 For a nineteenth century source concerning Orthodox reaction to Protestant missionaries, see K. H. N. Lamprylos, *Ο Μισσιοναρισμός και Προτεσταντισμός εις τας Ανατολάς: Ήτοι Διαγωγή των Προτεσταντών Μισσιοναρίων εις τα Μέρη μας, εις τινα τε άλλα της Γης Μέρη. Και Σχέσεις του Προτεσταντισμού προς την Μητέρα πασών των Εκκλησιών και το Ελληνικόν Έθνος*. For Greek scholarship portraying the rivalry between the missionaries and the Patriarchate, or the autocephalous Greek Church, see I. N. Karmiris, *Ορθοδοξία και Προτεσταντισμός*; K. Mamoni, Αγώνες του Οικουμενικού Πατριαρχείου κατά των Μισσιονάριων.
3 See U. Makdisi, *Artillery of Heaven: American Missionaries and the Failed Conversion of the Middle East*, pp. 61–62.
4 For "Turkish Protestants" and the curious case of the apostate Ahmet Tevfik, see S. Deringil, *Conversion and Apostasy in the Late Ottoman Empire*, pp. 78–84.
5 House of Commons Parliamentary Papers Online (1865) *Correspondence Respecting Protestant Missionaries and Converts in Turkey Presented to Both Houses of Parliament by Command of Her Majesty*. London: Harrison and sons, 1865. Retrieved May 21, 2015, from www.parlipapers.chadwyck.co.uk.
6 J. Richter, *A History of Missions in the Near East*, pp. 172–173.
7 S. Cobb, *The Real Turk*, p. 146.
8 J. Richter, *A History of Missions in the Near East*, p. 171.
9 H. H. Jessup, *The Greek Church and Protestant Missions or Missions to the Oriental Churches*, p. 6.
10 A. Rufus, *History of the Missions of the American Board of Commissioners for Foreign Missions to the Oriental Churches* (Vol. I), pp. 96–97.
11 V. Artinian, *Osmanlı Devleti'nde Ermeni Anayasası'nın Doğuşu: 1839–1863*, p. 55.
12 *An Answer to the Charges of the Greek Ecclesiastical Committee at Smyrna against the English and American Missionaries*, pp. 11–19.
13 Kyriakos Hatzi Nikolaou Lamprylos (1810–1883) was a publisher promoting the Orthodox resistance against the missionaries in Smyrna. He was publishing a newspaper called "Mnimosyni" (Μνημοσύνη, Commemoration). L. M. Marks, Οι ελληνικές εφημερίδες στην Οθωμανική Αυτοκρατορία, 1830–1862, pp. 442–445.
14 See K. H. N. Lamprylos, *Ο Μισσιοναρισμός και Προτεσταντισμός εις τας Ανατολάς: Ήτοι Διαγωγή των Προτεσταντών Μισσιοναρίων εις τα Μέρη μας, εις τινα τε άλλα της Γης Μέρη. Και Σχέσεις του Προτεσταντισμού προς την Μητέρα Πασών των Εκκλησιών και το Ελληνικόν Έθνος*.
15 C. Şişman, Failed Proselytizers or Modernizers? Protestant Missionaries among the Jews and Sabbateans/Dönmes in the Nineteenth-century Ottoman Empire, pp. 939–940.

16 Turkish Missions. (1884). *The Missionary Herald*, 426; Central Turkey Mission: The Revival at Adana. (1884). *The Missionary Herald*, 317.
17 Western Turkey Mission: Church Organized in Gemerek. (January 1904). *The Missionary Herald*, 28.
18 Letters from the Missions: Western Turkey mission: Joy at Ordoo. (May 1899). *The Missionary Herald*, 194.
19 I. Agapidis, *Ελληνικαί Ευαγγελικαί Κοινότητες του Πόντου*, p. 7.
20 I. Agapidis, *Ελληνικαί Ευαγγελικαί Κοινότητες της Μικράς Ασίας*.
21 H. Özsoy, *Kayseri'de Amerikan Misyoner Faaliyetleri ve Talas Amerikan Koleji*, p. 36.
22 G. Sabra, Orthodox-Protestant Relations: A View from the Middle East, p. 373.
23 For Maronite opposition to missionaries and for the curious case of an Arab reformer (and a convert), see U. Makdisi, *Artillery of Heaven*.
24 G. Sabra, Orthodox-Protestant Relations: A View from the Middle East, p. 374.
25 J. B. White, *Observations on Heresy and Orthodoxy*, p. 5.
26 G. R. Evans, *A Brief History of Heresy*, p. 159.
27 K. Nikolaidou-Danasi, *Καισάρεια Τόμος Α': Η Μονή Τιμίου Προδρόμου στο Ζιντζίδερε (Φλαβιανά). Το Πνευματικό και Εκπαιδευτικό Κέντρο της Καππαδοκίας Κερμίρα, Μερσίνα, Ποτάμια*, p. 70.
28 For the debates about the need to conduct religious services in Turkish, see S. Benlisoy, "Anatol Ahali–i Rumiyesi," Misyonerler ve Türkçe İbadet Meselesi.
29 Orthodoksia'nın Muhafazası. (February 12–14, 1894). *Anatoli*, 4773–4774.
30 E. Gazi, Revisiting Religion and Nationalism in Nineteenth-Century Greece, p. 99.
31 E. Riggs, Anatolia College, Western Turkey, p. 417.
32 G. L. Richards, Are Foreign Missions Worth While? p. 417.
33 Anatolia College was established in Merzifon in September 1886 and was sponsored by the Boston based ABCFM. The majority of the students were Armenians and Greeks with a few Russians and Bulgarians; the Muslim Turks were not officially allowed in foreign schools.
34 Anatolia was ordered closed in 1916 and most of the Americans left for the U.S. At the time the campus was turned into a Turkish Army Hospital. After the armistice in 1918, the campus became an American run orphanage. J. O. Iatrides, Missionary Educators and the Asia Minor disaster: Anatolia College's Move to Greece, p. 146. In 1924, after the Exchange of Populations between Greece and Turkey, Anatolia College was transferred to Thessaloniki, Greece (See https://anatolia.edu.gr/el/).
35 J. O. Iatrides, Missionary Educators and the Asia Minor Disaster: Anatolia College's Move to Greece, p. 145.
36 K. Mamoni, L. Istikopoulou, *Σωματειακή Οργάνωση του Ελληνισμού στη Μικρά Ασία (1861–1922)*, pp. 218–219.
37 E. Gazi, Revisiting Religion and Nationalism in Nineteenth-Century Greece, pp. 100–101.
38 S. Benlisoy, *Education in the Turcophone Orthodox Communities of Anatolia during the Nineteenth Century*, p. 256.
39 *Anatoli*, August 14, 1851, 30.
40 *Anatoli*, February 14, 1853, 104.
41 *Anatoli*, June 11, 1863, 638.
42 Mezhebe Tereddüt. (30 Iouliou 1888). *Terakki*, 6.
43 S. Benlisoy, *Education in the Turcophone Orthodox Communities of Anatolia During the Nineteenth Century*, pp. 267–268, 175.
44 Translation of the firman granted by Sultan Abd-ul Mejeed to his Protestant subjects. (1853). *Journal of the American Oriental Society*, 4, pp. 443–444. For the principal charter of Protestant community [Protestan Cemaati Nizamname-i

Esasiyesi], see V. Artinian, *Osmanlı Devleti'nde Ermeni Anayasası'nın Doğuşu: 1839–1863.*
45 E. Kleovoulos Mektupları. (August 31, 1888). *Terakki*, 8.
46 E. Kleovoulos Mektupları. (September 15, 1888). *Terakki*, 9.
47 E. Kleovoulos Mektupları. (September 30, 1888). *Terakki*, 10.
48 Ç. L. Çelebi, *Socio-economic Relations between Christian and Muslim Communities in the Sanjak of Kayseri in 1870–1880*, p. 319.
49 K. Nikolaidou-Danasi, Καισάρεια Τόμος Α': Η Μονή Τιμίου Προδρόμου στο Ζιντζίδερε (Φλαβιανά). Το Πνευματικό και Εκπαιδευτικό Κέντρο της Καππαδοκίας Κερμίρα, Μερσίνα, Ποτάμια, p. 39.
50 See J. Richter, *A History of Missions in the Near East*, p. 165.
51 U. Makdisi, *Artillery of Heaven: American Missionaries and the Failed Conversion of the Middle East*, p. 184.
52 E. Gazi, Revisiting Religion and Nationalism in Nineteenth-Century Greece, p. 99.
53 R. Clogg, Some Protestant Tracts Printed at the Press of the Ecumenical Patriarchate in Constantinople: 1818–1820, pp. 163–164.
54 H. S. Barnum, Periodical Literature from the Mission Press, p. 438.
55 J. K. Greene, The Jubilee of "Avedaper," p. 172.
56 *Angeliaforos*, May 7, 1904, 19.
57 U. Kocabaşoğlu, *Anadolu'daki Amerika*, pp. 21–22.
58 E. Gazi, Revisiting Religion and Nationalism in Nineteenth-Century Greece, p. 101.
59 G. Augustinos, "Englightened" Christians and the "Oriental" Churches: Protestant Missions to the Greeks in Asia Minor: 1820–1860, pp. 139–140.
60 U. Kocabaşoğlu, *Anadolu'daki Amerika*, p. 125.
61 O. H. Dwight, The Publication Department of the Western Turkey Mission, p. 52.
62 *Angeliaforos*, January 5, 1889, 1.
63 *Angeliaforos*, June 29, 1889, 26.
64 See Y. Bağceci, Osmanlı Devleti'nde Gregorian Ermenilerle Protestan Ermeniler Arasındaki İlişkiler.
65 *Angeliaforos*, March 2, 1889, 9.
66 C. Hamlin, *My Life and Times*, p. 140.
67 G. Augustinos, "Enlightened" Christians and the "Oriental" Churches: Protestant Missions to the Greeks in Asia Minor: 1820–1860, p. 140.
68 *Angeliaforos*, September 6, 1890, 36.
69 Letters from the Missions: Western Turkey Mission: Joy at Ordoo. (May 1899). *The Missionary Herald*, p. 195.
70 A Greek Protestant. (1856). *The Missionary Herald*, p. 291.
71 Western Turkey Mission: Smyrna: the Greek Work. (April 1886). *The Missionary Herald*, p. 146.
72 An American Oasis. (June 1902). *The Missionary Herald*, pp. 407–409.
73 A Typical Greek Village. (August 1904).*The Missionary Herald*, pp. 319–323.
74 *Angeliaforos*, January 30, 1830, 5.
75 Western Turkey Mission: A Visit to Ordu. (1886). *The Missionary Herald*, p. 219.
76 *Angeliaforos*, April 13, 1889, 15.
77 *Angeliaforos*, March 2, 1889, 9.
78 *Angeliaforos*, July 27, 1889, 30.
79 *Angeliaforos*, August 3, 1889, 31.
80 *Angeliaforos*, January 9, 1890, 2.
81 *Angeliaforos*, October 4, 1890, 40.
82 K. H. N. Lamprylos, Ο Μισσιοναρισμός και Προτεσταντισμός εις τας Ανατολάς: Ήτοι Διαγωγήτων Προτεσταντών Μισσιοναρίων εις τα Μέρη μας, εις τινα τε άλλα της Γης Μέρη. Και Σχέσεις του Προτεσταντισμού προς την Μητέρα Πασών των Εκκλησιών και το Ελληνικόν Έθνος,

154 Tolerating the heretics

83 As a defense against the missionary schools, these girls' schools were supported by the Philekpaideutiki Etaireia and named after Apostolos Arsakis. See P. Thanailaki, The American Protestant Missionary Schools in Greece in the Nineteenth Century and Greek Orthodox Education, p. 76.
84 CAMS, Cappadocia, Zincidere, Viktoria Seirinidou.
85 L. S. Crawford, For the Younger People: Trebizond and its People, p. 880.
86 CAMS, Cappadocia, Zincidere, Eleni Serafeimidou.
87 CAMS, Cappadocia, Zincidere, Nikolaos Haritonidis.
88 G. Sabra, Orthodox-Protestant Relations: A View from the Middle East, p. 373.
89 Personal communication with a family member.
90 P. S. Ladas, *The Exchange of Minorities: Bulgaria, Greece and Turkey*, p. 384.
91 A. G. Kalfas, P. A. Papageorgiou, *Ο Συνοικισμός Ευαγγελικών Της Κατερίνης (1923–2000). Τοπική Ιστορία και Κίνηση των Θρησκευτικών Ιδεών*, p. 38.
92 Compared to other Western powers, the US gave citizenship status to Ottoman Christians the most. Ortaylı claims that missionaries raised citizens for their country in missionary schools. İ. Ortaylı, Osmanlı İmparatorluğu'nda Amerikan Okulları Üzerine Bazı Gözlemler, p. 91.
93 CAMS manuscripts, Cappadocia, Gürümce, Georgios Karaoglanidis, 1958.
94 Interview with Sofia Kosmoglou, May 17, 2013.
95 Interview with Paris A. Papageorgiou, January 28, 2014.
96 CAMS, Cappadocia, Zincidere, Nikolaos Haritonidis.
97 A small group of Greek Catholics remained in Turkey. According to documents from the Vatican there were only 45 in 1998. The last priest of the Greek congregation, Thomas Varsamis, died in 1996. The remaining Greek Catholics currently do not have a separate church and they attend the services of Latin Churches. E. Macar, *İstanbul'un Yok Olmuş İki Cemaati: Doğu Ritli Katolik Rumlar ve Bulgarlar*.
98 "Prosorinon Politeuma tes Hellados," *The Epidaurus Constitution*, 1822.
99 There was a small Catholic community nurtured by Venetian authorities in the Ionian Islands. Adding to that, there were Latin Christian Communities on the islands of the Aegean Sea: Naxos, Tinos, Siros and Thira of the Cyclades and on the island of Chios. During the Greek Revolution, the Catholics on the islands held back since they had already been enjoying some degree of autonomy and freedom under the Ottoman rule. For Frazee, they did not see the future of the revolution and wanted conserve their existing position. For this reason they were insulted of being "Turk-worshippers." C. A. Frazee, The Greek Catholic Islanders and the Revolution of 1821, pp. 315, 320–321.
100 In the age of nationalism, religion seems to be the main marker of nationality in the Balkans. For this reason in Bulgaria as well, the activities of the Protestants were faced suspiciously and were thought to destroy the national unity which was based on the Orthodox faith. See L. J. Budilová, M. Jakoubek, *Bulgarian Protestants and the Czech Village of Voyvodovo*, pp. 28, 33.

Conclusion

As a student of nationalism studies, I have always wondered how nationalism drew people so powerfully into the Ottoman Empire. My readings about nationalism theories and case studies helped me to find several explanations for this question, but only one of them was all-encompassing. In almost all examples, nationalist revivals were inherently struggles against the political and economic hegemony of the local administrators or Ottoman authority itself. A nationalist flavor was added to these movements later on by intellectuals. When I started studying Cappadocia I initially thought that my hegemony theory was not applicable. The inhabitants of the region, including members of all religious groups, seemed to be equal parts of a whole with shared customs, similar socio-economic situation and, for many of them, even the same language. During the initial stages of my research, I was amazed by the syncretic behavior and friendly statements about Turks that I found in refugee testimonies. However, all these could not explain the nationalization of the Orthodox in the region. I knew that nationalist awakening happened quite late in Cappadocia, but sooner or later it sowed the seeds of suspicion and resentment, pitting communities against one another; it raised ethnic consciousness and made people believe that they could no longer live together.

After my research, I decided to include a debate about tolerance, in the hope of seeing the correlation between the scope of tolerance and nationalization, and I discovered Hayden's theory of "antagonistic tolerance." Adopting this theory was a real challenge because it was a seemingly negative perspective that argued that maintaining community borders against possible attacks by the religious Other was the reason for competition between faith groups. This would mean that the borders of social relations were drawn with a religiously defined Self and Other dichotomy. In this ecosystem of antagonistic tolerance, syncretic behaviors were the outcomes of the hegemony of one group over the others. All these arguments seem pessimistic but one has to keep in mind that the presence of antagonistic tolerance does not automatically mean that antagonism was prevalent in Cappadocia. As I stressed several times, antagonistic tolerance turned into antagonism only in times of crisis, when the hegemony could possibly be abolished. For Cappadocia, clashes between religious groups did not take place even during the years of the long war, not because there was peaceful cohabitation in the region but because of certain specificities in demographics and male emigration. Thus, the hegemony theory could apply to Cappadocia as well; its key indicators were competitive living together, imbalanced cosmopolitanism and syncretic behavior.

In addition to an analysis of the process of nationalization of the Anatolian Orthodox through an examination of the correlation between the cohabitation practices of neighboring faith groups, tolerance and nationalism, this book aimed to respond to Pax-Ottomana romanticism concerning Ottoman plurality using as a case study one of the most "peaceful" regions of the Empire, Cappadocia, since it provides a good setting to test the peaceful co-existence myth. I have asked various "why questions." One asked was why the Ottoman Empire dissolved into several nation-states if different faith groups lived together peacefully. To answer this question, I considered concepts like tolerance, inter-communality, plurality and multiculturalism, with reference to normative discussions in political philosophy, especially in view of the tendency of similar studies to employ these terms arbitrarily. Furthermore, I made an examination of competitive sharing between religious communities with an emphasis on the unequal and hegemonic aspect of religious syncretism. Sharing common customs and developing syncretic behaviors, in fact, do not mean that people were confused about their religion. To overcome any sort of romanticism, I also differentiated between testimonies that involved inter-personal and inter-communal relationships. Inter-personal encounters were neighborly relationships that included intimacy whereas at the inter-communal level the community borders were sharp, and the walls became higher or lower in line with the circumstances of the time. In times of peace the walls were more pervious, while in times of crisis, like wars and persecutions, community walls were higher.

This book also focuses on several misconceptions. For example, non-conflict or less conflict does not denote "peaceful cohabitation." In the case of Cappadocia, there were two parameters of cohabitation: one was a general rule according to which non-Muslims were secondary subjects in line with Islamic tradition, and the second was imbalanced cosmopolitanism in which Muslim Turks were the dominant group, both demographically and culturally. In this ecosystem of co-existence, the Cappadocian Orthodox tried to preserve their religion against conversion to Islam and mixed marriages with Turks, as well as, in the nineteenth century, the threat of missionaries, who proselytized among their co-religionists. In the Ottoman Empire, the Muslims were the ultimate tolerators who remained indifferent to their Others. The Orthodox, on the other hand, were the tolerated group who had no choice but to consent in their relations with the dominant group. Interestingly, they assumed the role of tolerators in their relations with the Greek Protestants because they were demographically stronger and more powerful with their established authorities and prestige in the Ottoman court. And all these parameters prove that Cappadocia could be a setting for Hayden's antagonistic tolerance.

Another question that this book hoped to address was the concept of whether or not there really was a glorious past to which we can refer to solve the problems of today. The answer is no from two different angles. If our reference point is managing diversity, the Ottoman Empire cannot be an example for today because contemporary diversity is much more complicated and multi-faceted. As I discussed in the second chapter, the reason for crediting Ottoman tolerance was an outcome of comparing it with its predecessors and contemporaries. It is true that the Ottomans were more flexible in handling diversity compared to other empires of its time, and must be judged within the limits of history. However, there were also times and places in which Ottomans arbitrarily limited non-Muslim liberties. The Ottoman world was not an ideal world about which we can romanticize and aspire to imitate today. Even the non-conflictual Cappadocia cannot be an example for us. The Ottoman Empire was a pre-modern imperial state that was run by Islamic doctrine and by the will of Sultans that could not possibly be questioned. In this system, justice was only a means to accommodate hegemony and to preserve the imperial domains. There were no individuals, only subjects of the Sultans and members of religious communities; in other words, individuals were confined to their communities. There was autonomy for faith groups, but no freedom for individuals. Heretics of all religions were persecuted. Cosmopolitanism in cities was imbalanced in favor of those who were demographically and economically dominant. Faith groups were often spatially separated, living in different neighborhoods and only coming together in marketplaces. Competitive sharing and competitive cohabitation were prevalent in inter-communal relations. All these cannot be a remedy for the minority problems and identity claims of today. Thus, naming Ottoman plurality as historical multiculturalism means mixing apples and oranges, since the pre-modern, imperial and Islamic Ottoman Empire is totally alien to contemporary discussions which take liberal democracies as givens. This last remark led me to a judgment: offering to imitate the past for resolutions to present-day problems and analyzing the past with modern concepts are both anachronistic behaviors; every phenomenon should be assessed in its time and place.

Throughout this book the modernist version of nationalism was adopted to explain Greek nationalism and the "Hellenization" of the Cappadocians. However, this was not a complete embracement since modernist theories of nationalism are mostly Eurocentric and remain inadequate for understanding the nationalisms of Southeastern Europe. Modernist theories focus on certain discontinuities to explain the emergence of nationalism. For some modernists, discontinuity meant revolutions in England, France and the U.S. and for some it was industrial capitalism. In the Ottoman Empire, there was no such discontinuity separating traditional from modern. To put it differently, nationalism was not a natural outcome of some indigenous political, cultural or economic transformation. Rather, it was exported from the West through the non-Muslim commercial class. Thus, nationalism spread through elite endeavor, especially when we are thinking of Greek nationalism.

After the Kingdom of Greece was established in 1832, the politicians of the newly founded country were torn between working for the welfare of its people and investing for irredentism to save the "unredeemed Greeks." Until its termination with a catastrophe on the Asia Minor shores, Greek irredentism used every possible means to revive Hellenism among the Orthodox of Macedonia and Asia Minor. As early as the 1830s, Greek nationalism turned out to be religious nationalism, and played on the religion card to save the Orthodox that were considered to be prospective nationals of the Kingdom. One of the targeted areas was Cappadocia, a region in which most Christians were Turcophone. The introduction of Greek nationalism to the Orthodox settlements of Cappadocia started in the 1870s, and various parties including the *syllogoi* (societies) and brotherhood organizations of the Orthodox settlements assumed roles in this process. During this period, as a result of Ottoman reforms (1839–1856), the traditional authority of the Patriarchate, which had been the sole authority in education, was curbed by the introduction of lay members to (mixed) councils that ran communal affairs. Subsequently, the middle class started to get involved in educational matters through the *syllogoi* founded in both Athens and Istanbul, two centers of Greek nationalism at the time. Being influenced by the activities of the *syllogoi*, the Cappadocian immigrants in big cities founded their own brotherhood organizations to help their hometowns. Except for a few examples, almost all Orthodox settlements of Cappadocia had brotherhood organizations overseas. These not only targeted the welfare of the remaining people in the hometowns, but also their enlightenment. As a result of all these endeavors, Cappadocian settlements rapidly progressed with the power and wealth of their expatriates abroad.

Throughout the nineteenth century there was a flow of the male population from Orthodox settlements of Cappadocia to places of economic opportunity like Istanbul, Izmir, Adana, Samsun, Cairo, Alexandria, Beirut, Odessa, Athens and even to America. Immigration had two contradictory outcomes in terms of the enlightenment and Hellenization of the Cappadocian Orthodox. On the one hand, due to increasing immigration rates, the Orthodox settlements were deserted, with mainly women, children and the elderly remaining at home; this made them vulnerable to the already dominant Muslim culture. In relatively poor villages this impact was especially high. In this way, in some Greek-speaking villages Turkish replaced Greek; women were exposed to the Turkish-Muslim culture more than in previous times since they were no longer isolated at home, but were instead running the daily business of the household and had to have some contact with Turks. Some women started to work in the fields of Turks as a result of poverty, and some even got married to them. The other side of the story is a flow of wealth from the male immigrants to their homelands. With the cash flow, new houses, infrastructures, churches, orphanages and schools were built. Children who received their education in these institutions developed a broader Community consciousness and proto-national ties. The successful ones went on to continue their education elsewhere, often in Athens or Istanbul, and became prominent intellectuals of their time. Emmanuil Emmanuilidis, Pavlos Carolidis, Ioakeim Valavanis and Evangelinos Misailidis were among the Cappadocia born intellectuals who graduated from the University of Athens. This shows that there was a connection between Athens and Cappadocia.

In terms of nationalization and the adoption of a national identity, the Cappadocian Orthodox represented different stances: there were educated people who were Greek nationalists like Valavanis; there were intellectuals who supported Ottomanism and Ottoman integrity, like Emmanuilidis and Carolidis; there were proto-nationalists who developed a broader Community consciousness; and there were the less educated or non-educated ordinary folk who still identified themselves by their religion. Interestingly, this last category of people regarded nationalist identity as an attack on their religious identity during the early years of the age of nationalism. Unquestionably, boundaries between these categories were not fixed, and they could change according to the prevailing circumstances. For instance, Emmanuilidis and Carolidis dropped Ottomanism right after the First World War as a reaction to the persecution of non-Muslims during the war. Later they became Greek nationalists.

I followed the stories of the ordinary people through refugee testimonies. For example, they expressed their view of the changing situation of nationalist policies in one phrase: "things spoiled." They often referred to a discontinuity. The peaceful atmosphere promising freedom and equality to everyone with the Young Turk Revolution (1908) rapidly came to an end, especially after the Balkan Wars. Tolerance was replaced with intolerance flavored by increasingly nationalistic policies. In refugee testimonies, years of hardship were explained with comparisons to previous years. According to their narrative, "things got spoiled" mostly due to external factors and groups like the Young Turks, the refugee Turks and the bandits. They hesitated to blame their neighbors, but stated that some of them became wild or opportunistic in this period.

Papa Efthim was the most prominent figure of the war years in Cappadocia. With the direct support of the Ankara government, he initiated the Turkish Orthodox Church project. His initiative, however, remained ineffective since the Anatolian Orthodox were abandoned by the Turkish politicians during the Lausanne negotiations. After their displacement, the Turkish Orthodox Patriarchate remained ineffective with a very small congregation, which included family members of Papa Efthim (the Erenerol family), who were exempted from the Exchange. Sadly enough, the Anatolian Orthodox were also abandoned by Greek politicians at Lausanne. Under the pressure of the flow of refugees expelled from Asia Minor during and after the war, Greece was reluctant to receive thousands of new refugees. As a result of the give and take politics that were carried out to break the deadlock of the Greek Orthodox Patriarchate, the Anatolian Orthodox population was eventually exchanged with the Muslims residing in Greece. This was another rupture for the Anatolian Orthodox, and accelerated their process of "nationalization" as citizens of the Greek state.

The last chapter of this book was reserved for the Greek Protestants previously disregarded in the historiography of non-Muslims in the Ottoman Empire. The case of the Greek Protestants is interesting in the sense that they had kinship relations with the Orthodox. For this reason, although they were sometimes persecuted at the hands of the Orthodox, they were not totally alienated from the Orthodox Community. In other words, despite the fact that there was antagonism at an inter-communal level to protect the Orthodox from proselytization, inevitable kinship relations existed at an inter-personal level. As for inter-communal relations, the boundaries between Protestants and the Orthodox ostensibly faded away during the long war; the Protestants preferred to leave Turkey either for Greece or the U.S., although they were not included in the Exchange Protocol. We could propose several reasons for their departure: they might not have known that they were in fact outside the Protocol; they might have followed their Orthodox relatives; they might have left due to a fear of persecution at the hands of the Turkish authorities; or they might have already left when the Protocol was signed as was the case in Pontus where Christians were sent into exile. The reception of the Protestants by Greek nationalists was not pleasant, as Orthodox Christianity was the main indicator of Greek national identity and conversion meant *denationalization*.

Visiting Greece regularly, I might be able to claim that the difference between inter-communal and inter-personal relationships has not disappeared even today. Ayşe and Eleni might be good friends stripped of their national identity just as essential human beings. They might exchange recipes, sing a common song and address together the politicians as scapegoats constantly fueling enmity but they still have a nonpermeable inter-communal border especially apparent in the interpretation of history, be it in school, on television, on social media or at home. I remember a friend of mine once told me that the Ottoman Empire is still dissolving.[1] He seems to be right. Adding to the competitive structure of inter-communal (or international) encounters in the neighborhood, the Kurdish question at the heart of the historical Empire, Syria's downfall and subsequent flow of Syrian refugees to Turkey and all over the world makes me feel like the nineteenth century is continuing. To overcome the "disease of the nineteenth century," we should demand free representation of self both in public and private spheres, and no domination of one group over another. The ultimate solution is respect rather than tolerance and what we need to promote is inter-personal relations until when inter-communal is permeable. I am not pessimistic. We have the key to untie this tight knot; that is, history is a lesson to be learned, not a model to be imitated.

Note

1 I have to give credit to my friend Anastas Vangeli.

Bibliography

Archives and Libraries

Greece

Centre for Asia Minor Studies.
Oral Tradition Archives of the Centre for Asia Minor Studies (CAMS).
Photography Archive of the Centre for Asia Minor Studies (CAMS).
Greek Historical Evangelical Archive.
The Gennadius Library.

Turkey

National Library of Turkey.

Newspapers and periodicals

Anatoli 1851–1854; 1891–1897.
Terakki 1888.
Angeliaforos 1889–1890; 1903–1904.
The Missionary Herald 1870–1922.

Almanacs and Regulations of Brotherhood Organizations

Kalfoglou, I. H. (1894). *Ημερολόγιον «Η Ανατολή»*.
(1905). *Κανονισμός της εν Κωνσταντινουπόλει Αδελφότητος της Κώμης Αραβάν: Ο Άγιος Γεώργιος*. Constantinople: Patriarhikou Tipografeiou.
(1909). *Κανονισμός της εν Κωνσταντινουπόλει Φιλεκπαιδευτικής Αδελφότητος Καρβάλης: Ναζιανζός, Ιδρυθείσης τω 1884*. Constantinople: Tipografeiou Pl. Misailidou.

Books and Articles

Agapidis, I. (1948). *Ελληνικαί Ευαγγελικαί Κοινότητες του Πόντου*. Thessaloniki: Nikos Z. Zlatanos Publication House.
Agapidis, I. (1950). *Ελληνικαί Ευαγγελικαί Κοινότητες της Μικράς Ασίας*. Thessaloniki: Nikos Z. Zlatanos Publication House.
Ahladi, E. (2008). Izmir'de Ittihatçılar ve Rumlar: Yunan-Rum Boykotu (1908–1911). *Kebikeç*, 26, 188–190.

Bibliography

Aktar, A. (2007). Debating the Armenian Massacres in the Last Ottoman Parliament, November–December 1918. *History Workshop Journal*, *64(64)*, 240–270.
Aleksov, B. (2005). Perception of Islamization in the Serbian National Discourse. *Southeast European and Black Sea Studies*, *5(1)*, 113–127.
Alpan, A. S. (2013). But the Memory Remains: History, Memory and the 1923 Greco-Turkish Population Exchange. *The Historical Review/La Revue Historique*, *9*, 199–232.
Anagnostopoulou, S. (2013). *Μικρά Ασία: 19ος Αιώνας -1919: Οι Ελληνορθόδοξες Κοινότητες. Από το μιλλέτ των Ρωμιών στο Ελληνικό Έθνος*. Athens: Pedio.
Anderson, B. (2006). *Imagined Communities: Reflections on the Origin and Spread of Nationalism*. New York, NY; London: Verso.
Anestidis, S. T. (2002). Introduction. In I. Kalfoglou (Ed.), *Ιστορική Γεωγραφία της Μικρασιατικής Χερσονήσου* (S. Anestidis, Trans.). Athens: Centre for Asia Minor Studies. (Original work published 1899), pp. 13–34.
Anestidis, S. T. (2014). Yunan ve Türk Edebiyatında Erken Karamanlı Tiplemeleri. In E. Balta (Ed.), *Cultural Encounters in the Turkish-speaking Communities of the Late Ottoman Empire* (pp. 29–40). Istanbul: The Isis Press.
Anhegger, R. (2001). Evangelinos Misailidis ve Türkçe Konuşan Dindaşları. *Tarih ve Toplum*, *XXXV(209)*, 11–18.
Anonymous. (1905–1906). Στατιστική της Επαρχίας Ικονίου. *Xenophanes*, *3*, 44–47.
Anonymous. (1905–1906). Στατιστική της Επαρχίας Καισαρείας (Στατιστικός Πίνακας). *Xenophanes*, *3*, 230–233.
(1836). *An Answer to the Charges of the Greek Ecclesiastical Committee at Smyrna against the English and American Missionaries*. Smyrna: Harlow American Press.
Arendt, H. (1998). *The Human Condition*. Chicago, IL: University of Chicago Press.
Artinian, V. (2004). *Osmanlı Devleti'nde Ermeni Anayasası'nın Doğuşu: 1839–1863*. Istanbul: Aras Yayıncılık.
Augustinos, G. (1986). "Englightened" Christians and the "Oriental" Churches: Protestant Missions to the Greeks in Asia Minor: 1820–1860. *Journal of Modern Greek Studies*, *4(2)*, 129–142.
Augustinos, G. (1992). *The Greeks of Asia Minor: Confession, Community, and Ethnicity in the Nineteenth Century*. Kent, OH: Kent State University Press.
Baer, M. D. (2008). *Honored by the Glory of Islam: Conversion and Conquest in Ottoman Europe*. Oxford: Oxford University Press.
Bağçeci, Y. (2008). Osmanlı Devleti'nde Gregorian Ermenilerle Protestan Ermeniler Arasındaki İlişkiler. *Turkish Studies*, *3(7)*, 169–192.
Balta, E. (1987a). *Karamanlidika: Additions (1584–1900): Bibliographie Analytique*. Athenes: Centre D'Études De'Asie Mineure.
Balta, E. (1987b). *Karamanlidika: Nouvelles Additions et Complements I*. Athenes: Centre D'Études De'Asie Mineure.
Balta, E. (1990). Karamanlıca Kitapların Önsözleri. *Tarih ve Toplum*, *74*, 18–20.
Balta, E. (1997). *Karamanlidika: XXE Siècle: Bibliographie Analytiqu*. Athenes: Centre D'Études De'Asie Mineure.
Balta, E. (2003). Gerçi Rum isek de Rumca Bilmez Türkçe Söyleriz: The Adventure of an Identity in the Triptych: Vatan, Religion and Language. *Türk Kültürü İncelemeleri Dergisi*, *8*, 25–44.
Balta, E. (2010). Karamanli Press Smyrna 1845- Athens 1926. In *Beyond the Language Frontier. Studies on the Karamanlis and the Karamanlidika Printing*. Analecta Isisiana CX, Istanbul: The Isis Press, pp. 107–122.

Balta, E. & Kappler, M. (Eds.). (2010). *Cries and Whispers in Karamanlidika Books*. Wiesbaden: Harrassowitz Verlag.

Bardakjian, K. B. (1982). The Rise of the Armenian Patriarchate of Constantinople. In B. Braude & B. Lewis (Eds.), *Christians and Jews in the Ottoman Empire (Vol. 1)*. New York, NY: Holmes and Meier Publishers, pp. 87–98.

Barkey, K. (2008). *Empire of Difference: The Ottomans in Comparative Perspective*. New York, NY: Cambridge University Press.

Barnum, H. S. (1903). Periodical Literature from the Mission Press. *The Missionary Herald*, 15, 436–439.

Barth, F. (1969). Introduction. In F. Barth (Ed.), *Ethnic Groups and Boundaries: The Social Organization of Culture Difference*. Boston, MA: Little, Brown and Company, pp. 9–38.

Benhabib, S. (1997). The Embattled Public Sphere: Hannah Arendt, Juergen Habermas and Beyond. *Theoria*, 90(1), 1–24.

Benlisoy, F. & Benlisoy, S. (2000). 19. Yüzyılda Karamanlılar ve Eğitim: Nevşehir Mektepleri. *Toplumsal Tarih*, 74, 24–33.

Benlisoy, F. & Benlisoy, S. (2010). "Karamanlılar," "Anadolu Ahalisi" ve "Aşağı Tabakalar": Türkdilli Anadolu Ortodokslarında Kimlik Algısı. *Tarih ve Toplum Yeni Yaklaşımlar*, 11, 7–22.

Benlisoy, F. & Benlisoy, S. (2016). *Türk Milliyetçiliğinde Katedilmemiş bir Yol: "Hıristiyan Türkler" ve Papa Eftim*. İstanbul: İstos.

Benlisoy, S. (2003a). İstanbul'a Göçmüş Ürgüplü Ortodoksların Kurduğu Bir Cemiyet: "Areti" Maarifperveran Cemiyeti. *Tarih Ve Toplum*, 233, 4–9.

Benlisoy, S. (2003b). İstanbul'da Yaşayan Nevşehirli Ortodokslar Tarafından Kurulan Papa Yeorgios Nam Cemiyet-i Islahiyyesi. *Tarih ve Toplum*, 236, 35–41.

Benlisoy, S. (2010). Education in the Turcophone Orthodox Communities of Anatolia during the Nineteenth Century (Unpublished Doctoral Dissertation, Boğaziçi University).

Benlisoy, S. (2019). "Anatol Ahali-i Rumiyesi," Misyonerler ve Türkçe İbadet Meselesi. *Toplumsal Tarih*, 306, 28–34.

Ben-Naeh, Y. (2009). *Sultanlar Diyarında Yahudiler: 17. yüzyılda Osmanlı Yahudi Toplumu*. Istanbul: Goa Basım Yayın.

Bjørnlund, M. (2008). The 1914 Cleansing of Aegean Greeks. *Journal of Genocide Research*, 10(1), 41–57.

Bosworth, C. E. (1982). The Concept of *Dhimma* in Early Islam. In B. Braude & B. Lewis (Eds.), *Christians and Jews in the Ottoman Empire (Vol. 1)*. New York, NY: Holmes and Meier Publishers, pp. 37–54.

Boura, C. (1999). The Greek Millet in Turkish Politics: Greeks in the Ottoman Parliament (1908–1918). In D. Gondicas & C. Issawi (Eds.), *Ottoman Greeks in the Age of Nationalism*. New Jersey: The Darwin Press, pp. 193–206.

Bowman, G. (2002). Comment on R. Hayden, Antagonistic Tolerance: Competitive Sharing of Religious Sites in South Asia and the Balkans. *Current Anthropology*, 43(2), 219–220.

Braude, B. (1982). Foundation Myths of the Millet System. In B. Braude & B. Lewis (Eds.), *Christians and Jews in the Ottoman Empire (Vol. 1)*. New York, NY: Holmes and Meier Publishers, pp. 69–88.

Bringa, T. (1995). *Being a Muslim the Bosnian Way: Identity and Community in a Central Bosnian Village*. Princeton, NJ: Princeton University Press.

Brown, W. (2006). *Regulating Aversion: Tolerance in the Age of Identity and Empire*. Princeton, NJ and Oxford: Princeton University Press.

164 Bibliography

Budilová, L. J. & Jakoubek, M. (2017). *Bulgarian Protestants and the Chech Village of Voyvodovo*. Sofia: New Bulgarian University.

Cahen, C. D. (2012). Dhimma. In P. Bearman, T. Bianquis, C.E. Bosworth, E. van Donzel & W.P. Heinrichs (Eds.), *Encyclopedia of Islam Second Edition*. Leiden: Brill, pp. 227–231, Online Publication.

Campos, M. (2011). *Ottoman Brothers: Muslims, Christians, and Jews in Early Twentieth-Century Palestine*. Stanford, CA: Stanford University Press.

Carter, I. (2013). Are Toleration and Respect Compatible? *Journal of Applied Philosophy*, 30(3), 195–208.

Caunce, S. (2011). *Sözlü Tarih Ve Yerel Tarihçi*. Istanbul: Tarih Vakfı Yurt Yayınları.

Çelebi, Ç. L. (2009).Socio-economic Relations between Christian and Muslim Communities in the Sanjak of Kayseri in 1870–1880 (Unpublished Doctoral dissertation, National and Kapodistrian University of Athens).

Çetinkaya, Y. D. (2014). *The Young Turks and the Boycott Movement: Nationalism, Protest and the Working Classes in the Formation of Modern Turkey*. London; New York, NY: I. B. Tauris.

Clogg, R. (1968). Some Protestant Tracts Printed at the Press of the Ecumenical Patriarchate in Constantinople: 1818–1820. *Eastern Churches Review*, 2(2), 152–164.

Clogg, R. (1978). Some Karamanlidika Inscriptions from the Monastery of the Zoodokhos Pigi, Balıklı. *Byzantine and Modern Greek Studies*, 4, 55–67.

Clogg, R. (1982). The Greek Millet in the Ottoman Empire. In B. Braude & B. Lewis (Eds.), *Christians and Jews in the Ottoman Empire: The Functioning of a Plural Society (Vol. 1)*. New York, NY: Holmes & Meier Publishers, pp. 185–207.

Clogg, R. (1996). Anadolu Hıristiyan Karındaşlarımız: The Turkish-Speaking Greeks of Asia Minor. *Anatolica: Studies in the Greek East in the 18th and 19th Centuries*. Hampshire; Vermont: Variorum, pp. 65–91.

Clogg, R. (1999). A Millet within a Millet: The Karamanlides. In D. Gondicas & C. Issawi (Eds.), *Ottoman Greeks in the Age of Nationalism*. New Jersey: The Darwin Press, pp. 115–132.

Cobb, S. (1914). *The Real Turk*. Boston, MA; New York, NY; Chicago, IL: The Pilgrim Press.

Cohen, A. (2004). What Toleration Is. *Ethics*, 115(1), 68–95.

Crawford, L. S. (1906). For the Younger People: Trebizond and its People. *The Missionary Herald*.

Daniel, E. L. (2012). Manicheanism. In T.B. Bearman, C.E. Bosworth, E. van Donzel, W. P. Heinrichs (Eds.), *Encyclopedia of Islam Second Edition*. Leiden: Brill, pp. 428–429.

Davison, R. H. (1982). The Millets as Agents of Change in the Nineteenth-Century Ottoman Empire. In B. Braude & B. Lewis (Eds.), *Christians and Jews in the Ottoman Empire (Vol. 1)*. New York, NY: Holmes and Meier Publishers, pp. 187–208.

Dawkins, R. (1916). *Modern Greek in Asia Minor: A Study of the Dialects of Silli, Cappadocia and Pharasa with Grammer, Texts, Translations and Glossary*. Cambridge: Cambridge University Press.

Dean, M. (1999). *Governmentality: Power and Rule in Modern Society*. Thousand Oaks, CA: Sage Publications.

Deringil, S. (2000). There is No Compulsion in Religion: Conversion and Apostasy in the Late Ottoman Empire 1839–1856. *Comparative Studies in Society and History*, 40, 547–575.

Deringil, S. (2012). *Conversion and Apostasy in the Late Ottoman Empire*. New York, NY: Cambridge University Press.

Doumanis, N. (2013). *Before the Nation: Muslim-Christian Co-existence and its Destruction in Late Ottoman Anatolia*. Oxford: Oxford University Press.
Dwight, O. H. (1898). The Publication Department of the Western Turkey Mission. *The Missionary Herald*.
Dyke, V. V. (1985). *Human Rights, Ethnicity, and Discrimination*. London: Greenwood press.
Ekmečić, M. (1989). *Stvaranje Jugoslavije 1790–1818*. Belgrade: Prosteva.
Eldem, E. (1999). Istanbul: From Imperial to Peripheralized Capital. In E. Eldem, D. Goffman & B. Masters (Eds.), *The Ottoman City between East and West*. New York, NY: Cambridge University Press, pp. 135–206.
Emmanuilidis, E. (2014). *Osmanlı İmparatorluğunun Son Yılları*. Istanbul: Belge Yayınları. (Orijinal work published 1924).
Epstein, M. A. (1982). The Leadership of the Ottoman Jews in the Fifteenth and Sixteenth Centuries. In B. Braude & B. Lewis (Eds.), *Christians and Jews in the Ottoman Empire (Vol. 1)*. New York, NY: Holmes and Meier Publishers, pp. 101–115.
Erdem, H. (2005). "Do Not Think of the Greeks as Agricultural Laborers": Ottoman Responses to the Greek War of Independence. In F. Birtek & T. Dragonas (Eds.), *Citizenship and Nation-State in Greece and Turkey*. Oxon; New York, NY: Routledge, pp. 67–84.
Ergene, T. (1951). *İstiklal Harbinde Türk Ortodoksları*. Istanbul: İ. P. Neşriyat Servisi.
Erol, M. (2004). Evangelinos Misailidis. *Toplumsal Tarih*, *128*, 70–71.
Erol, M. (2014). Cultural Manifestations of a Symbiosis: Karamanlidika Epitaphs of the Nineteenth Century. In E. Balta (Ed.), *Cultural Encounters in the Turkish-Speaking Communities of the Late Ottoman Empire*. Proceedings of the III International Workshop of Karamanlidika Studies. İstanbul: Isis Press, pp. 77–104.
Ertuğrul, H. (1998). *Azınlık ve Yabancı Okullarının Türk Toplumuna Etkisi*. Istanbul: Nesil Yayınları.
Evans, G. R. (2008). *A Brief History of Heresy*. Hoboken: Wiley.
Exertzoglou, H. (1999). The Development of a Greek Ottoman Bourgeoisie: Investment Patterns in the Ottoman Empire, 1850–1914. In D. Gondicas & C. Issawi (Eds.), *Ottoman Greeks in the Age of Nationalism*. New Jersey: The Darwin Press, pp. 89–114.
Foucault, M. (1991). Governmentality. In A. Burchell, C. Gordon & P. Miller (Eds.), *The Foucault Effect: Studies in Governmentality with Two Lectures by and an Interview with Michel Foucault*. Chicago, IL: The University of Chicago Press, pp. 87–104.
Frazee, C. A. (1979). The Greek Catholic Islanders and the Revolution of 1821. *East European Quarterly*, *13*(3), 315–326.
Friedmann, Y. (2003). *Tolerance and Coercion in Islam: Interfaith Relations in the Muslim Tradition*. New York, NY: Cambridge University Press.
Gazi, E. (2009). Revisiting Religion and Nationalism in Nineteenth-Century Greece. In R. Beaton & D. Ricks (Eds.), *The Making of Modern Greece*. Surrey: Ashgate, pp. 95–106.
Gellner, E. (1983). *Nations and Nationalism*. Oxford: Basil Blackwell.
Georgelin, H. (2012). Armenian Inter-community Relations in Late Ottoman Smyrna. In R. G. Hovannisian (Ed.), *Armenian Smyrna/Izmir: The Aegean Communities*. Costa Mesa: Mazda Publishers, pp. 177–190.
Gingeras, R. (2009). *Sorrowful Shores: Violence, Ethnicity, and the End of the Ottoman Empire, 1912–1923*. New York, NY: Oxford University Press.

Bibliography

Goffman, D. (1999). Izmir: From Village to Colonial Port City. In E. Eldem, D. Goffman & B. Masters (Eds.), *The Ottoman City between East and West*. New York, NY: Cambridge University Press, pp. 79–134.

Göktürk, G. (2017). Zalim Gurbet Sana Yol Vermiyor mu? Geride Kalan Ortodoks Kadınların Gözünden Gurbetliğe Bakış. *Toplum ve Bilim, 141*, 122–140.

Greene, J. K. (1905). The Jubilee of "Avedaper." *The Missionary Herald*.

Grigoriadis, I. N. (2013). *Instilling Religion in Greek and Turkish Nationalism: A "Sacred Synthesis"*. New York, NY: Palgrave Macmillan.

Gülsoy, U. (2010). *Cizyeden Vatandaşlığa: Osmanlı'nın Gayrimüslim Askerleri*. İstanbul: Timaş Yayınları.

Gutmann, A. (2004). *Identity in Democracy*. Princeton, NJ: Princeton University Press.

Hacısalihoğlu, M. (2007). Osmanlı İmparatorluğunda Zorunlu Askerlik Sistemine Geçiş: Ordu-Millet Düşüncesi. *Toplumsal Tarih, 164*, 58–64.

Hamlin, C. (1893). *My Life and Times*. New York, NY; Chicago, IL; Toronto: Fleming H. Revell Company (Publishers of Evangelical Literature).

Hanley, W. (2008). Grieving Cosmopolitanism in Middle East Studies. *History Compass, 6(5)*, 1346–1367.

Harakopoulos, M. (2014). *Ρωμιοί της Καππαδοκίας: από τα Βάθη της Ανατολής στο Θεσσαλικό Κάμπο. Η Τραυματική Ενσωμάτωση στη Μητέρα Πατρίδα*. Athens: Pedio.

Hasluck, F. W. (1929). *Christianity and Islam under the Sultans*. Oxford: Clarendon Press.

Hatziiosif, H. (2005). *Συνασός: Ιστορία Ενός Τόπου Χωρίς Ιστορία*. Heraklion: University Press of Crete.

Haydaroğlu, I. P. (1990). *Osmanlı İmparatorluğunda Yabancı Okullar*. Ankara: Kültür Bakanlığı.

Hayden, R. M. (2002). Antagonistic Tolerance: Competitive Sharing of Religious Sites in South Asia and the Balkans. *Current Anthropology, 43(2)*, 205–231.

Hayden, R. M. (Ed.). (2016). *Antagonistic Tolerance: Competitive Sharing of Religious Sites and Spaces*. Oxon; New York, NY: Routledge.

Hayden, R. M. & Naumovic, S. (2013). Imagined Commonalities: The Invention of a Late Ottoman "Tradition" of Coexistence. *American Anthropologist, 115(2)*, 324–334.

Hayden, R. M., Sözer, H., Tanyeri-Erdemir, T. & Erdemir, A. (2011). The Byzantine Mosque at Trilye: A Processual Analysis of Dominance, Sharing, Transformation and Tolerance. *History and Anthropology, 22(1)*, 1–17.

Hirschon, R. (1998). *Heirs of the Greek Catastrophe: The Social Life of Asia Minor Refugees in Piraeus*. New York, NY; Oxford: Berghahn Books.

Hirschon, R. (2006). Knowledge of Diversity: Towards a More Differentiated Set of "Greek" Perceptions of "Turks." *South European Society and Politics, 11(1)*, 61–78.

Hobsbawm, E. (1992). *Nations and Nationalism Since 1780: Programme, Myth, Reality*. Cambridge; New York, NY: Cambridge University Press.

Huntington, S. P. (1997). *The Clash of Civilizations and the Remaking of World Order* (1st Touchstone ed.). New York, NY: Touchstone.

Iatrides, J. O. (1986). Missionary Educators and the Asia Minor Disaster: Anatolia College's Move to Greece. *Journal of Modern Greek Studies, 4(2)*, 143–157.

Iğsız, A. (2008). Documenting the past and Publicizing Personal Stories: Sensescapes and the 1923 Greco-Turkish Population Exchange in Contemporary Turkey. *Journal of Modern Greek Studies, 26*, 451–487.

Iğsız, A. (2018). *Humanism in Ruins*. Stanford, CA: Stanford University Press.

İnalcık, H. (1991). The Status of the Greek Orthodox Patriarch under the Ottomans. *Turcica*, XI-XII, 195–219.

Jessup, H. H. (1891). *The Greek Church and Protestant Missions or Missions to the Oriental Churches.* New York, NY: Christian Literature Co.
Kalfas, A. G. & Papageorgiou, P. A. (2001). *Ο Συνοικισμός Ευαγγελικών της Κατερίνης (1923-2000). Τοπική Ιστορία και Κίνηση των Θρησκευτικών Ιδεών.* Katerini: Ελληνική Ευαγγελική Εκκλησία Κατερίνης.
Kamouzis, D. (2013). Elites and the Formation of National Identity. In B. C. Fortna, S. Katsikas, D. Kamouzis & P. Konortas (Eds.), *State-nationalisms in the Ottoman Empire, Greece and Turkey: Orthodox and Muslims, 1830–1945.* London; New York, NY: Routledge, pp. 13–46.
Kapoli, E. (2008). Archive of Oral Tradition of the Centre for Asia Minor Studies: Its Formation and its Contribution to Research. *Ateliers d'anthropologie, 32.* Retrieved March 22, 2020, from http://journals.openedition.org/ateliers/1143.
Kapoli, P. P. (2004). *Πόλη και Μετανάστευση στην Οθωμανική Αυτοκρατορία: Κωνσταντινούπολη και Καππαδόκες Μετανάστες (1856–1908).* (Unpublished MA thesis, National and Kapodistrian University of Athens, 2004).
Karalidis, K. I. (2005). *Τσαρικλί Νίγδης Καππαδοκίας.* Athens: Έκδοση του Συλλόγου Καππαδοκών Μαυρολόφου «Ο Άγιος Γεώργιος-Τσαρικλί».
Karmiris, I. N. (1937). *Ορθοδοξία και Προτεσταντισμός.* Athens.
Kazamias, A. (1991). The Education of the Greeks in the Ottoman Empire, 1876–1923: A Case Study of Controlled Toleration. In J. J. Tomiak (Ed.), *Schooling, Educational Policy and Ethnic Identity.* New York, NY: New York University Press, pp. 343–367.
Kechriotis, V. (2014). Osmanlı İmparatorluğu'nun Son Döneminde Karamanlı Rum Ortodoks Diasporası: İzmir Mebusu Emmanouil Emmanouilidis. *Toplumsal Tarih, 251,* 38–43.
Kechriotis, V. (2015a). Ottomanism with a Greek Face: Karamanli Greek Orthodox Diaspora at the End of the Ottoman Empire. In M. Isabella & K. Zanou (Eds.), *Mediterranean Diasporas: Politics and Ideology in the Long 19th century.* London: Bloomsbury, pp. 189–204.
Kechriotis, V. (2015b). Atina'da Kapadokyalı, İzmir'de Atinalı, İstanbul'a Mebus: Pavlos Karolidis'in Farklı Kişilik ve Aidiyetleri. *Toplumsal Tarih, 257,* 28–35.
King, P. (1998). *Toleration.* London: Frank Cass Publishers.
Kirtsoglou, E. & Sistani, L. (2003). The Other *Then,* the Other *Now,* the Other *Within*: Stereotypical Images and Narrative Captions of the Turk in Northern and Central Greece. *Journal of Mediterranean Studies, 13*(2), 189–213.
Kitromilides, P. M. (Ed.) (1982). *Η Έξοδος. Τόμος Β'. Μαρτυρίες από τις επαρχίες της Κεντρικής και Νότιας Μικρασίας.* Athens: Centre for Asia Minor Studies.
Kitromilides, P. M. (1990). Greek Irredentism in Asia Minor and Cyprus. *Middle East Studies, 26*(1), 3–17.
Kitromilides, P. M. (1994). *Enlightenment, Nationalism and Orthodoxy: Studies in the Culture and Political Thought of Southeastern Europe.* Aldershot; Hampshire: Variorum.
Kitromilides, P. M. (2013). *Enlightenment and Revolution: The Making of Modern Greece.* Cambridge, MA: Harvard University Press.
Kocabaşoğlu, U. (2000). *Anadolu'daki Amerika.* Ankara: İmge Yayınları.
Kojève, A. (1980). In Place of an Introduction. In A. Bloom (Ed.), *Introduction to the Reading of Hegel.* Ithaca, NY; London: Cornell University Press, pp. 3–30.
Konortas, P. (1999). From Ta'ife to Millet. In D. Gondicas & C. Issawi (Eds.), *Ottoman Greeks in the Age of Nationalism: Politics, Economy, and Society in the Nineteenth Century.* Princeton, NJ: The Darwin Press, pp. 169–180.

Koraes, A. (1970). Report on the Present State of Civilization in Greece. In E. Kedourie (Ed.), *Nationalism in Asia and Africa*. New York, NY: World Pub. Co, pp. 153–188.

Kritikos, G. (1999–2000). Motives for the Compulsory Exchange. *Deltio: Bulletin of the Centre for Asia Minor Studies*, *13*, 209–224.

Kritovulos. (2013). *İstanbul'un Fethi: Tarih-i Sultan Mehmet Han-ı Sani*. İstanbul: Kapı Yayınları.

Kymlicka, W. (1996). Two Models of Pluralism and Tolerance. In D. Heyd (Ed.), *Toleration: An Elusive Virtue*. Princeton, NJ: Princeton University Press, pp. 81–105.

Ladas, S. P. (1932). *The Exchange of Minorities: Bulgaria, Greece and Turkey*. New York, NY: The Macmillan Company, pp. 81–105.

Lafi, N. (2008). The Ottoman Cosmopolitan Hypothesis in the Light of Pheng Cheah's Critical Explorations of Cosmopolitanism. *Transnationalism and Colonialism. EUME Summer School*. Istanbul.

Lamprylos, K. H. N. (1836). *Ο Μισσιοναρισμός και Προτεσταντισμός εις τας Ανατολάς: Ήτοι Διαγωγή των Προτεσταντών Μισσιοναρίων εις τα Μέρη μας, εις τινα τε άλλα της Γης Μέρη. Και Σχέσεις του Προτεσταντισμού προς την Μητέρα Πασών των Εκκλησιών και το Ελληνικόν Έθνος*. Smyrna.

Layoun, M. N. (2001). *Wedded to the Land? Gender, Boundaries and Nationalism in Crisis*. Durham; London: Duke University Press.

Lessersohn, N. (2015). "Provincial Cosmopolitanism" in Late Ottoman Anatolia: Livanio an Armenian Shoemaker's Memoir. *Comparative Studies in Society and History*, *57(2)*, 528–556.

Lewis, B. (2002). *The Emergence of Modern Turkey*. New York, NY: Oxford University Press.

Liakos, A. (2008). Hellenism and the Making of Modern Greece: Time, Language, Space. In K. Zacharia (Ed.), *Hellenisms: Culture, Identity, and Ethnicity from Antiquity to Modernity*. Hampshire; Burlington: Ashgate, pp. 201–236.

Livanios, D. (2003). Making Borders, Unmaking Identities: Frontiers and Nationalism in the Balkans, 1774–1913. *Seminar Paper Delivered at the Watson Institute for International Studies*. Brown University.

Locke, J. (2010). A Letter Concerning Toleration. In R. Vernon (Ed.), *Locke on Toleration*. Cambridge: Cambridge University Press, pp. 3–46.

Loukopoulos, D. (1984–1985). Η Ξενιτειά. *Deltio: Bulletin of the Centre for Asia Minor Studies*, *5*.

Macar, E. (2006). *İstanbul'un Yok olmuş İki Cemaati: Doğu Ritli Katolik Rumlar ve Bulgarlar*. Istanbul: İletişim.

Mackridge, P. (2009). *Language and National Identity in Greece 1766–1976*. New York, NY: Oxford University Press.

Makdisi, U. (2008). *Artillery of Heaven: American Missionaries and the Failed Conversion of the Middle East*. New York, NY: Cornell University Press.

Mamoni, K. (1980–1981). *Αγώνες του Οικουμενικού Πατριαρχείου κατά των Μισσιονάριων*. Μνημοσύνη.

Mamoni, K. & Istikopoulou, L. (2006). *Σωματειακή Οργάνωση του Ελληνισμού στη Μικρά Ασία (1861–1922)*. Athens: Βιβλιοπωλείον της Εστίας.

Manousaki, S. A. (2002). *Μνήμες Καππαδοκίας*. Athens: Centre for Asia Minor Studies.

Marks, L. M. (2005). Οι Ελληνικές Εφημερίδες στην Οθωμανική Αυτοκρατορία,1830–1862. In L. Droulia (Ed.), *Ο Ελληνικός Τύπος 1784 ως Σήμερα: Ιστορικές καιΘεωρητικές Προσεγγίσεις: Πρακτικά Διεθνούς Συνεδρίου. 23–25 Μαΐου 2002*. Athens: Ινστιτούτο Νεοελληνικών Ερευνών Εθνικού Ιδρύματος Ερευνών, pp. 442–447.

Masters, B. (2001). *Christians and Jews in the Ottoman Arab World: The Roots of Sectarianism*. New York, NY: Cambridge University Press.
Mazower, M. (2000). *The Balkans*. New York, NY: Modern Library.
McCarthy, J. (2001). *The Ottoman Peoples and the End of Empire*. New York, NY: Arnold Publishers.
McKinnon, C. (2006). *Toleration: A Critical Introduction*. London; New York, NY: Routledge.
Ménage, V. L. (1979). The Islamization of Anatolia. In N. Levtzion (Ed.), *Conversion to Islam*. New York, NY: Holmes and Meier, pp. 52–67.
Merlie, M. L. (1977). Οι Ελληνικές Κοινότητες στη Σύγχρονη Καππαδοκία. *Deltio: Bulletin of the Centre for Asia Minor Studies, 1*.
Mill, J. S. (2009). *On Liberty*. Auckland, New Zealand: The Floating Press (from a 1909 edition).
Miller, D. (1999). Group Identities, National Identities and Democratic Politics. In J. Horton & S. Mendus (Eds.), *Toleration, Identity and Difference*. New York, NY: Palgrave Macmillan, pp. 103–125.
Monk, I. H. (1999). Toleration and Moral Will. In J. Horton & S. Mendus (Eds.), *Toleration, Identity and Difference*. New York, NY: Palgrave Macmillan, pp. 17–37.
Mourelos, Y. G. (1985). The 1914 Persecutions and the First Attempt at an Exchange of Minorities Between Greece and Turkey. *Balkan Studies, 26(2)*, 389–413.
Nikolaidou-Danasi, K. (2017a). *Καισάρεια Τόμος Α': η Μονή Τιμίου Προδρόμου στο Ζιντζίδερε (Φλαβιανά). Το Πνευματικό και Εκπαιδευτικό Κέντρο της Καππαδοκίας. Κερμίρα, Μερσίνα, Ποτάμια, Τόμος Α*. Thessaloniki.
Nikolaidou-Danasi, K. (2017b). *Καισάρεια Τόμος Β': Η Κατά Καισάρειαν Ροδοκανάκειος Ιερατική Σχολή. Ανδρονίκιο, Μουταλάσκη, Στέφανα*, Thessaloniki.
Orakçı, M. (2014). Karamanlıca Bir Gazete: *Terakki*. In E. Balta (Ed.), *Cultural Encounters in the Turkish-speaking Communities of the Late Ottoman Empire*. Istanbul: The Isis Press, pp. 411–428.
Ortaylı, İ. (1981). Osmanlı İmparatorluğu'nda Amerikan Okulları Üzerine Bazı Gözlemler. *Amme İdaresi Dergisi, 14(3)*, 87–96.
Ortaylı, İ. (2008). *Osmanlı'da Milletler ve Diplomasi*. İstanbul: Türkiye İş Bankası Kültür Yayınları.
Öz, M. (2013). Zındık. *İslam Ansiklopedisi*. Diyanet İşleri Başkanlığı. Retrived March 22, 2020, from https://islamansiklopedisi.org.tr/zindik.
Özdemir, E. R. (2006). Borders of Belonging in the "Exchanged" Generations of Karamanlis (Unpublished MA Thesis, Koç University).
Ozil, A. (2013). *Orthodox Christians in the Late Ottoman Empire: A Study of Communal Relations in Anatolia*. New York, NY: Routledge.
Özkırımlı, U. & Sofos, S. A. (2008). *Tormented by History: Nationalism in Greece and Turkey*. London: Hurst Publishers.
Özsoy, H. (1996). *Kayseri'de Amerikan Misyoner Faaliyetleri ve Talas Amerikan Koleji*. Kayseri: Talas Belediyesi Kültür Yayınları.
Özyürek, E. (2007). *The Politics of Public Memory in Turkey*. Syracuse; New York, NY: Syracuse University Press.
Papa Efthim. (1925). *Papa Efthim Efendi'nin Orthodoxos Ahaliye Müracaatı Ve Patrikhaneye Karşı Müdafaanamesi*. Centre for Asia Minor Studies. *Karamanlidika* book collection.
Papailias, P. (2004). *Genres of Recollection: Archival Poetics and Modern Greece: Anthropology, History, and the Critical Imagination*. New York, NY: Palgrave Macmillan.

Bibliography

Parekh, B. (2006). *Rethinking Multiculturalism: Cultural Diversity and Political Theory*. New York, NY: Palgrave Macmillan.

Pashalidou, A. P. D. (1996). *Η Λύση του Γάμου στο Μουσουλμανικό Δίκαιο: με Ειδική Αναφορά στα Προβλήματα των Μεικτών Γάμων*. Lefkosia: MAM.

Patsavos, L. J. & Joanides, C. J. (2000). Interchurch Marriages: An Orthodox Perspective. *Greek Orthodox Theological Review, 45(1/4)*.

Petropoulou, I. (2002). Foreword. In I. Kalfoglou (Ed.), *Ιστορική Γεωγραφία της Μικρασιατικής Χερσονήσου* (S. Anestidis, Trans.). Athens: Centre for Asia Minor Studies. (Original work published 1899).

Philipp, T. (2004). Bilād Al-šām in the Modern Period: Integration into the Ottoman Empire and New Relations with Europe. *Arabica, 51(4)*, 401–418.

Phillips, A. (1999). The Politisation of Difference: Does This Make for a More Intolerant Society? In J. Horton & S. Mendus (Eds.), *Toleration, Identity and Difference*. New York, NY: Palgrave Macmillan.

Portelli, A. (2002). What Makes Oral History Different? In R. Perk & A. Thomson (Eds.), *Oral History Reader*. New York, NY: Routledge.

Psomiades, H. J. (1960). The Oecumenical Patriarchate under the Turkish Republic: The First Ten Years. *Greek Orthodox Theological Review, 6(62)*, 56–80.

Quataert, D. (1997). Clothing Laws, State, and Society in the Ottoman Empire, 1720–1829. *International Journal of Middle East Studies, 29(3)*, 403–425.

Richards, G. L. (1919). Are Foreign Missions Worth While? *The Missionary Herald*.

Richter, J. (1910). *A History of Missions in the near East*. Edinburgh: Oliphant, Anderson & Ferrier.

Riggs, E. (1886). Anatolia College, Western Turkey. *The Missionary Herald*.

Roudometof, V. (1998). From Rum Millet to Greek Nation: Enlightenment, Secularization, and National Identity in Ottoman Balkan Society, 1453–1821. *Journal of Modern Greek Studies, 16*.

Rufus, A. (1873). *History of the Missions of the American Board of Commissioners for Foreign Missions to the Oriental Churches (Vol. 1)*. Boston, MA: Congregational Publishing Society.

Sabra, G. (1999). Orthodox-Protestant Relations: A View from the Middle East. *The Ecumenical Review, 51(4)*, 372–375.

Samouilidis, Ch. (2010). *Καραμανίτες: οι Τελευταίοι Έλληνες της Καππαδοκίας*. Athens: Estia.

Sennett, R. (2004). *Respect: The Formation of Character in an Age of Inequality*. London: Penguin.

Shaw, S. (1976). *History of the Ottoman Empire and Modern Turkey: Empire of the Gazis: The Rise and Decline of the Ottoman Empire, 1280–1808 (Vol. 1)*. Cambridge, New York, NY: Cambridge University Press.

Sigler, A. J. (1983). *Minority Rights: A Comparative Analysis*. Connecticut: Greenwood press.

Şimşek, Ş. Ş. (2010). The Anatoli Newspaper and the Heyday of the Karamanlı Press. In E. Balta & M. Kappler (Eds.), *Cries and Whispers in Karamanlidika Books*. Wiesbaden: Harrassowitz Verlag.

Şişman, C. (2015). Failed Proselytizers or Modernizers? Protestant Missionaries among the Jews and Sabbateans/Dönmes in the Nineteenth-century Ottoman Empire. *Middle Eastern Studies, 51(6)*, 932–949.

Smith, A. D. (1986). *The Ethnic Origins of Nations*. New York, NY: Basil Blackwell.

Smith, A. D. (1998). *Nationalism and Modernism: A Critical Survey of Recent Theories of Nations*. London; New York, NY: Routledge.
Stamatopoulos, D. (2006). From *Millets* to Minorities in the 19th Century Ottoman Empire: An Ambiguous Modernization. In S. G. Ellis, G. Halfdanarson & A. K. Isaacs (Eds.), *Citizenship in Historical Perspective*. Pisa: Pisa University Press.
Tanc, B. (2001). Where Local Trumps National: Christian Orthodox and Muslim Refugees since Lausanne. *Balkanologie, 5(2)*, 273–289.
Tarinas, S. (2007). *Ο Ελληνικός Τύπος της Πόλης*. İstanbul: Tempo.
Tatsios, T. G. (1984). *The Megali Idea and the Greek-Turkish War of 1897: The Impact of the Cretan Problem on Greek Irredentism, 1866–1897*. New York, NY: East European Monographs, Boulder, CO, distributed by Columbia University Press.
Taylor, C. (1994). The Politics of Recognition. In A. Gutmann (Ed.), *Multiculturalism*. Princeton, NJ: Princeton University Press, pp. 25–73.
Thanailaki, P. (2004). The American Protestant Missionary Schools in Greece in the Nineteenth Century and Greek Orthodox Education. *Greek Orthodox Theological Review, 49 (1/2)*, 75–87.
Theodoridou, Ch. (1976). *Διακριθέντες του Ξεριζωμένου Ελληνισμού: Μικράς Ασίας - Πόντου - Αν. Θράκης – Κωνσταντινουπόλεως, Τόμος Β'*. Athens: Εκδ. Συλλόγων Εθνικής Μνημοσύνης και Φοιτησάντων εις την Ευαγγελικήν Σχολήν Σμύρνης.
Thompson, P. (2000). *The Voice of the Past*. New York, NY: Oxford University Press.
Thornberry, P. (1991). *International Law and the Rights of Minorities*. New York, NY: Clarendon Press.
Tilly, C. (2005). *Identities, Boundaries & Social Ties*. Boulder, CO: Paradigm Publishers.
Tsolainos, K. P. (1923). Greek Irredentism. *Annals of the American Academy of Political and Social Science, 108*, America's relation to the European Situation.
Tsolakidis, K. (2007). *Belki Bir Gün Dönerim* (B. Myisli, Trans.). Istanbul: Literatür Yayınları. (Original work published 2001).
Tuckerman, C. K. (1872). *The Greeks of To-day*. New York, NY: G. P. Putnam & sons.
Tyler, A. (2008). *Islam, the West, and Tolerance: Conceiving Co-existence*. New York, NY: Palgrave MacMillan.
Valensi, L. (1997). Inter-communal Relations and Changes in Religious Affiliation in the Middle East (Seventeenth to Nineteenth Centuries). *Comparative Studies in Society and History, 39(2)*, 251–269.
Van der Veer, P. (1994). *Religious Nationalism*. Berkeley, CA; Los Angeles, CA: University of California Press.
Van der Veer, P. (2003). Syncretism, Multiculturalism si Discursul Tolerantei (Syncretism, Multiculturalism and the Discourse of Tolerance). *Journal for the Study of Religions and Ideologies, 2(5)*, 4–20.
Vassiadis, G. (2007). *The Syllogos Movement of Constantinople and Ottoman Greek Education 1861–1923*. Athens: Center for Asia Minor Studies.
Vryonis, S. Jr. (1971). *The Decline of Medieval Hellenism in Asia Minor and the Process of Islamization from the Eleventh through the Fifteenth Century*. Berkeley, CA; Los Angeles, CA: University of California Press.
Vryonis, S. Jr. (1982). Religious Change and Continuity in the Balkans and Anatolia from the Fourteenth through the Sixteenth Century. In S. Vryonis, Jr (Ed.), *Byzantina Kai Metabyzantina: Studies on Byzantium, Seljuks, and Ottoman*. Malibu: Undina Press.
Walder, D. (2011). *Post-colonial Nostalgia: Writing, Representation, Memory*. Abingdon; New York, NY: Routledge.
Walzer, M. (1997). *On Toleration*. New Haven, CO: Yale University Press.

172 Bibliography

White, J. B. (1835). *Observations on Heresy and Orthodoxy*. London: J. Mardon.
Yesari, M. (2017). *Bir Namus Meselesi*. İstanbul: İstos Yayınları.
Yıldırım, O. (2006). *Diplomacy and Displacement: Reconsidering Turco-Greek Exchange of Populations 1922–1934*. New York, NY: Routledge.
Yıldırım, Y. & Karpat, K. H. (Eds.). (2012). *Osmanlı Hoşgörüsü*. İstanbul: Timaş Yayınları.
Zandi-Sayek, S. (2012). *Ottoman Izmir: the Rise of a Cosmopolitan Port, 1840/1880*. London; Minneapolis: University of Minnesota Press.
Zürcher, E. J. (1998). The Ottoman Conscription System in Theory and Practice, 1844–1918. *International Review of Social History, 43*(3), 437–449.

Electronic Resources

A Balkan Tale. Retrieved January 15, 2015, from www.balkantale.com/
Halsall, P. (1996). Pact of Umar, 7th century? The Status of non-Muslims under Muslim Rule. *Medieval Sourcebook*. Retrieved June 6, 2015, from http://legacy.fordham.edu/hal sall/source/pact-umar.asp
House of Commons Parliamentary Papers Online. (1865). *Correspondence Respecting Protestant Missionaries and Converts in Turkey Presented to Both Houses of Parliament by Command of Her Majesty*. London: Harrison and sons, 1865. Retrived May 21, 2015, from www.parlipapers.chadwyck.co.uk
"Prosorinon Politeuma Tes Hellados," *The Epidaurus Constitution, 1822*. Retrieved July 18, 2019, from www.hellenicparliament.gr/UserFiles/f3c70a23-7696-49db-9148-f24dce6a27c8/syn06.pdf
Winter, J. *Sites of Memory, Sites of Mourning*. Retrieved April 13, 2015, from Open Yale courses Web site: http://oyc.yale.edu/history/hist-202/lecture-18

Index

American missionaries 132–141; schools and orphanages 136, *137*, 139, 140–141, 143–144, *144*, 146
Anagnostopoulou, S. 7, 53, 89
Anatolia College, Merzifon 136, *144*
Anatoli newspaper 13–14; education promotion 99–100, 104–106; readership and finances 106–107; on religious issues 65–66, 135, 136; Turkish language promotion 96
Anderson, B. 41, 75, 89–90, 108
Angeliaforos newspaper 14, 139, 141–142; on education issues 146; on Protestant life 143, 144
antagonistic tolerance 4, 15, 42, 57, 59, 61, 155
apostasy, in Islam 29, 33, 37, 142
Arab Christians 134, 148
Arabic 14, 62, *63*, 96, 107, 141
Arendt, H. 27
Areti (Αρετή) 94, 99
Armenians: *dhimmi* status of 30; persecution of 48, 115; Protestant proselytism and 128, 133, 134, 142
Augustinos, G. 33, 140

"Balkan Tale, A" 44
Balkan Wars 46–47, 116, 122
Barkey, K. 34
Barth, F. 43, 52, 53, 54
Before the Nation (Doumanis) 45–46
Bektashism 61
Benlisoy, F. 5, 124, 125
Benlisoy, S. 5, 124, 125, 136
Bor (Niğde) 87
Bowman, G. 61–62
boycott movement 118–121
Braude, B. 31–32
Bringa, T. 55–56

brotherhood organizations 87, 90, 94, 95, 98–99, 108, 158
Brown, W. 24, 25

Camcean, Mikayel 31
Campos, M. 36
Cappadocia, defined 7–8
Carolidis, Pavlos 101–102, 158
Carter, I. 26
Centre for Asia Minor Studies (CAMS): Oral Tradition Archives 10–13
Christianity and Islam under the Sultans 63–64
Christians: inter-church competition 82, 94, 100, 133–139, 142–145, 148–151; inter-marriage with Muslims 65–69, *69*; religious syncretism and 57–65, *63*
church and state, separation of 22–23
"clash of civilizations" theory 57
Clogg, Richard 5
clothing, Ottoman restrictions on 34–35
communal identity 52–54; religious syncretism and 57–65
cosmopolitanism 48–49, 156, 157
cultural societies *(syllogoi)* 90, 97–98, 108, 158
Curzon, Lord 127

denationalization 67, 131, 132
Deringil, S. 67, 68, 132
dhimmis (zımmi), status of 29–30, 34–37
dimotika (Greek vernacular) 90, 101
djizya tax *(cizye)* 29, 30, 37
Doumanis, N. 45–48, 55, 58, 115

economy 85–89, 91, 118–121
education: of girls 99, 100, 140–141; Greek intelligentsia promoting 88–89, 90, 96,

174 Index

97–100, 107–108; immigration and 88–89; missionary contribution to 135, 136, *137*, 139, 140–141, 143–144, *144*, 146–147; religious 135–136; school system in Greek Orthodox communities 89–97
Emmanuilidis, Emmanuil 101, 119, 158
Enlightenment, influence of 78
ethnicity, national identity and 41, 43, 53–54, 81–82
ethnie concept 41, 43
Exchange of Populations (1923) 79, 89, 120, 127, 149–150, 160
exile of Greek Christians 120–121, 125, 126, 149

French Revolution, influence of 78
Friendly Society (Φιλική Εταιρεία) 78

Gavoustima 1–2, *3*
Gazi, E. 135
Gellner, E. 74–75
Gennadius II, Patriarch 30, *32*
Georgelin, H. 48
Greco-Turkish Population Exchange 79, 89, 120, 127, 149–150, 160
Greek irredentism 80–82, 90, 157–158
Greek language: education and linguistic "rehellenization" 90, 92, 95–96, 100, 117; *Katharevoussa* 90, 92; supplanted by Turkish 6, 84, 89; vernacular 6, 90, 101
Greek nationalism 77–82; education and 82–86, 89–90, 95–96, 97–100; ethnic identity and 43, 53–54, 81–82; Greek Orthodox Church and 78–79, 81, 82, 90, 116; of Greek Protestants 148–149, 150–151; intellectuals promoting 90, 97–100, 102–103, 104; inter-marriage and 67; linguistic "rehellenization" 90, 92, 95–96, 100, 117; in the long war (1912–1922) 116–117, 123, 128, 148–151; *millet* system and 33; popular indifference to 42, 102, 117; printed press and 104–108; prominent Greek Orthodox figures and 100–104; religious identity and 53–54, 57, 67, 75–79, 102, 117, 150
Greek Orthodox Church: education promotion and 82, 90, 94, 97, 135; Greek nationalism and 78–79, 81, 82, 90, 116; illiteracy of clergy 94, 135; mixed marriages and 67–68; Protestantism and 82, 94, 100, 133–139, 142–145, 148–151; status under Ottomans 31, *32*, 33
Greek Orthodox Community, organizational structure of 33, 91
Greek Protestants: lives of converts 141–148, *144*; missionary activities and emergence of 132–141, *137*, *138*, *140*; nationalism and inter-communal relations 143–144, 148–151; socio-economic motivations of 146–147
Grigoriadis, I. N. 79

Hamidian years, as a *belle époque* 13, 48, 115
Hamlin, Cyrus 142
Hasluck, W. F. 60–61, 63–64
Hayden, R. M. 4, 42, 57, 58, 59–60, 61–62, 64, 65, 155
Hegelian Master-Slave dialectic 52
Hellenic Literary Society of Constantinople (EFSK) 97, 98
heretics 29, 30, 33, 37; Greek Protestants as (*see* Greek Protestants)
Hirschon, R. 53, 64–65
Hoare, Samuel 122
Hobsbawm, E. 41, 43, 75, 90
Huntington, Samuel P. 57

identity politics 19–20
immigration 6, 49, 82–89, 91, 103–104, 116, 147–148, 158
İnalcık, Halil 30
Indian nationalism 42
intellectuals, promotion of education by 88–89, 90, 96, 97–100, 107–108
inter-communality: Christian communities in wartime (1912–1922) 148–151; *vs.* inter-personal relations 45–46, 50, 55–56, 158, 160; mixed marriages as evidence of 65–69; non-Muslim communities 35–36
inter-marriages 56, 65–70, *69*, *70*, 89
inter-personal *vs.* inter-communal relations 45–46, 50, 55–56, 158, 160
irredentism 80–82, 90, 157–158
Islam: apostasy in 29, 33, 37, 142; mixed marriages in 67, 68; non-Muslims and heretics in 29–30, 37; religious syncretism and 57–65, *63*
Islamization 57, 64; in Young Turk program 118
İsmet Paşa (İnönü) 127
Izmir 35, 49, 85, 86, 87, 134

Jewish community: *millet* system and 33;
  Protestant proselytism and 133;
  restrictions concerning 34

Kalfoglou, Ioannis 103, 106
Kapoli, E. 11
Karamanlidika 6, 14, 103, 135; press 103, 104–108
Karamanlı, use of term 5–6, 7
Katharevoussa 90, 92
Kayabaşı (Niğde) *51*
Kayseri 7, 8, 85, 91, 134
King, Jonas 139
King, P. 25–26, 36
Kleovoulos, Efstathios (Metropolitan) 137–138
Konya 7, *8*, 91
Korais, Adamantios 78, 90
Kymlicka, W. 29

Lamprylos, Kyriakos H. N. 133
language, Greek nationalism and 41–42, 81–82, 84, 89–90, 99–100
Layoun, M. N. 65
Letter Concerning Toleration, A 22
Lewis, Bernard 30
Livanios, D. 89
Locke, John 22–23
long war (1912–1922) 116–117, 121–123, 128, 148–151; inter-communal relations during 148–151
Lutheran-Calvinists 139

marriages, mixed *see* inter-marriages
Marsovan (Merzifon): Protestant-Orthodox relations in 143–144, *144*
Master-Slave dialectic (Hegel) 52
Mazower, M. 61
Megali Idea 80, 81, 98
Mehmed II 30–31, *32*
memory, oral history and 12–13
Ménage, V. L. 57
Merlie, Melpo Logotheti 10, 11
military conscription 121–123
Miller, D. 23
millet system 28–33, 91; Protestant status recognized in 134, 137
Mill, John Stuart 23
Misailidis, Evangelinos 13, 99–100, 102–103, 105, 106, 108
missionaries, Protestant 131, 132–141, *137*, *138*, *140*
Missionary Herald, The 14–15, 139, 143

missionary schools 136, *137*, 139, 143–144, *144*, 146–147
Monk, I. H. 23, 25
Mourelos, Y. G. 118
multiculturalism, contemporary approaches to 4–5, 15, 20–21, 44–45

nationalism: ethnic identity and 41–42, 43, 53–54, 81–82; ethnoreligious segregation and 35; religious identity and 4, 42, 53–54, 57, 75–79, 82, 150, 158–159; theories on the emergence of 41–43, 74–77
Nevşehir 10, 14, *69*, 91, 92–93, *93*, 99, 107
Niğde 7, 8–10, *51*, 86, 91; St. Vasilis Church of Misti 70
non-Muslim communities: *dhimmitude* 29–30, 34–37; military service in wartime (1912–1922) 121–122; *millet* system and 28–38; restrictions concerning 30, 34–36; segregation of 35; taxation of 29, 30, 121; Young Turk revolution and 120–121

Oral Tradition Archives, CAMS 10–13
Other, concept of 52–54
Ottoman state: attitude to religious conversion 33, 35, 37, 81, 139, 142; Greek Orthodox loyalty to 101–102, 103; non-Muslim communities in 29–30, 34–37; plurality in 44–52; *see also* tolerance, Ottoman
Ozil, A. 33
Özsoy, H. 134

Papa Efthim 124–127, 159
Papailias, P. 11
Parekh, B. 29
peaceful co-existence 4–5, 44–52, 55–56, 155–156
"People of the Book" 29–30
Pheraios, Rhigas (Velestinlis) 78
Phillips, A. 24, 25
Population Exchange (1923) 79, 89, 120, 127, 149–150, 160
print press 13–15, 102–103, 104–108, 139, 141
Prokopi (Ürgüp), Nevşehir 87, 94
Protestant Greeks *see* Greek Protestants
Protestantization 135–136, 140
Protestant missionaries 131–141, *137*, *138*, *140*

religious conversions: inter-marriage and 65–68; Ottomans and 33, 35, 37, 81; Protestant 131–148; syncretism and 62–64
religious identity, nationalism and 4, 42, 53–54, 57, 67, 76–79, 82, 150, 158–159
religious segregation 34–35, 49–50
religious syncretism 57–65, *63*
respect *vs.* toleration 26–27
Russian Empire 33–34, 78

schools *see* education
Shaw, Stanford 30
Şimşek, Ş. Ş. 106
Smith, Anthony 41, 43
syllogoi (societies) 90, 97–98, 108, 158
syncretism, religious 57–65, *63*

Talas, Kayseri 86–87, 93, 134, 137–138; American College in *137*; American Hospital in *140*
taxation 29, 30, 76, 121
Taylor, C. 52
Terakki magazine 14, 88, 95, 107–108, 136
Theological Seminary, Kayseri 94–95, *95*
Thornberry, P. 28
Tilly, C. 42, 52, 53
tolerance 22–28; antagonistic 4, 15, 42, 57, 59, 61, 155; Christian denominations and 142–144, 150–151; contemporary *vs.* historical understandings 4–5, 15, 20–22, 37–38, 44–45; inter-communality *vs.* 55–56; John Locke on 22–23; "negative" 29, 36, 42, 50–51; power relations and 51–52; respect *vs.* 26–27; theories on 22–28
tolerance, Ottoman: anachronistic understandings of 20–22, 37–38, 44–45; cosmopolitanism and 48–49; *millet* system myth 28–38, *32*; misconceptions about plurality 44–52

trade 85–88, 118–121
Tsouhour, Kayseri 49, 87
Tuckerman, Charles K. 80
Turco-Greek Population Exchange 79, 89, 120, 127, 149–150, 160
Turco-Greek War (1919–1922) 124–128
Turkification policies 118–121
Turkish language: church services in 135; in Greek Orthodox schools 94, 95–96; immigration and linguistic Turkification 6, 84, 89; *Karamanlidika* publications 6, 13–14, 103, 104–108, 106–108, 141; as mother tongue of Greek Orthodox 6, 94, 95–96, 100, 117
Turkish Orthodox Patriarchate 124–127, 159
Tyler, A. 27, 29

Valavanis, Ioakeim 102, 158
Valensi, L. 59
Van Der Veer, P. 4, 42, 64
Velestinlis (Rhigas Pheraios) 78
Venizelos, Eleftherios 127
Vryonis, S. Jr. 57

Walzer, M. 23–24, 25, 28–29
wars: Balkan Wars 46–47, 116, 122; Greek nationalism and 116–117, 128; long war (1912–1922) 116–117, 121–123, 128, 148–151; military conscription during 121–123; Turco-Greek War and Papa Eftim 124–128

Young Turk Revolution 118–121, 128

Zincidere, Kayseri: Greek Protestant life in *138*, 138–139, 141–142, 146–148; as religious and educational center 8, 93, 94, 125, 138–139; in wartime 116